A
CATHOLIC
Pilgrimage
through American
HISTORY

"Few people realize the rich Catholic heritage we have in the United States. Fewer still know the vital role Catholics of all kinds have played in key moments in our American history. Kevin Schmiesing does a masterful job of bringing US history and Catholic history together in an informative, entertaining, and essential book. Every Catholic in America should own a copy!"

Marge Steinhage Fenelon
Author of *My Queen, My Mother*

"The story of Catholicism in the United States today cannot be told without sharing the centuries of adventures of saints and soon-to-be-saints who have characterized the American Church. But that story also must include the accounts of the parishes and parish priests, the religious sisters and scientists and politicians, the converts and other quirky personalities whose Catholic faith has been an indispensable part of the American Experiment. And Kevin Schmiesing is most certainly the person to tell that story. I've been waiting for this book since we first started doing *This Week in Catholic History* segments with him on the radio back in 2007."

Matt Swaim
Cohost of the *Sonrise Morning Show*

"Kevin Schmiesing's *A Catholic Pilgrimage through American History* is an eye-opening look at a past—often inspiring and occasionally scandalous—about which many American Catholics know far too little. From Spanish missionaries in sixteenth-century Florida to American astronauts in outer space, the author introduces us to people and events spanning nearly half a millennium and to the places where these historic events occurred. Informative and exciting, this trip is a journey you'll learn from and richly enjoy."

Russell Shaw
Author of *American Church*

"While American Catholics contest with one another over the Church of the future, they would be wise to get acquainted with the Church of the past. Kevin Schmiesing gives us the perfect pilgrimage through the American Catholic past: we sojourn to places we've never entered, greet personalities we've never met, and explore institutions we've never understood. History textbooks have usually told the American story as a fundamentally Protestant story that grows increasingly secular over time. Catholic contributors and institutions are asides, placed tidily in boxes on the margins. Rarely is Catholic America integrated into our national macro-narrative. When you finish your trip through Catholic American history you'll know just how wrong has been the traditional telling of our story and you'll find new possibilities for our future."

Al Kresta
President and CEO of Ave Maria Radio
Host of *Kresta in the Afternoon*

"This book is a guide for travelers willing to go in any direction in search of the truth about themselves, because that's what we're looking for when we pursue history."

From the foreword by **Mike Aquilina**
Editor of the Reclaiming Catholic History series

"American history has been taught and learned in many different ways. Kevin Schmiesing offers us a new perspective by looking at the history of the United States through the lens of our Catholic faith. You'll learn more about Catholic America and the stories behind some well-known and out-of-the way places to visit and the people who made them such. And you'll be inspired by the heroic men and women and their invaluable contributions to Catholic America."

Fr. Edward Looney
Author of *A Heart Like Mary's*

A

CATHOLIC
Pilgrimage
through **American**
HISTORY

People and Places that Shaped the
Church in the United States

KEVIN SCHMIESING

AVE MARIA PRESS **AVE** Notre Dame, Indiana

Nihil Obstat: Reverend Monsignor Michael Heintz, PhD
Censor librorum

Imprimatur: Most Reverend Kevin C. Rhoades
Bishop of Fort Wayne-South Bend

Given at: Fort Wayne, Indiana on 22 November 2022

Foreword © 2022 by Mike Aquilina

Founded in 1865, Ave Maria Press is a ministry of the United States Province of Holy Cross.

www.avemariapress.com

Paperback: ISBN-13 978-1-64680-090-2

E-book: ISBN-13 978-1-64680-091-9

Cover images © Getty Images.

Cover and text design by Christopher D. Tobin.

Printed and bound in the United States of America.

Library of Congress Cataloging-in-Publication Data.
Names: Schmiesing, Kevin E., author.
Title: A Catholic pilgrimage through American history : people and places
   that shaped the church in the United States / Kevin Schmiesing.
Description: Notre Dame, Indiana : Ave Maria Press, [2022] | Includes
   bibliographical references and index. | Summary: "Kevin Schmiesing
   chronologically draws out Catholic contributions to the major events and
   themes in American history through examining a fascinating array of
   twenty-seven shrines, memorials, and other historic places"-- Provided
   by publisher.
Identifiers: LCCN 2021048223 (print) | LCCN 2021048224 (ebook) | ISBN
   9781646800902 (paperback) | ISBN 9781646800919 (ebook)
Subjects: LCSH: Catholic Church--United States--History. | Sacred
   space--United States.
Classification: LCC BX1406.3 .S36 2022 (print) | LCC BX1406.3 (ebook) |
   DDC 282/.73--dc23/eng/20211208
LC record available at https://lccn.loc.gov/2021048223
LC ebook record available at https://lccn.loc.gov/2021048224

In memory of John J. Carrigg, 1921–2015

Contents

Foreword

There's something deeply American about a road trip, both the ones we actually take and those we read about.

It's the setting of some of our great works of literature, from Mark Twain's *Adventures of Huckleberry Finn* to Jack Kerouac's *On the Road*.

When we tire of responsibility, it's what we do. We light out for the territory. We hitch a ride.

The road trip is the plot device of favorite American movies. Bob Hope and Bing Crosby dominated the box office as they sang and joked along the roads to Bali, Morocco, Zanzibar, Singapore, and even Utopia.

No one expressed the free spirit of the road trip better than Walt Whitman:

> Afoot and light-hearted I take to the open road,
> Healthy, free, the world before me,
> The long brown path before me leading wherever I choose.

Does it get any more American than that?

Kevin Schmiesing captures that spirit in the pages of this book. It's a guide for travelers willing to go in any direction in search of the truth about themselves, because that's what we're looking for when we pursue history. It's what people go digging for in archeology. It's what they pay for in genealogy. And it's really what we're all doing when we set out on the road.

The road trip Kevin proposes is not for the squeamish. Even if we set out lighthearted and patriotic, we can be crestfallen when we discover that Catholics were not always welcome here. There were sincere Americans who wondered if our clergy had horns. There were nativist mobs eager to burn our churches and convents.

Nor were we Catholics always welcoming. In the itineraries of this book we find that some of our leaders habitually used racist speech and others did their level worst to thwart their own coreligionists.

History takes us on that kind of road trip. We may not always like what we see, but we're better off for having seen it.

A well-read Catholic might argue that the road trip is actually more Catholic than American. There is abundant literature that predates the conquest of this continent. You can start with the fourth-century pilgrim diary of Egeria, proceed to the medieval *Fioretti* of the first Franciscans, and then frolic in the pages of Dante's *Divine Comedy* and Chaucer's *Canterbury Tales*. These are, in general, more lighthearted than the American books, which tend to have an anxious undercurrent of homesickness and fatigue.

I think of poor Sal Paradise in Kerouac's *On the Road*. Hardly more than a hundred pages in, he finds himself marooned and just wanting "to get home." He confesses to the reader:

> I didn't know who I was — I was far away from home, haunted and tired with travel, in a cheap hotel room I'd never seen, hearing the hiss of steam outside, and the creak of the old wood of the hotel, and footsteps upstairs, and all the sad sounds. . . . I was halfway across America, at the dividing line between the East of my youth and the West of my future.

But the faith has a way of accounting for such moments of ship-wreck, not to mention the endless dark stretches of back roads archaeology and the ominous craters that pock the pavement. The faith shows us ways of dealing with things, forgiving, and moving forward— arriving at the destination, seizing the grace of the moment, whatever it may be, and then heading home.

Healing can happen on the pilgrimages in this book. Just a bit of history will teach us that there's always been a certain tension between Catholicism and Americanism. As isms, they're both demanding, and each keeps a wary eye on the other. We can learn from our spiritual ancestors how they managed to accomplish so much in spite of mis-understandings and entrenched bigotry.

And what we learn can give us the courage to hit the road our-selves, again and again, to set out upon the highways that await us. Thus I am grateful to Kevin Schmiesing for writing a book that's so American and so Catholic, with its natures seamlessly and hypostat-ically united.

The last word belongs to the author's mother, who speaks truth: "Every time we step out the door, we're on pilgrimage to somewhere."

Mike Aquilina
Editor of the Reclaiming Catholic History series

Acknowledgments

The research for this book took me across regions and periods that lay outside the areas of my own expertise in American Catholic history, so it was imperative that I solicit the assistance of scholars with more local and specialized knowledge. That process, which might have been laborious and unpleasant, was instead an edifying education in both the expanse and the goodwill of the community that comprises historians of American Catholicism. With a few exceptions, I had no personal connection to the individuals in question, yet the victims targeted by my requests for help were polite and obliging.

The following people read and commented on chapters in their areas of expertise, as indicated by their affiliations: Fr. Warren Murrman (St. Vincent Archabbey); Fr. David Endres (Mount St. Mary's of the West Seminary and School of Theology); John Waide (Saint Louis University); Patrick Jamieson (*Island Catholic News*); Fr. Thomas Blantz, CSC (University of Notre Dame); Sr. Judith Metz, SC (Sisters of Charity of Cincinnati); Fr. Michael Savelesky (Diocese of Spokane); Thomas Lynch (Boys Town); Fr. Michael F. Steltenkamp, SJ; Peter Schmid, Loretta Greene, and Elizabeth Russell (Providence Archives, Mother Joseph Province); Cornel Rosario (University of Wisconsin–Milwaukee); Don Rosenbeck and Matt Hess (Shrine of the Holy Relics); Richard Fossey (*Catholic Southwest*); Gilberto Quezado; Tim Tomes, Fr. Dale Cieslik, and Fr. Clyde Crews (Archdiocese of Louisville); and Fr. Thomas Willis (Cathedral Basilica of St. Augustine).

Henry Miller (Historic St. Mary's City), Tony Falcon (Mission San Diego), and my cherished friend Adam Tate (Clayton State University) deserve special mention for their extraordinary generosity in reading chapters closely and contributing so substantially to their improvement.

Others who assisted in various ways include Nathan Tate, Matthew Bunson, Dominic Aquila, Virgil Riethman, D. Michael Barhorst, Michael Krom, and Dan LeRoy. Librarians at Amos Memorial Library, the Maly Library of Mount St. Mary's Seminary of the West, and the US Catholic Collection at the University of Dayton assisted me on several occasions. I am grateful to John Vella and *Crisis Magazine* .com for inviting me to contribute articles on important figures in American Catholic history and for granting permission to use that material, which appears in a few chapters. I am also grateful to Matt Swaim and Annie Egan of the *Son Rise Morning Show* and the entire Sacred Heart Radio family for providing a venue for *This Week in Catholic History* reports over the past fourteen years. The research for those segments provided the foundation for several chapters. Susan McGurgan, director of the Archdiocese of Cincinnati's Lay Ecclesial Ministry Program, invited me many years ago to teach a class on Church history. The class not only became a rewarding biannual tradition; it also spurred a deeper exploration of our American Catholic past and thus contributed to this book as well.

Thanks are due also to Jayme Stuart Wolfe, Mike Amodei, and the rest of the team at Ave Maria Press for their advice, encouragement, and contributions to the book's final form.

Remaining errors, as well as opinions and interpretations expressed here, are mine alone and should not be imputed to those who graciously helped to make the book more accurate and refined than it otherwise would have been.

Finally, thank you to my family, who have not only tolerated but often encouraged my enthusiasm for all things historical. Anne went beyond the call of duty by reading carefully and commenting helpfully on the entire manuscript—one more entry in a ledger tracking a debt of gratitude so immense that it can never be repaid.

Introduction

You could say that this book began as a family joke. During my childhood, our parents took us traveling nearly every summer and visited places that will be familiar to many vacationing middle-class American families: Niagara Falls, Myrtle Beach, Washington, DC. For my mother, however, a trip to the ocean or to a national monument did not provide adequate justification for the expense and effort put into a vacation. The journey was therefore also a "pilgrimage." This meant that religious sites—on the way, out of the way, or near our destination—must be given their due. The National Shrine of the North American Martyrs lay between Ohio and Niagara Falls, for example, in upstate New York. It was inserted into the itinerary.

Mom took it to extremes sometimes. Even a trip to Grandma's house half an hour away might become a pilgrimage if we could make a stop at the nearby Shrine of the Holy Relics (see chapter 12). This mentality gave rise to half-serious complaints from my siblings and me that every time we stepped out our door we must be on a "pilgrimage" to somewhere.

Upon reflection and with the wisdom of years, I see that Mom's notion was not only defensible but also consistent with a long tradition of thought on the character of Christian life. St. Augustine's approach to faith has been called a "spirituality of pilgrimage." Our very existence on this earth, to use his terminology, is a brief sojourn in the City of Man as we prepare for citizenship in the City of God.

The movement of pilgrim travel reminds us that this world is not our final home. "Just as the beginning of wisdom is the fear of the Lord," writes John Paul Meenan, "we might say that the first step on the road to sanctity is the realization that we are in exile, strangers and sojourners, knowing somehow, someway, we belong somewhere else."[1] Life is a journey toward our ultimate destination, which lies beyond the passageway of death. The same is true for the Church itself, of which the early theologian Tertullian said, "She knows that she is a pilgrim on this earth."[2]

To travel to holy places is not a requirement of Christian life, a point made early and decisively by Church Father Gregory of Nyssa (d. 394). "Change of place does not effect any drawing nearer unto God," he wrote, "but wherever you may be, God will come to you, if the chambers of your soul be found of such a sort that He can dwell in you and walk in you."[3] Nonetheless, for countless faithful throughout the centuries, the experience of travel to religious destinations has been a source of inspiration and edification. Pilgrimage thus plays a large role in the history of Christian devotion.

The Camino de Santiago—featured in the 2010 film *The Way*, starring Martin Sheen—is the most famous of many venerable pilgrimage routes, but the sojourns of religious pilgrims are an important facet of European history more generally. One of the classics of English literature, Geoffrey Chaucer's *Canterbury Tales*, is a description of characters on pilgrimage to the tomb of St. Thomas Becket near London. One of the motivations for the medieval Crusades was provision for the safety of pilgrims on their way to the Holy Land. Neither the concept nor the historical significance is exclusively Catholic or even Christian. One need only think of the importance of Muslims' *hajj*— their pilgrimage to the heart of the Islamic religion at Mecca—for an example from another faith tradition.

History, spirituality, and the lives of the saints are all bound up in the idea and the practice of Christian pilgrimage. The Catholic Church, it has often been noted, places a high value on material things such as bread and wine, the warm colors and subtle texture of a church fresco, the aged fragments of bone from the earthly remains of martyrs. For some, this emphasis on earthly things seems misplaced, but understood properly, its theological justification becomes clear. Through the Incarnation, the union of God with physical man, Christ restored the goodness of creation announced in Genesis but ruined by the Fall. This side of heaven, the material world retains its danger as a source of temptation, but it is also the foundation for majestic art that raises the spirit to heaven, for sacrificial generosity that provides for those in need, and for sacramental actions that serve as conduits for the grace of God. In these ways, the earth is sanctified, and things created by human hands become items and places of spiritual value.

The idea, again, is not restricted to Catholicism. A similar understanding was reflected in a collection of essays published a few years ago titled *Why Place Matters*, which strove to swim "against the principal currents" of our cosmopolitan, digital, disembodied times. For "whether we like it or not, we are corporeal beings, grounded in the particular, in the finite conditions of our embodiment, our creatureliness."[4] *A Catholic Pilgrimage through American History* is grounded in the idea that "place still does matter."

Thus, certain places acquire profound meaning. They have been sanctified by divine grace channeled through human activity. Usually this human action involves sacrifice of some kind: labor, charity, or—frequently—the spilling of blood. This makes etymological sense, because the word *sacrifice* comprises the Latin roots *sacer* and *facio*: to make sacred. (The same sensibility accounts for Catholic reverence toward a church altar as the place where the Holy Sacrifice of the Mass is enacted every day.) Many Americans have experienced the movement of spirit elicited by physical presence at national landmarks: the sting of tragedy at the battlefields of Gettysburg; humbling awe at the majestic display of nature in the Grand Canyon; anger and sadness at the 9/11 memorial in New York. How much more should American Catholics take notice of those places that witnessed extraordinary moments in the ongoing saga of salvation, the Church's history in our nation?

As Pope Benedict XVI said in an address at Santiago de Compostela,

> To go on pilgrimage is not simply to visit a place to admire
> its treasures of nature, art or history. To go on pilgrimage
> really means to step out of ourselves in order to encounter
> God where he has revealed himself, where his grace has

> shone with particular splendor and produced rich fruits of
> conversion and holiness among those who believe.[5]

Not every place in this book is a pilgrimage site in the way Benedict describes, but all have significance as markers of the American Catholic experience. I have included addresses to help you locate a central point of the site being described in each chapter. Typically there are several other points of interest located near these central sites. There are also hundreds more such places in this country that are not detailed in this book, equally rich in meaning and history. There's no substitute for being there bodily, and I hope that you will find the opportunity to visit one or more of them. (Perhaps it can be fit into a family vacation . . .) But if physical presence is impossible, reading about these places might at least provide some vicarious benefit. Either way, happy travels!

1.

The First Parish of an Emerging Nation

Cathedral Basilica of St. Augustine
38 Cathedral Place
St. Augustine, Florida 32084

*Did you know that the state of Florida
is named after the Feast of Easter?*

As every schoolchild used to know, "In 1492, Columbus sailed the ocean blue." The Italian-born explorer, sailing under the banner of Their Catholic Majesties Ferdinand and Isabella of Spain, got his first glimpse of the New World in the islands of the Caribbean. His last stop on that maiden voyage was Hispaniola (today, Haiti and the Dominican Republic), where his flagship, the *Santa Maria*, ran aground.

Some six hundred miles northwest of Hispaniola was an enormous peninsula jutting out from the American mainland. Spanish explorers may have touched land in Florida as early as 1502. The first official expedition to the future state was directed by Juan Ponce de León, to whom the Crown had granted a charter to explore and settle a purported island to the north of the Bahamas. He arrived at the Atlantic coast of North America during Easter Week, known as the Feast of Flowers. This new land—which turned out not to be an island after all—was thus called Pascua Florida (Easter Flower), or simply Florida.

Forming a Catholic Parish

Fifty years after Ponce de León's explorations, the Spanish decided to colonize east Florida in an attempt to keep French aspirations in the region at bay. The first European colonists in Florida had been a sect of French Calvinists, called Huguenots, whose faith was persecuted in their home country and who thus sought a new beginning and religious freedom in the New World. When King Philip II of Spain learned of the colony, he was determined for reasons of both state and church to drive the French Calvinists out of Florida.

Pedro Menéndez de Avilés led the initial expedition in 1565, which expelled the Huguenots from their fort on the St. John's River and planted the settlement named after St. Augustine, on whose feast day (August 28) the fleet had sighted the Florida coast. The Spanish implemented their usual model for settlement, with religious missionaries accompanied by civil authorities. Diocesan priests immediately founded a mission, Nombre de Dios, the first Catholic parish within the bounds of what would eventually become the United States. The Church community was formally founded on September 8, the Feast of the Nativity of Mary. Fr. Francisco López de Mendoza Grajales erected a cross, and all of the Spanish, led by General Menéndez, venerated it, after which the priest offered Mass dedicating the new colony to God.

Jesuits staffed the earliest missions in Florida and built St. Augustine's first church building, but they soon abandoned the field in the face of intense opposition from the native inhabitants. Franciscans, arriving in 1578, faced the same obstacles as had the Jesuits. Initial efforts to extend the missions across Florida and north into Georgia and the Carolinas ended in violence and retreat but gained for the American Church some of its earliest martyrs.

In typical Spanish fashion, the heart of St. Augustine was its central plaza, anchored by a church and government buildings. The first church, Nuestra Señora de los Remedios, was built of wood planks, though its interior was "furnished richly enough with an ornate, painted retablo, costly altar hangings, a gilded cross and candlesticks, and bright-colored banners." Unfortunately, this humble yet dignified edifice was short-lived, burned down in a raid by Sir Francis Drake, the most famous privateer in English history. His raid was but one episode in a centuries-long battle between England and Spain for control of the Caribbean and its surroundings.[1]

In 1597, Fr. Ricardo Artur (or Richard Arthur) arrived to take up the pastorate of St. Augustine, becoming the first of many Ireland-born priests to minister to the Church in America. Exactly how Artur came into the service of Spain is unclear; possibly he had been part of the Irish "Wild Geese" brigade that fought in the Spanish-Dutch wars of the sixteenth century.

A second church at St. Augustine also burned to the ground in 1599, although the 1594 records of the first baptism and marriage survived, making them the oldest extant written documents in the Americas north of Mexico. Parishioners decided to build the third church with an eye to durability. It lasted ninety-five years as the hub of the colony's activity. The number of baptisms recorded in the parish rose steadily from seven in 1596 to more than one hundred in 1761. Franciscans and other missionaries started to succeed among the local inhabitants as well. By the late seventeenth century there were more than twenty-five thousand Native American Christians attached to more than thirty missions in Florida. Earlier in the century, in yet another first, the nearby chapel of Nuestra Señora de La Leche y Buen Parto (Our Lady of the Milk and Happy Delivery) was built, making it the first Marian shrine within what would become the United States.

"Nearly every aspect of life in colonial St. Augustine," the historian Kathleen Deagan writes, "like that in all New World Spanish colonies, was influenced by the Catholic Church." The Church provided a source of unity in what gradually became a "melting pot of ethnic groups" that were "loosely bound together by a common Catholic faith, Castilian tongue, and the political dominion of the Spanish Crown." There were *peninsulares* (Spanish from various provinces of the Iberian Peninsula), *criollos* (those of Spanish/Indian mixed ancestry), full-blooded Native Americans, and *morenos* (Africans from the Antilles or escaped from the Carolinas). Beginning in the 1680s, there were also English, who were permitted to settle in the region. A 1696 journal reported an encounter with an Englishman married to a Spanish woman; they were parents of seven children.

Colonial St. Augustine was never profitable for Spain. It was neither rich in precious metals nor agriculturally promising (though the Spanish did introduce thriving orange and fig trees). Instead, according to Deagan, military concerns and the presence of the Franciscan missions "remained the primary reason for St. Augustine's existence." The year 1675 marked the apogee of Spanish Florida, with St. Augustine anchoring a mission chain that stretched across the peninsula into what is today the Florida panhandle. But Catholicism in St. Augustine faced grim days ahead.

An English Interlude at St. Augustine

The English again proved to be the bane of St. Augustine's Catholics. By 1700, the flourishing British colonies just to the north set their sights on the Spanish stronghold of Florida. James Moore led a sortie from South Carolina with the object of capturing St. Augustine. The expedition failed, but in the melee the town's church was once again reduced to ashes.

Fr. Agustín Ponce de León—namesake of both the parish and the heralded explorer—was serving a mission near St. Augustine when it was raided by the English and their Creek allies in 1705. Learning of the capture of two of his native altar boys, the Franciscan friar pursued the captors and offered himself in place of the young Christians. The raiders killed the boys and the priest, adding three more names to the long list of Florida's martyrs.[2]

In 1740, James Oglethorpe, a member of the British Parliament and the founder of the Georgia colony (see chapter 26), led another assault, this time from Georgia. His force laid siege to St. Augustine for a month but withdrew in mid-July after the British navy failed to sustain its blockade.

Spain managed to keep hold of Florida through the first half of the eighteenth century by protecting its colony from behind the bulwarks of the Castillo San Marcos, the fort that guards the Atlantic approach to St. Augustine. The fortification was constructed in the late seventeenth century and, as one description put it, "has dominated the town ever since." Log and earth walls extended from the fort to encompass the city. But the Spanish Empire was waning, and funds could not be spared for rebuilding the church. Mass was said in makeshift locations until 1763, when control of St. Augustine finally passed into British hands. Within a year, all the priests had abandoned Florida for Cuba and there were few Catholics left in the already historic parish of St. Augustine.

There is one peculiar Catholic twist to this British interlude. After the English took control of Florida, a Scottish aristocrat was given a land grant south of St. Augustine and initiated a colonial venture to raise cotton and olives. To populate his colony, Andrew Turnbull recruited a hundred Italian men, who gathered at the Mediterranean island of Minorca to prepare for their transatlantic expedition. In the meantime, many found wives among the Minorcans, and so, to work his Florida farms, Turnbull ended up with dozens of budding Catholic families, who had brought along with them a Minorcan priest. In 1777, Turnbull's little colony failed, and the band of Catholics, led by their pastor, settled in St. Augustine, bringing Catholicism back to the First Parish. The American poet William Cullen Bryant, visiting St. Augustine in 1843, found this group's ethnic customs still in evidence, including an Easter procession in honor of the Virgin Mary, accompanied by a hymn sung in a Minorcan dialect.

A New Church, A New Country

By the time the Minorcan immigrants arrived, St. Augustine had become a refuge of another sort. Loyalists from the British colonies to the north, finding life intolerable among their patriot neighbors as the strife of the American Revolution intensified, fled south to the English outpost. Most of them didn't stay long. As part of the settlement of the Treaty of Paris ending the American Revolution in 1783, Florida was returned to Spanish control. The Tory refugees then migrated again.

It was during this second and final Spanish period that plans were made for the construction of a monumental edifice to serve the Catholics of Florida. The façade of the new church was reminiscent of the mission style that dominates the American Southwest, but it also incorporated neoclassical elements such as its pediment resting on Doric columns. The walls were made of coquina—a local masonry standby composed of a sedimentary rock formed from seashells. The building was completed in 1797.

At about this time, a young boy arrived in Florida from Cuba, accompanying his father, a Spanish military officer. Félix Varela spent eight years in St. Augustine before returning to Cuba to continue his education. He went on to an illustrious career as a priest, professor, and advocate for Cuban independence. Driven out of Cuba, he labored as a parish priest and diocesan official in New York (where he spent time at Old St. Peter's; see chapter 6) before retiring to St. Augustine, where he assisted at the First Parish until his death in 1853.

As Spain's empire continued to recede during the nineteenth century, the maintenance of the Florida outpost became untenable. American "filibusters"—freelance fighters trying to expand US control in Spanish America—invaded Florida in 1812, sparking the "Patriot War." In St. Augustine, a diverse force of Hispanic, Black, and mixed-race defenders refused to surrender. But Florida's destiny was to be American, not Spanish. The Adams-Onís Treaty of 1819 ceded the colony to the US and also created a class of free Blacks in the Deep South by guaranteeing all former Spanish subjects the full rights of American citizenship.

The transfer of Spanish territory to the United States ushered in yet another difficult period for St. Augustine Catholicism. Insisting that the property had been the possession of the Spanish Crown rather than the Church, American officials confiscated Catholic holdings in Florida, including the churches of St. Augustine and Mission Nombre de Dios. Worse yet, the vulnerable Catholics of the region were bereft of episcopal leadership, as it was not immediately clear which bishop should now have authority over what had been part of the Archdiocese of Havana.

Bishop John England of Charleston took Florida Catholics under his wing while the situation was sorted out. The articulate and well-respected Bishop England fired off a missive to President James Monroe asserting the property rights of St. Augustine's Catholics under American law. The administration ruled in favor of the Church, Congress confirmed the decision, and St. Augustine's Catholics were once again in possession of their own church.[3]

Secession and Beyond

In 1845, Florida became the twenty-seventh state in the Union. The days of Catholic dominance under Spanish rule were long past. By 1850 Protestant churches in the state outnumbered Catholic ones by a ratio of more than thirty to one. St. Augustine, the former capital of an imperial district, had been superseded by other Florida cities. It was now a backwater, described by an 1858 observer as "dilapidated in appearance, with the stillness of desolation hanging over it." Then, just sixteen years after statehood, Florida withdrew from the Union and joined the Confederate States of America.

The opinions of southern Catholics, including priests and bishops, on matters such as slavery and secession generally mirrored those of the non-Catholic majority. One prelude to secession was an eloquent sermon delivered in the Church of St. Augustine on January 4, 1861. The preacher was Augustin Verot, vicar apostolic of Florida. Bishop Verot began by citing the Church Father St. Augustine to make the point that a nation's prosperity and success depend on its virtue and that an unjust nation is sure to founder. Verot identified slavery as the cause of the strife threatening to destroy the Union, but his aim was not to condemn slavery. Finding support in scripture, natural law, and even Church teaching for the institution of slavery, Verot instead chastised abolitionists, calling them "fanatical preachers whose only object is to inflame the wicked passions of their hearers." Northern abolitionists were further tainted, Verot observed, by their association with Know-Nothingism (of the type that cast the pope's stone into the Potomac; see chapter 13).

Yet Verot was no crass apologist for slavery. He went on to enumerate the "wrongs which the South ought to acknowledge and confess." If slavery in theory enjoyed the sanction of natural law (in the bishop's view), slavery in practice was often a violation of human dignity. Citing

Pope Gregory XVI, Verot condemned the slave trade and similarly decried the violation of the rights of free Blacks (often former slaves) as well as slaveholders' abuse of slave women, failure to respect the integrity of slave families, and indifference to the religious welfare of enslaved persons.

As historian Frank Marotti points out, Verot faced a difficult dilemma. Recent papal teaching and the fact that many of the area's slaves were Catholic favored a strong stand against slavery. But a thundering denunciation of slavery risked raising the ire of the dominant white, Protestant population. The Minorcans still made up a sizable portion of St. Augustine's parishioners, and identifying the Church too closely with slave rights would make "this already suspect Hispanic population less 'Southern' and less 'white.'"

Yet Verot's attempt to split the difference between North and South was destined to fail. While he was preaching in St. Augustine, delegates from around the state were deliberating in Tallahassee; six days later they voted to secede from the United States.

In March 1862, Union gunboats appeared off the coast of north Florida. The news arrived at the Church of St. Augustine during Mass as a handwritten note—"The Yankees are landing"—and circulated rapidly. Heedless of the priest's protests, the worshippers rushed out of church to grab their belongings and flee the city. Federal troops landed at St. Augustine the next day, and the city remained under Northern control for the duration of the war. The city's early discomfiture may have saved its historic church: several other Florida Catholic churches were sacked and burned by Union troops on their rampage through the South as the war drew to a close.

Shortly after the state was accepted back into the Union following the Civil War, St. Augustine became the official seat of Florida Catholicism. Verot, who had in the meantime been appointed bishop of Savannah, Georgia, was selected as the inaugural bishop of the Diocese of St. Augustine in March of 1870. The Church of St. Augustine was now a cathedral.

Fire, that perennial terror, struck again in 1887, but the coquina skeleton survived, and the church was restored and expanded. The

Standard Oil magnate Henry Flagler, who was responsible for developing Florida's east coast, provided major funding. James Renwick, the architect of the new St. Patrick's Cathedral in New York, was enlisted to oversee the renovation, which added the six-story bell tower as well as the transept that gives the church its cruciform shape.[4]

The Gilded Age boom reflected in Flagler's largesse was but the first in a succession of waves of economic prosperity and massive immigration from Europe, Latin America, and northern states. The Catholic Church expanded commensurately. The Diocese of St. Augustine was gradually partitioned, and today Florida is home to seven dioceses.

St. Augustine, with its cathedral, its fortress, and its sparkling beach, became a tourist attraction. Even in its dark days in the nineteenth century, "Moss-grown and shattered," historian George Fairbanks wrote, it appealed to "our instinctive feelings of reverence for antiquity." More than 150 years later, that sense of antiquity has only intensified. Millions of visitors each year connect with the rich history of La Florida by ambling along the cobblestone streets of "America's Ancient City."

In the midst of it all, through many highs and lows, the First Parish has endured. In 1976, in recognition of its historic significance, the cathedral was granted minor basilica status by Pope St. Paul VI. This church and its predecessors have witnessed the passage of a succession of characters: brown-robed Franciscan friars, mail-shirted Spanish soldiers, blue-coated Union troopers, short-panted American vacationers. Heaven only knows what's in store for the future of Florida Catholicism, but it's a safe bet that the Basilica of St. Augustine will be at its heart.

Sources

Barnes, Mark R. "Cathedral of St. Augustine: Taking Another Look." *El Escribano: The St. Augustine Journal of History* (2008): 48–85, npshistory.com/publications/nhl/st-augustine-cathedral.pdf.

Deagan, Kathleen, ed. *America's Ancient City: Spanish St. Augustine, 1565–1763.* New York: Garland, 1991.

_____. *Spanish St. Augustine: The Archaeology of a Colonial Creole Community*. New York: Academic Press, 1983.

Fairbanks, George F. *The History and Antiquities of the City of St. Augustine, Florida*. New York: Charles B. Norton, 1858.

Gannon, Michael V. *The Cross in the Sand: The Early Catholic Church in Florida, 1513–1870*. Gainesville: University of Florida Press, 1965.

"Historical Timeline." Diocese of St. Augustine, www.dosafl.com/timeline.

Marotti, Frank. *The Cana Sanctuary: History, Diplomacy, and Black Catholic Marriage in Antebellum St. Augustine, Florida*. Tuscaloosa: University of Alabama Press, 2012.

"The Martyrs of La Florida." Martyrs of La Florida Missions, martyrsoflafloridamissions.org/martyrs.

Milanich, Jerald T., and Charles Hudson. *Hernando de Soto and the Indians of Florida*. Gainesville: University Press of Florida/Florida Museum of Natural History, 1993.

"Our Story." Shrine of Our Lady of La Leche, missionandshrine.org/our-story/.

They Might Be Saints: The Martyrs of La Florida. Film. EWTN, 2018.

Verot, The Right Reverend A. [Augustine]. *Slavery & Abolitionism, Being the Substance of a Sermon Preached in the Church of St. Augustine, Florida, on the 4th Day of January, 1861*. New Orleans: Catholic Propagator Office, 1861.

Vollbrecht, John L. *St. Augustine's Historical Heritage as Seen Today*. St. Augustine: J. Carver Harris, 1952.

2.

The Catholic Plymouth Rock

Brick Chapel of 1667
18751 Hogaboom Lane
St. Mary's City, Maryland 20686

Did you know that in the thirteen American colonies, the first law granting religious freedom was passed in Maryland, the only Catholic colony?

Barbados, St. Lucia, Montserrat, Nevis. It sounds like the itinerary of a Caribbean cruise, and in a way it was. But the ship was made of wood, there weren't any all-you-can-eat buffets, and the entertainment consisted of tales the passengers shared with one another. It was 1634, and the first Catholic settlers of British North America were on their way, destined for the brand-new colony of Maryland.

Two sailing vessels, the *Ark* and the *Dove*, both departed the Isle of Wight off England's western coast on St. Cecilia's Day, November 22, 1633. A few days into the journey, the larger merchant ship, the *Ark*, was separated from the little pinnace, and the colonists aboard the *Ark* feared that the *Dove* had perished in a storm.[1] In January 1634, while the *Ark* was berthed in Barbados, the *Dove* suddenly appeared! She had weathered the storm in Plymouth and then set out again for

America. Together the ships traveled on to the north, passing by the Caribbean islands and arriving in Chesapeake Bay in March.

Entering the Potomac

Aboard the *Ark* were the pioneers of the colony of Maryland, including George and Leonard Calvert, and at least one Jesuit priest, Fr. Andrew White. The Calvert brothers were grandsons of George Calvert, the first Lord Baltimore, who had reverted to the Catholicism of his ancestors in part through the influence of Fr. White.[2] The elder George Calvert sought the king's approval for the founding of a colony that would not enforce the establishment of the Church of England and thereby steer clear of the religious conflict that plagued the mother country—and, incidentally, provide a hospitable environment for Catholics.

George's son Cecil finally obtained a charter from King Charles I, who granted the second Lord Baltimore a tract of land on the Atlantic coast between the colony of Virginia to the south and the Dutch settlement of New Amsterdam to the north. When Charles proposed to Cecil Calvert that the colony be named "Mariana" in honor of the king's wife, Henriette Marie, Calvert demurred. He reminded Charles that the famous Spanish Jesuit theorist with a similar name, Juan de Mariana, had written a treatise that was widely perceived to justify rebellion against monarchies. The pair settled on "Maryland" instead.

Fr. Andrew White had been banished from England in the anti-Catholic backlash caused by the Gunpowder Plot—the botched 1605 assassination conspiracy against King James I[3]—but then returned to continue his clandestine ministry. He accepted the Calverts' invitation to provide spiritual support to the new colony. White explained the primary purpose of the colony in his 1633 tract describing the venture: "First and chiefly, to convey into the said land and neighboring parts the light of the Gospel and of the truth."

Fr. White and the Calverts were obliged to chart a careful course through the treacherous religious waters of seventeenth-century Britain. When the *Ark* and *Dove* set sail, all passengers on board were administered the Oath of Allegiance, a measure enacted by the king in 1606, following the Gunpowder Plot. Catholics disagreed among themselves as to whether the oath could be legitimately taken. To circumvent the requirement, after the ships publicly departed, they made an unofficial stop at the Isle of Wight to pick up the Jesuit and perhaps other Catholic settlers.[4] They then continued their journey across the Atlantic, bearing the seeds of an experiment in religious pluralism.

When the ships reached a small island a short way up the mouth of the Potomac River, they called it St. Clement. There the passengers debarked, and Fr. White presided over the first Mass ever celebrated in British North America. It was March 25, 1634, the Feast of the Annunciation. Following the Mass, White recounted later, the group gathered around a "great cross which we had hewn from a tree" and "erected it as a trophy to Christ the Savior, while the litany of the holy cross was chanted humbly on the bended knees, with great emotion of soul." Only a minority of the new colonists were Catholic, but all joined in giving thanks for reaching their destination. For Catholics, the occasion held special significance. Even as the annunciation marked the proclamation of a birth that would change the history of the world by bringing God to earth, the English Catholics kneeling on the soil of St. Clement's Island envisioned a new birth of freedom in America—a place where Catholics might enjoy the full rights of citizenship.

English Anti-Catholicism in Maryland

Ever since King Henry VIII divorced Catherine of Aragon and the English Reformation began, Catholics and Protestants in the British Isles had been at loggerheads. Both sides discriminated against, persecuted, and sometimes even killed their religious counterparts, but Catholics had the worst of it. Despite a brief renewal of Catholic rule under Queen Mary I ("Bloody Mary") and the relative tolerance of the seventeenth-century monarchs James and Charles, Catholics by and large lived as second-class citizens. Under Elizabeth I, the situation grew worse. Dozens of Andrew White's predecessor Jesuits and other priests were martyred under the queen's authority.

Maryland represented a new beginning. Leonard Calvert, the first governor, immediately instituted religious liberty. The motivations of the Calverts are difficult to ascertain fully because of a dearth of sources—either they didn't write about their reasons or those writings didn't survive. Some historians maintain that their apparently noble experiment in religious freedom owed more to self-interest than to any high ideals of toleration. Catholics were a minority in Maryland from the beginning and resided there at the whim of the British monarch and Parliament back in London. The earliest surviving census records indicate a Catholic population representing just 10 percent of the colony's white inhabitants, though that portion rises to more than 30 percent in places such as St. Mary's County. Cecil's instructions to Leonard included an admonition that all Catholic activities be done "as privately as they may be" and that Catholics should be "silent upon all occasions of discourse concerning matters of religion." If Catholics were to be able to worship, to participate in public affairs, and to hold political office in Maryland, religious toleration and Catholic deference had to be the ordering principles of the colony.

Others point out that the Calverts' actions demonstrate a real commitment to freedom of conscience. They exploited the omission of a church-establishment clause in the colony's charter to push for a maximum of religious freedom. During drafting of the colony's 1649 Act Concerning Religion, Cecil Calvert advocated language that would grant freedom in religious matters to all Christians and Jews, but Protestants in control of the legislature passed a more restrictive version that excluded both Jews and non-Trinitarian Christians (the "Unitarians" of the day). Throughout his proprietorship, Cecil championed "liberty of conscience" for the settlers of his colony.

The Birth of Maryland

A few days after the Annunciation Mass on St. Clement's Island, the colonists crossed over to the mainland, bought thirty miles of river-front property from the local chief in exchange for some tools, and founded the first permanent settlement in Maryland, St. Mary's, on a bluff overlooking the river that would later go by the same name.[5] St. Mary's City was the capital of the colony until 1694. The Jesuit missionary White was heartened by the colony's prospects. The rich soil, thick woods, and abundant wildlife led him to conclude that "there is not wanting to the region whatever may serve for commerce or pleasure."

During the 1630s, Catholics, although a minority, were proportionately overrepresented among the wealthy landowners who exerted political influence in the colony. The Calverts established a manorial system, the arrangement that had permitted English Catholic gentry to preserve the practice of their faith in post-Reformation England by hosting priests and sacraments in their private chapels. Fr. White enjoyed some evangelistic success among the native population, baptizing a Piscataway chief into Christianity in 1640 and converting many other Indigenous people over the course of the decade that he spent in Maryland. Several chapels were built, and the Catholic settlers practiced their faith publicly—a unique privilege for Catholic subjects of the English Crown in the seventeenth century.

Unfortunately, this early experiment in religious freedom did not last. Just ten years into the colony's life, strife developed between Maryland and the neighboring colony of Virginia. It was on the surface a commercial dispute, but it became a colonial version of the religious and political conflict of the English Civil War—the struggle between "Roundheads" and "Cavaliers" that toppled the monarchy and brought Oliver Cromwell to power. Leonard Calvert expelled from Maryland a Virginia merchant, Richard Ingle, who had established a trading post without Calvert's permission. Ingle, operating with a letter of marque issued by the British Parliament against royalists and accompanied by British soldiers, retaliated by attacking St. Mary's, which he took and set afire. Ingle's band abducted Fr. White and deported him to England, where, unlike Maryland, it was illegal for Catholic priests to minister.[6] White having already been banished once, this repeat infraction became a capital crime. The Jesuit successfully argued that he had been brought into Britain against his will and thus escaped the death penalty. He was unable to gain permission to return to Maryland, however, and died in England in 1656.[7]

Calvert partisans recaptured the city in 1647, and the Maryland Assembly passed a Toleration act two years later, which ushered in another period of peace. Catholic freedom in the colony was decisively curtailed, however, following the enthronement of William and Mary in England in the aftermath of the Glorious Revolution of 1688. When Maryland Protestants revolted against the Calverts, the king and queen stripped the Calvert family of their authority and put the colony in the hands of a Protestant governor. Catholics lost the rights to vote and to worship in public. The capital of Maryland was moved from St. Mary's to Annapolis, and anti-Catholicism became part and parcel of the transatlantic British Empire. "By the mid-eighteenth century," the historian Francis Cogliano writes, "it was impossible for Englishmen in Britain or America to divorce anti-popery from their notion of what it was to be English."

Despite the failure of religious freedom in Maryland, British Catholics had made a beginning in the colonies, and the faith would endure. Fr. White's baptism of the *tayac* Kittamaquund inaugurated the conversion of the entire Piscataway tribe to Catholicism. A twenty-first-century American prelate called it "the moment when the Catholic faith became part of the New World." Descendants of those seventeenth-century Piscataway still worship at St. Mary's parish in Prince George's County—a place once known as the "Piscataway Church."

The Maryland-based Carroll family would give to America one of its wealthiest and most enthusiastic patriots, Charles, as well as its first Catholic bishop, John. When Charles Carroll passed away in 1832 at the age of ninety-five, President Andrew Jackson shut down the federal government; the only other Revolutionary-era hero so honored had been George Washington. John Carroll, the first bishop of Baltimore, founded the first Catholic college at Georgetown, established the country's first Catholic seminary—St. Mary's in Baltimore—and began construction of the nation's first Catholic cathedral.

A Catholic Past Unearthed

In 1790, Pennsylvania Founding Father James Wilson rued the "ungracious silence" that characterized the treatment of the Calverts' role in the creation of the American nation—especially their contribution to the ideal of religious freedom. History textbooks in the centuries since have not done much to rectify that neglect, but changes are afoot. In recent decades, St. Mary's has begun recovering and displaying its significance as the original site of Catholic settlement in the British colonies and as the first capital of Maryland. A replica of the *Dove* can be explored at a dock on the river near the town center. The site of Leonard Calvert's home has been excavated.

The brick, cruciform foundation of the long-lost "Brick Chapel of 1667," which had been one of the principal buildings of the seventeenth-century town, was first located in 1938. Later in the century, extensive historical and archaeological research revealed more details. Three coffins were discovered at the site and determined to be Phillip (d. 1682), the youngest son of George Calvert (Lord Baltimore), Phillip's wife, and an unknown child. Ground-penetrating radar detected some five hundred other graves around the chapel. Reconstruction of the chapel commenced in 2002 and proceeded over the next five years. Today, the cross once again sits atop the tile roof of the brick chapel, a testament to the Jesuits and their congregants who brought the faith to the thirteen colonies.

St. Mary's City is the Jamestown or Plymouth Rock for American Catholics—the place where Catholic forebears landed in the New World and planted a colony in the face of manifold challenges. The *Ark* was our *Mayflower*, the ship that brought a group of brave adventurers seeking freedom and opportunity.

Sources

Cogliano, Francis D. *No King, No Popery: Anti-Catholicism in Revolutionary New England*. Westport, CT. Greenwood Press, 1995.

Curran, Robert Emmett. *Papist Devils: Catholics in British North America, 1574–1783*. Washington, DC: Catholic University of America Press, 2014.

Farrelly, Maura Jane. *Anti-Catholicism in America, 1620–1860*. Cambridge: Cambridge University Press, 2018.

_____. *Papist Patriots: The Making of an American Catholic Identity*. New York: Oxford University Press, 2012.

Gerber, Scott D. "Law and Catholicism in Colonial Maryland." *Catholic Historical Review* 103 (Summer 2017): 465–90.

Historic St. Mary's City. hsmcdigshistory.org/.

Hoffman, Ronald, with Sally D. Mason. *Princes of Ireland, Planters of Maryland: A Carroll Saga, 1500–1782.* Chapel Hill: University of North Carolina Press, 2000.

Ives, J. Moss. *The* Ark *and the* Dove: *The Beginning of Civil and Religious Liberties in America.* London: Longmans, Green, 1936.

Krugler, John D. *English and Catholic: The Lords Baltimore in the Seventeenth Century.* Baltimore: Johns Hopkins University Press, 2004.

Sharpe, James. *Remember, Remember: A Cultural History of Guy Fawkes Day.* Cambridge, MA: Harvard University Press, 2005.

Starr, Kevin. *Continental Ambitions: Roman Catholics in North America: The Colonial Experience.* San Francisco: Ignatius Press, 2016.

Sutto, Antoinette. *Loyal Protestants and Dangerous Papists: Maryland and the Politics of Religion in the English Atlantic, 1630–1690.* Charlottesville: University of Virginia Press, 2015.

Szczepanowski, Richard. "New Faith in the New World." *Catholic Standard,* July 16, 2015.

White, Andrew. *A Relation of the Colony of the Lord Baron of Baltimore in Maryland* (1847), rpr. in *American History Told by Contemporaries.* Vol. 1, ed. Albert Bushnell Hart, 252–57. New York: Macmillan, 1898.

3.

The Abenaki Tribe and Fr. Râle's War

Sébastien Râle Memorial
470 Father Rasle Road
Madison, Maine 04950

Did you know that Harvard University's library contains the original Abenaki dictionary created by the Jesuit missionary Sébastien Râle in the early 1700s?

About fifteen miles off of Interstate 95 as it tracks northeast across the state of Maine is the town of Norridgewock. The area used to be the home of the Abenaki tribe, which was by the early eighteenth century almost entirely Christian. Nearby is a monument marking the site of the "first Native American school in the region now known as the state of Maine." In what is now the neighboring town of Madison stands a modest granite obelisk surmounted by an iron cross. Its inscription in Latin reads, in part: "Rev. Sebastian Rasle . . . . a true apostle in the faith and love of Christ among the Abenakis." The monument was erected in 1833 and dedicated before a crowd of five thousand by Bishop Benedict Joseph Fenwick, who came from Boston for the occasion. One hundred and nine years before this event, American colonists made the same trek from Boston and murdered Fr. Râle, the founder of the Abenaki school.

Missions to Maine

The conversion of the Native Americans in this part of the world was the ambitious project of the Jesuit and Recollect fathers who served in New France from the time of Sts. Isaac Jogues, Jean de Brébeuf, and their companions—collectively known as the North American Martyrs. More than three hundred Jesuits came from France during the seventeenth and eighteenth centuries to labor in the North American vineyard. Jogues didn't see much fruit from his efforts during his lifetime, but some of the tribes were indeed receptive to the Gospel, and even among the more intractable, such as the Mohawks, there were spectacular successes such as St. Kateri Tekakwitha. The Abenakis, one of the receptive tribes, were evangelized over the course of the seventeenth century by Jesuit missionaries.

Not unlike the Franciscan friars in California and Florida, who were emissaries of both Christianity and the Spanish Crown, the Jesuits of New France were not only evangelists for the Catholic faith but also "enthusiastic, enterprising empire-builders for the Bourbon state." These missionaries were, as one recent historian put it, "planted knee-deep in an untidy world of politics, social pressures, and war." This muddy reality could be seen clearly in the life—and especially the death—of Fr. Sébastien Râle.

The Jesuits were present in what would become the state of Maine as early as 1611, when Fr. Pierre Biard explored the Kennebec River and offered Mass at its mouth on the Gulf of Maine. A harbinger of the conflict to come, the earliest Jesuit mission was destroyed by English colonists from Virginia, and a Jesuit brother was killed in the attack. Protestant hostility was a strong deterrent to Catholic missions all along the Eastern Seaboard.

The Leadership of Sébastien Râle

The Jesuits resumed their mission in Maine in the 1630s. The respected "black robe" of the Abenakis in the 1700s was Sébastien Râle, a French native who had come to the New World in 1689. After an initial post in an Abenaki village near Quebec, Râle worked among the Illinois tribe at Kaskaskia on the Mississippi River. In 1694, he returned to minister to the Abenakis, this time at a mission already established on the Kennebec River, at what is now the town of Norridgewock. The Catholic community there was the fruit of the evangelization of an Algonquin catechist, who spread the Gospel among the amenable Abenakis. By the time Râle's predecessor, Fr. Gabriel Druillettes, finished his stint there in 1652, "all, or nearly all were Christians."

The sporadic nature of priestly ministry and the tumult of ongoing Native American and colonial battles, however, prevented the flourishing of a stable Christian community. It was Fr. Druillettes who had been commissioned a few years earlier by the French authorities in Quebec to seek an alliance with New England against the Iroquois tribes who had been the scourge of French Canada and her Indian friends (including the Abenakis). Druillettes's diplomatic mission to Boston and New Haven failed. The Puritans had no wish to incite the hostility of the powerful Iroquois. Had it succeeded, the fate of Fr. Râle would likely have been different.

Râle aimed to stabilize the native Christian community by establishing a permanent home there. The Jesuit priest became a fixture in the Abenaki tribe. He strove mightily to learn their language, whose dissimilarity to European tongues presented a formidable challenge. In such a situation, it was important to keep a sense of humor. "Not being accustomed to the trick of their guttural sounds," he noted in one of his letters, he sometimes repeated words inaccurately and "thereby gave them cause for laughter."

Fr. Râle adapted his ministry to the rhythms of Abenaki life, and the people in turn made accommodations to enable the practice of their faith. He wrote of the annual Abenaki excursion to the seashore, "where they pass some months in hunting the ducks, bustards, and birds which are found there in large numbers." During this period, he reported, "they build on an island a church which they cover with bark, and near it they erect a little cabin for my residence." Grateful for this kindness, he ministered to the tribe at their seasonal hunting ground: "I take care to transport thither a part of our ornaments, and the service is performed with the . . . same crowds of people as at the village."

The extent of Fr. Râle's familiarity with Abenaki life may be judged by the thoroughness of the Abenaki dictionary he compiled with diligence over the course of several years. Fr. Râle did not disdain to record and translate "indecent words"—important for a confessor, after all—that required delicate treatment in a dictionary that might be made public. So, he employed a venerable tactic among learned Catholic confessors, describing the meaning of such words and phrases using Latin instead of the vernacular French.

Unfortunately, Fr. Râle and his congregation would not be left in peace to laugh, study, hunt, and pray. The Abenakis were one important piece on the chessboard of European imperialism in North America, and their pastor would not survive the game.

France and Britain at Odds over Maine

Maine was disputed territory in the eighteenth century. The descendants of the Pilgrims and Puritans in Massachusetts were pushing north, while the allies of New France sought to advance their sphere of influence among the Indigenous peoples on New England's northern frontier. Politics, economics, and religion all played roles in this conflict. At the same time that the kings of England and France vied for supremacy in Europe, the two empires' fur companies sought to dominate the lucrative North American trade, and Protestant and Catholic missionaries spread different versions of the Gospel among the unchurched inhabitants of the continent.

In the various conflicts between England and France in North America, New Englanders suspected French priests, including Fr. Râle, of inciting Native Americans against the English. There is evidence for this in the testimony of some Abenakis, though Râle was accused of the opposite offense (indifference) by French officials. During Queen Anne's War (1702–1713), the Abenakis of Norridgewock joined with other French allies in fighting against the army and colonists of Britain. Again, the role of Fr. Râle is disputed. An English account claims that the Abenakis agreed to a treaty that sealed an alliance with the English, while Râle insisted that they rejected the British overture and remained neutral while promising to come to the defense of France in the event of war.

In any case, the Abenakis were soon involved in the conflict, raiding the New England frontier. Convinced of their disloyalty and the priest's nefarious influence, the British decided to deal with the Abenakis forcibly. A detachment of British soldiers attacked Norridgewock in 1705 and burned the village and its church. Râle had been warned in time. He fled into the woods and hid from his would-be assassins.

The Treaty of Utrecht in 1713 brought violence to a temporary end, but tension remained. Under the terms of the treaty—whether the Abenakis actually agreed to those terms is another disputed point—the English gained rights to tribal territory. Moreover, individual New Englanders bargained with tribal chiefs to purchase tracts of land.[1] Whatever the validity of these agreements, it is certain that colonists continued to advance into Maine, confident in their cause. As they did, Abenaki resistance grew.

Râle continued to lead the mission at Norridgewock and evidently urged the Abenakis to resist control by the English. He may have been motivated by genuine concern for the well-being of his flock; it was already clear that the future of native communities was threatened by colonial settlement, and he tried to dissuade the New England colonists from promoting the rum trade, which did enormous damage to the Indigenous people's way of life. He may have also been motivated by religious concerns; the practice of the Catholic faith was proscribed in the New England colonies and priests were entirely forbidden. Finally, he may have been motivated by patriotic sentiment; it was important for the French to hold Maine so as to prevent the English from overrunning Canada altogether (as eventually happened). Likely, his motivation was a mixture of all of these.

From the British perspective, meanwhile, such insubordination could not be tolerated so near their borders. Another attempt was made at eliminating Râle in 1722, but he again escaped into the wilderness. The soldiers managed to collect some booty, however. They confiscated the priest's three-volume Abenaki dictionary, written in his own hand.[2]

The Battle of Norridgewock

This incident was one of the early salvos in what is now known as "Dummer's War" or, sometimes, "Father Râle's War." As lieutenant governor of the Massachusetts colony, William Dummer oversaw the campaign. Râle's superior urged him to flee the dangerous scene and return to Quebec, but the missionary refused to leave. In August 1724, more than two hundred New England troops paddled by whaleboat from Fort Richmond in southern Maine up the Kennebec River to Norridgewock, determined to put an end to the Abenaki threat.

The Abenakis were outmanned and outgunned, and resistance was brief. The villagers scattered into the woods, leaving behind their homes and their church. Between twenty and thirty Indians died in the Battle of Norridgewock. Fr. Sébastien Râle was among the slain.

Râle's exact manner of death is disputed. One account says that he was killed in his cabin as he defended himself with a musket. In other reports, he selflessly drew attention to himself in an effort to give the villagers time to flee. Louise Ketchum Hunt, whose Abenaki ancestors were among the survivors of the attack, has recorded the tribe's oral tradition, which supports the latter version. Fr. Râle hurried to the center of the village, where a large cross stood, with arms raised in a gesture of peace, hoping to negotiate with the raiders. Seven village chiefs, alerted by the church bells and observing Râle, rushed to his side. The priest, the chiefs, and two altar servers were gunned down at the foot of the cross. The colonists harvested scalps from Râle and many of his flock, returning to Boston to collect the bounty attached to them. Surviving Abenakis rescued the seven-foot steel cross, erected by Râle when he arrived at Norridgewock, and carried it along as they fled north. Today it stands at St. Anne's Catholic Church in Old Town, Maine, on the Penobscot Indian Reservation.

The Maine Indians, forced to flee their ancient Kennebec River home after Râle's death, found shelter in French Canada. During the

American Revolution, they were granted some land by the state of Massachusetts (which controlled Maine). Resolutely true to their faith through it all, they were beneficiaries of the priestly exodus caused by the French Revolution: three French priests ministered to them in the 1790s, including Jean Louis Lefebvre de Cheverus, who would later become the first bishop of Boston. When Maine achieved statehood in 1820, it broke from its Puritan past by granting full religious freedom to Catholics, among whom were the Christian Abenakis who worshipped in the shadow of Fr. Râle's cross.

Râle's legacy was as divisive as his life. For some Abenakis and Catholic admirers, he is a hero and a martyr who gave everything for his beloved flock. Other Native Americans blame his intransigence as one of the causes of their destruction. There was even an unsubstantiated rumor that Râle had sold out his village to the English in exchange for a hat full of gold coins. To the British colonists he was a "bloody incendiary" who put allegiance to France above his calling as a Christian minister. A non-Catholic historian, who dismissed hagiographic accounts of Râle's life and death, nonetheless concluded that he was "an exceptionally able and devoted man, who spent his life in unselfish, hazardous work."

In 1808, Boston became one of the earliest dioceses of the United States, encompassing all of New England. Its second bishop was Benedict Joseph Fenwick, who, like Râle, was a Jesuit. A member of the Society of Jesus, so despised by the New England colonists, thus became the leader of the region's growing Catholic community. It was Fenwick who dedicated the memorial to Fr. Râle—a remarkable, provocative figure in life, death, and memory.

Sources

Clarke, William A., SJ. "The Church at Nanrantsouak: Sébastien Râle, SJ, and the Wabanaki of Maine's Kennebec River." *Catholic Historical Review* 92, no. 3 (July 2006): 225–51.

Connolly, Arthur T. *Fr. Sebastian Rasle*. Boston: New England Catholic Historical Society, 1906.

Eckstorm, Fannie Hardy. "The Attack on Norridgewock, 1724." *New England Quarterly* 7, no. 3 (Sept. 1934): 541–78.

Hunt, Louise Ketchum. *In the Shadow of the Steel Cross: The Massacre of Father Sebastién Râle, S.J. and the Indian Chiefs*. Phoenix: Amor Deus, 2015.

Lapomarda, Vincent A., SJ. "The Jesuit Heritage in Maine." Chap. 1 in *The Jesuit Heritage in New England*. Worcester, MA: Jesuits of Holy Cross College, 1977. crossworks.holycross.edu/nen-provhistory/6/.

Lucey, William Leo, SJ. *The Catholic Church in Maine*. Francestown, NH: Marshall Jones, 1957.

McShea, Bronwen. *Apostles of Empire: The Jesuits and New France*. Lincoln: University of Nebraska Press, 2019.

O'Neel, Brian. *150 North American Martyrs You Should Know*. Cincinnati: Servant, 2014.

Schuyler, H. C. "The Apostle of the Abnakis: Father Sebastian Rale, S.J. (1657–1724)." *Catholic Historical Review* 1, no. 2 (1915): 164–74.

Sprague, John Francis. *Sebastian Ralé: A Maine Tragedy of the Eighteenth Century*. Boston: Heintzemann Press, 1906.

4.

A Franciscan Adventure in Alta California

Mission San Diego de Alcalá
10818 San Diego Mission Road
San Diego, California 92108

*Did you know that major league
baseball's San Diego Padres are
named after Franciscan missionaries?*

Northeast of downtown San Diego, just across the interstate from the football stadium built in the 1960s, stands an adobe church, gleaming white in the brilliant sun that shines most of the time in this part of the country. To say that the church is built in the mission style isn't quite right—it was churches such as this that gave the mission style its name. The stadium used to be home to the Chargers—the city's professional football team until its move to Los Angeles in 2017—but the more pertinent team is the local major league baseball club, which also played there for a number of years. They're the Padres, and that nickname has a lot to do with the church across the highway.

Fr. Juniper Goes to America

The story begins an ocean away, off the southern coast of Spain, on the island of Majorca. There, on November 24, 1713, a child was born who

would become, in the words of historian Kevin Starr, "an action hero
of Catholic history." Miguel Joseph Serra grew up on the family farm
in the village of Petra. The devout boy decided to enter the Franciscan
order and took the name Junípero, after one of the first companions
of St. Francis.

Like so many Franciscans during the Age of Exploration, he was
smitten by the idea of evangelizing the millions of New World inhabitants who had not yet heard the Good News of salvation. During
Junípero's novitiate year, two Franciscan missionary-martyrs, Peter
Dueñas and John of Cetinas, were beatified. A few years earlier, the
Franciscan apostle to Peru, Francisco Solanus, had been canonized.
The novice was enthralled by the chronicles of the Franciscan order
and read them intensely. This reading stirred in him "a strong desire
to be a missionary and to emulate those who so appealed to him."

Junípero was also a brilliant student, and he earned a doctorate
in theology from the Catholic university on Majorca. During a brief
stint teaching philosophy at the Franciscan seminary there, he taught
seven young Franciscans, two of whom, Francisco Palóu and Juan
Crespí, would later be his companions in the American mission field.

In 1749, a delegation of reinforcements prepared to leave for New
Spain, but by the time Serra applied, the quota was full. A few of the
young, little-traveled friars, however, reconsidered and withdrew,
opening a spot for Serra. His wish was finally granted.

Mexico was the crown jewel of New Spain. The province was a
heady and sometimes combustive mixture of Spanish and Indigenous
cultures—the legacy of the discoveries of Christopher Columbus, the
military exploits of the conquistador Hernán Cortés, and the evangelistic marvel accomplished by the apparition of Mary on Tepeyac Hill.
In the fifteen years following Juan Diego's report of the appearance
of Our Lady of Guadalupe, some nine million Mexicans converted
to Christianity—an astounding religious transformation of an entire
culture.

By Serra's time, the Franciscans had been working in New Spain
for two centuries. They were engaged, in both Mexico and across the
Catholic world, in a not-always-friendly rivalry with the other great

missionary orders of the day, Jesuits and Dominicans. The Society of Jesus held sway in the far western and northern reaches of New Spain, but their position was precarious. Shortly after Serra came to Mexico, the Jesuits were suppressed in the Spanish Empire (1768), a prelude to the order's universal disbanding by the pope's command in 1773. The Church and the world had not heard the last of the Jesuits, but their temporary discomfiture furnished just enough room for Franciscans to take their place in the missions of northwest Mexico. Thus, the coast of California is dotted with the names of Franciscan rather than Jesuit saints: Santa Clara and San Juan Capistrano might have been instead San Ignacio and San Luis de Gonzaga.

A Mission for California

The Franciscans were thereby charged with bringing Christianity to the remote Pacific shores of Alta California. Heading the enterprise was a surprising figure, the diminutive Junípero Serra.

Serra's task was made more challenging by physical disability. During his journey from the port of Vera Cruz to Mexico City, where he would teach at San Fernando University, Serra sustained an injury—possibly an insect or snake bite—and the wound failed to heal properly. It caused him pain and hampered his ability to walk for the rest of his life.

But he never let it interfere with his ministry. In mission work among the Pame Indians of the Sierra Gorda near Mexico City, Fr. Serra had already demonstrated skill with languages, endurance in the face of hardship, and outstanding management instincts. Foremost, however, was his zeal for souls, a quality that seems to have been poured out in generous measure to the Catholics of western Europe during the Age of Exploration. Serra's main purpose was to bring the light of Christ to the peoples of America.

The history of the Church is bound up with the history of the world, though. The California missions had a dual purpose: to share the Good News but also to extend Spanish political and cultural dominance in the region. The Spanish had been in Mexico since the conquest of the Aztec Empire in 1521, and the explorer Juan Rodríguez

Cabrillo had first sheltered at San Diego Bay in 1542. Yet it was only in the 1740s, when rumor of British and Russian activity in the North Pacific reached the Spanish Crown, that orders were issued to establish footholds in Alta California. The coastal region where Spanish settlement would focus was densely populated: it's estimated that as many as three hundred thousand Native Americans lived there on the eve of Spanish contact. Approximately one-third of them perished over the next half century, primarily due to disease.

The tension between the aims of the Church—Serra's concern—and the aims of the Spanish government was one of the thorniest problems that Serra had to confront. It was a source of friction almost from the beginning of the first California mission: San Diego de Alcalá, established July 16, 1769.

The general pattern for missions was that a presidio, or military compound, would initially be constructed—a logical move on a frontier where the result of Indigenous-European encounter was uncertain at best. At San Diego, the presidio and the mission shared a space until 1774. Frs. Serra, Fernando Parrón, and Juan Vizcaíno were the friars initially stationed at San Diego, although Vizcaíno would soon leave after being injured in the mission's first violent encounter.

That happened just a month after the mission was founded. Several tribesmen were killed when, in a show of force against the newcomers, they entered the compound and began ransacking it. The mission's history would long be troubled by the inability to maintain peace with the surrounding people.

Battles with the local inhabitants were not the only threat to the infant mission's existence. San Diego was nearly abandoned in early 1770, when the community ran out of supplies and faced starvation. Serra insisted on staying, but he enjoyed little support from the civil authorities. They struck a deal: Serra agreed to pull up stakes if the mission was not resupplied by the time his novena was finished. On the final day of his nine-day prayer, the Feast of St. Joseph, the Spanish freighter *San Antonio* made a seemingly miraculous appearance off the coast and the mission was saved.

The friars repeatedly complained about the pillages of the Indigenous people by the Spanish soldiers, including the forcible seizure and assault of women. Fr. Luis Jayme declared that many of the soldiers "deserve to be hanged" for their treatment of nearby inhabitants. The friars had challenges enough in climate, language, and cultural difference; adding to the mix their identification in the local people's minds with their abusive countrymen meant that evangelization would be a steep uphill climb.

In 1772, Fr. Jayme reported fifty-five native converts. By 1774, when the mission moved inland, some four hundred Native Americans had been baptized, and there were ninety-seven in residence. Yet even this modest success proved illusory. In 1775, two of the recently baptized converts left the mission and returned to their tribes to organize a rebellion against the Spanish colonials. On November 5, 1775, some eight hundred tribesmen from forty rancherias (villages) attacked the mission compound. As they were burning the church and other buildings, Fr. Jayme approached, stunned that the people he knew and loved could be perpetrating such a deed. The attackers brutally killed him; another friar only recognized him "by the whiteness of his skin and the tonsure on his head." Fr. Luis Jayme was California's first Christian martyr.

Mission San Diego survived this crisis, and the Franciscans exhibited extraordinary mercy in the rebellion's aftermath. Although a number of tribesmen were arrested and punished by the Spanish military, the padres consistently counseled forgiveness. The men at the center of the revolt turned themselves in, were granted asylum by the friars, and "became model neophytes at the mission." Many other former rebels became Christian and received the sacraments from the friars whose confrere they had slaughtered not long before.

The End of the Missions?

The Franciscans of California never thought of the faith as a purely spiritual phenomenon. Material aid and practical training were part and parcel of the mission project, a fact that has led some observers to characterize the Franciscan method as "bribing" Indigenous people to convert to Catholicism. This understandable misapprehension fails to appreciate the missionaries' faith on its own terms. For friars such as Serra and his collaborators, the material dimension was not separate from the spiritual dimension, even as the human nature of Christ was intimately united with his divinity. The friars recognized that providing material benefits to the local people might induce them to listen more willingly to their preaching, but the benefits were not conferred as a reward for doing so. The willingness of Catholic missionaries and charities throughout history to offer assistance to people of every faith bears witness to the falsity of viewing missionary activity as a quid pro quo transaction.

Native Californians who engaged the missions did benefit materially. The friars taught agriculture in crops such as corn, wheat, barley, and beans. They also introduced livestock and plant species such as olives and grapes, which were the basis for the wine production for which the state is known today.

Even as the American Revolution raged on the other side of the continent, Serra presided over the foundation of nine missions. Eventually, a mission station was established along the coast at intervals of every twenty miles or so, a day's journey by foot. Twenty-one missions were constructed during the period of Franciscan supervision. The original plan for the missions, which was reflected in the laws of New Spain, was that they would exist for just ten years—long enough to Christianize and equip the inhabitants for life under European rule—after which they would be "secularized" (placed under the control of a diocesan bishop and his priests) and the resources given over to the devout new subjects of the Spanish Crown.

In reality, none of the missions in Alta California followed that pattern. Following Mexican independence in 1821, the new government took a hostile stance toward the Catholic Church and confiscated the missions. The Franciscans were removed from their administrative functions, and the local people soon withdrew from the missions' communal system. The churches fell into disrepair and were abandoned. The mission lands, which Serra and his successors always intended to give back to the inhabitants when both people and land were, in their estimation, adequately prepared, were acquired by the rich and powerful of Mexican society. The years of hard labor at risk of life and limb had been wasted, it seemed.

An American State

But the story of the missions didn't end there. In 1847, the last Franciscan at Mission San Diego was still writing letters to his superiors, complaining about the activities of soldiers—only now it was not the Spanish or Mexican military but the United States Army. The missions had entered a new stage.

Native Californians who had learned skills at the mission thrived in the market economy that came with American rule after 1846. Under the religious freedom granted by the United States, many mission properties gradually reverted to their original purpose. Today, most of the missions have been restored, and many are centers of active Catholic parishes. The geography of California, moreover, is imprinted indelibly with the long-ago labors of Fr. Serra and his confreres. The names of places such as San Diego, San Jose, and Santa Barbara tacitly attest to the Franciscan missionaries who chose these sites and christened them with the names of their revered saints.

As for Fr. Serra, his name will live on in the annals of Church history. On September 23, 2015, in the first canonization to take place on American soil, the Jesuit Pope Francis canonized the Franciscan Junípero Serra, calling him "one of the founding fathers of the United States."[1]

Sources

Archibald, Robert. *The Economic Aspects of the California Missions.* Washington, DC: Academy of American Franciscan History, 1978.

Brown, Alan K., trans. and ed. *With Anza to California, 1775–1776: The Journal of Pedro Font, O.F.M.* Norman, OK: Arthur H. Clark, 2011.

DeNevi, Don, and Noel Francis Moholy. *Junípero Serra: The Illustrated Story of the Franciscan Founder of California's Missions*. San Francisco: Harper & Row, 1985.

Engelhardt, Zephyrin. *San Diego Mission*. San Francisco: James H. Barry, 1920.

Geiger, Maynard J. *The Life and Times of Fray Junípero Serra, O.F.M.* 2 vols. Washington, DC: Academy of American Franciscan History, 1959.

Newell, Quincy D. *Constructing Lives at Mission San Francisco: Native Californians and Hispanic Colonists, 1776–1821*. Albuquerque: University of New Mexico Press, 2009.

Phillips, George Harwood. *Chiefs and Challengers: Indian Resistance and Cooperation in Southern California, 1769–1906*. 2nd ed. Norman: University of Oklahoma Press, 2014.

Sandos, James A. *Converting California: Indians and Franciscans in the Missions*. New Haven, CT: Yale University Press, 2008.

Starr, Kevin. *Continental Ambitions: Roman Catholics in North America: The Colonial Experience*. San Francisco: Ignatius Press, 2016.

5.

Catholic Gateway to the West

Basilica of St. Louis, King of France
209 Walnut Street
St. Louis, Missouri 63102

*Did you know that the children of
William Clark (of the Lewis and Clark
Expedition) were baptized in this
historic St. Louis church?*

As sightseers in St. Louis look down from the Gateway Arch, soaring more than six hundred feet above the Mississippi River, a striking stone structure can be seen just to the west, within the grounds of the park that surrounds the Arch. Unmistakably one of the principal buildings in the oldest quarter of the city, it is a Catholic church—the home to a faith community that's been watching Americans move west for more than 250 years.

City of the Saint-King

The city of St. Louis has its origins in 1763, when the French merchant Pierre Laclède established a trading post on the western banks of this Upper Mississippi River location. Laclède and his business partner, Gilbert Maxent, were granted an Indian trade monopoly by the French government, providing them with the foundation for a prosperous commercial enterprise. Laclède was living in a common-law marriage with Marie Chouteau. (Her neighbors called her a "widow," though her husband had deserted her and decamped to France.)

The settlement was named after the patron saint of the Bourbon Kings Louis of France: between them, Louis XIV and Louis XV ruled the country for more than a hundred years. Their patron was the crusader-king Louis IX. Laclède's original plan for the city included an area at the center that would be reserved for "its most important spaces and buildings," including the church block.

The founding fathers of St. Louis understood well that Christianity provided a necessary civilizing influence on the frontier and that the growth and prosperity of the new city depended on it. Yet at the time it was hard to imagine that a magnificent cathedral would one day rise from the patch of dirt. The first church constructed in St. Louis was a one-room log hut, which would serve as the region's sole Catholic church until it was replaced during the American Revolution. During that period, the small Catholic community was served irregularly by French missionary priests based in Illinois.

In the 1770s, the French settlers of St. Louis were ambivalent about the political strife roiling the Eastern Seaboard. They had no love for the British, as they and their mother country had concluded their own conflict, the French and Indian War (in which Great Britain sided with the Indians), just a decade earlier. Yet the principal loyalty among many of the French in the Mississippi Valley was to French Canada, which was also their ecclesiastical authority—most missionaries originated in Quebec—and which, following the French and Indian War, had become part of the British Empire. The bishop of Quebec, concerned to mollify his English rulers, imposed a cautious neutrality on his priestly charges, including the missionary priests of the Mississippi region. So, Canada rejected the overtures of the American colonies—overtures tendered by a partially Catholic delegation—to join their rebellion against the British Crown.[1]

Not far from St. Louis, however, in the frontier settlement of Kaskaskia, Illinois, a French-speaking Catholic priest made a momentous decision to disregard the directive of the distant bishop with whom he already had a strained relationship. In 1778, Fr. Pierre Gibault and a delegation of Kaskaskians met with the patriot officer George Rogers Clark, whose contingent of militia was angling for control over the continent's interior. Gibault and his colleagues agreed that the area's French residents would not resist American forces, and Clark promised that their persons, property—and religious practice—would be respected. Gibault further offered to treat on Clark's behalf with the people of Vincennes, the French outpost on the Wabash River, which likewise pledged its support to the rebellion. (Today, a statue of Gibault, the "Patriot Priest," stands in George Rogers Clark National Historical Park in Vincennes.)

While the American armies in the east were struggling to survive and turn the tide of war in favor of the colonies, the Catholic settlers of St. Louis were building their second church. Although it was also made of logs, the 1776 construction was larger and more dignified than the original structure.

In an unusual twist, the second church became a cathedral before St. Louis became the seat of a diocese. New Orleans was the headquarters of the Diocese of Louisiana and the Floridas when Louis DuBourg was appointed as its second bishop. Finding an unsettled situation in New Orleans, which had a reputation for "anticlerical laypeople and questionably loyal priests," DuBourg decided to reside in St. Louis, which was at the time part of the same diocese.

By 1818, the second church was also inadequate. DuBourg lamented that it was "a kind of miserable barn falling in ruins." The new church DuBourg built, ready to host Mass by 1820, served the parish of St. Louis until 1834.

Under DuBourg, St. Louis became a center of Catholic activity in the Mississippi Valley. He invited the Sisters of the Sacred Heart, who arrived from France in 1818 with St. Rose Philippine Duchesne at their head. He also founded the academy that would develop into Saint Louis University. DuBourg's ecclesiastical career ended in France, where he died as the archbishop of Besançon. In 1826, St. Louis was made a diocese in its own right, and Italy-born Joseph Rosati became its first bishop.

The Chouteaus

By the early nineteenth century, the city no longer resembled the motley collection of cabins that Laclède had planted in the 1760s. Pierre Laclède and Marie Chouteau had children of their own, who adopted their mother's surname. Among them were Auguste (1786–1838) and Pierre (1789–1865), who inherited their father's firm. In 1803, the Louisiana Purchase made St. Louis part of the United States, but the Chouteau brothers continued to prosper, building a private economic empire based on their status as liaisons between Native Americans, fur companies, and the US government. Under the Chouteaus' guidance, St. Louis served as a "peaceful free trade zone" among the various European and American (Indigenous and Anglo) nations intersecting at the Mississippi River. The Chouteaus' diverse commercial activities included transportation and supply, milling, mining, and banking, and their trade reached markets far beyond St. Louis, from New Orleans to Montreal to Le Havre, France. They were major figures in the development of not only St. Louis but also another midwestern hub, Kansas City.

The Chouteaus remained committed if irregular Catholics. Though Auguste, for example, fathered a number of children by Osage mothers—an indication of the extent of the Chouteaus' inculturation into Native American ways—this flouting of orthodox Christian morality was combined with solicitude that all such offspring be baptized into the Catholic Church. His children's baptisms were performed by the local Jesuit missionaries.

When Meriwether Lewis and William Clark began their famous trek in 1804, it was the Chouteaus who supplied the expedition. (Later, Clark's children would be baptized in the parish church of St. Louis, as would the child of the explorers' Native American guide, Sacagawea.) The Lewis and Clark Expedition stimulated interest in the lands west of the Mississippi, elevating St. Louis's importance even higher. Positioned at the confluence of the Missouri and Mississippi Rivers, St. Louis enjoyed an unparalleled position as the gateway to the Midwest and West. Even those traveling by wagon rather than river, such as the pioneers who trudged the Oregon Trail all the way to the Pacific

Northwest, would pass through St. Louis on their way to the "jump-ing-off" points of Independence, St. Joseph, or Kansas City.

A Grand New Church

When Bishop Rosati arrived in St. Louis, he was dismayed at the con-dition of the cathedral, resorting to the same agrarian comparison his predecessor had made of the previous church: "only half-finished, rather rustic inside, and looking much like a hay-barn." In 1831, he oversaw the laying of the cornerstone for an ambitious new church constructed in the Greek Revival style. It would not be completed until 1853, when the limestone façade, pillared front entrance, and soaring single steeple struck an impressive pose amidst central St. Louis.

By that time, Rosati had died, passing away during a visit to Rome, where he was buried. His grave remained there for more than a hun-dred years, until, in 1971, his remains were transferred to the church that he had built at the Gateway to the West. They are marked by a simple plaque located away from public access beneath the main altar.

The cathedral, meanwhile, continued to serve a growing church in a growing city. During Rosati's tenure, Sisters of Charity arrived to serve a new hospital provided for by the Irish American philanthropist John Mullanphy, who had settled in St. Louis after a career in the army.

Rosati's successor was Peter Richard Kenrick. Peter, like his brother Francis, was a native of Dublin who came to serve the burgeoning American Church after his ordination. Francis, after a stretch teaching at the infant St. Thomas Seminary in Bardstown (see chapter 9), went on to become bishop of Philadelphia and finally archbishop of Balti-more. Peter, whom Francis lured to America to teach at his seminary in Philadelphia, was also raised to the rank of archbishop when St. Louis was made an archdiocese in 1847. The explosive growth of the American West, and with it the Church in the West, gave rise to the suffragan dioceses of Dubuque, Nashville, Chicago, Milwaukee, and St. Paul. All told, forty-five dioceses would eventually be formed from what had been Upper Louisiana, the vast territory once overseen by the bishop of St. Louis.

Kenrick witnessed the city's darkest days, when the cholera epidemic of 1849 wiped out 10 percent of the total population of seventy-seven thousand, while thousands more fled to outlying areas. During the contagion's peak in the summer, there were at least two hundred funerals a day. The students and the Jesuit faculty at Saint Louis University remained on campus and held vigil in the college church, praying before a statue of the Blessed Virgin Mary. Not a single student or Jesuit contracted the disease, and when students returned for classes in the fall, they fulfilled a pledge to honor their intercessor by crowning the statue with a silver coronet.

The golden anniversary of Kenrick's ordination in 1882 and his funeral fourteen years later were two of the last grand ceremonies performed at what would soon be known as the "Old Cathedral." By 1904, St. Louis was the fourth-largest city in the country, with a population of nearly six hundred thousand. It flaunted its world-class status by staging the seven-months-long Louisiana Purchase Exposition— popularly known as the St. Louis World's Fair. Meanwhile, shifting demographics had decimated the number of regular parishioners at the downtown cathedral parish. At the same time, its once-impressive size had faded in comparison, as the massive Catholic immigration of the late 1800s swelled other urban parish populations throughout the country. Plans were begun during Kenrick's tenure for a new, larger mother church for the archdiocese. Kenrick's second successor, Archbishop (later Cardinal) John Glennon, oversaw construction of the mosaic-rich new church at a site farther west of the river. In 1914, the monumental edifice officially replaced the original cathedral as the new Cathedral of St. Louis.

Yet, as a history written shortly after the inauguration of the new cathedral insisted, "The Old Cathedral will and must remain the great religious shrine of the city." The Old Cathedral was granted basilica status by Pope St. John XXIII in 1961. It is the oldest building in St. Louis and was the only structure in the old-city area that was not sacrificed to the construction of the Arch. Its parish records bear witness to its historic role as a sanctuary for new beginnings and new life: more than 15,000 weddings and nearly 19,000 baptisms are listed there. It continues to stand as a reminder of the Catholic role in the westward expansion of the American nation.

Sources

Berger, Henry W. *St. Louis and Empire: 250 Years of Imperial Quest & Urban Crisis*. Carbondale: Southern Illinois University Press, 2015.

Christian, Shirley. *Before Lewis and Clark: The Story of the Chouteaus, the French Dynasty That Ruled America's Frontier*. New York: Farrar, Straus and Giroux, 2004.

Cleary, Patricia. *The World, the Flesh, and the Devil: A History of Colonial St. Louis*. Columbia: University of Missouri Press, 2011.

Holloman, Joe. "Spotlight: Rosati Remains Resting in Rightful Recess." *St. Louis Post-Dispatch*, July 2, 2016.

Hyde, Anne Farrar. *Empires, Nations, and Families: A New History of the North American West, 1800–1860*. New York: Ecco Press, 2012.

Pasquier, Michael. *Fathers on the Frontier: French Missionaries and the Roman Catholic Priesthood in the United States, 1789–1870*. Oxford: Oxford University Press, 2010.

Rothensteiner, John. *History of the Archdiocese of St. Louis: In Its Various Stages of Development from A.D. 1673 to A.D. 1928*. St. Louis: Blackwell Wielandy, 1928.

Slama, Joe. "A Sickness and a Silver Crown: How Saint Louis University Survived the Cholera Epidemic of 1849." *Catholic World Report*, March 25, 2020.

Souvay, Charles M., CM. *The Cathedrals of St. Louis: An Historical Sketch*. N.p., n.d.

Starr, Kevin. *Continental Achievement: Roman Catholics in the United States: Revolution and Early Republic*. San Francisco: Ignatius Press, 2020.

6.

Ground Zero for Catholic New York

St. Peter's Church, Manhattan
22 Barclay Street
New York, New York 10007

*Did you know that St. Elizabeth Ann
Seton, the first American-born saint,
became Catholic at St. Peter's Church
in Manhattan?*

All Americans of the generation born in the nineties and before know the date September 11, 2001, just as their parents' generation know November 22, 1963, and their grandparents know December 7, 1941. On September 11, 2001, the landing gear from one of the doomed airliners came crashing into the roof of a building that stood near the World Trade Center in lower Manhattan. A while later, firefighters bore the lifeless body of a Catholic priest into the same building, placing it before the altar within, above which hung a painting of Christ bleeding on the Cross. Franciscan friar Mychal Judge, chaplain to the New York Fire Department, was killed by falling debris as he accompanied firefighters into the North Tower. Longtime New York pastor Fr. George Rutler captured the spiritual drama of the scene: "For those who had forgotten, the Eucharist is a sacrifice of blood, and it is the priest who offers the sacrifice. September 11 gave an indulgent world . . . an icon of the priesthood."

The building is St. Peter's Catholic Church, and its role on 9/11 was only the latest chapter in a remarkable history as the oldest Catholic parish in the nation's largest city.

A Diverse Congregation

There were few Catholics in New York during the colonial period. The first Catholic priest to set foot on Manhattan Island may have been St. Isaac Jogues, who was rescued from his Mohawk captors by New Netherlands traders, in a generously ecumenical act on the part of the Reformed Dutch.

In New York, as elsewhere in British North America, colonial politics reflected developments back home. When the Catholic Thomas Dongan became governor of the New York colony in 1682, he introduced toleration for the Church and founded a Catholic school. But the New York edition of England's Glorious Revolution of 1688, which dethroned Catholic king James II and installed Protestants William and Mary on the throne, derailed Catholic hopes for favor. New York's version of the Glorious Revolution—the 1691 Leisler's Rebellion—stifled the colony's toleration of Roman Catholicism. From that point through the American Revolution, Catholics in New York lacked full rights. In the 1770s, the Jesuit missionary Ferdinand Steinmeyer (also known as Ferdinand Farmer) held secret Masses for the city's tiny Catholic population. By the time of the Revolution, there were perhaps only two hundred Catholics in the city of twenty thousand.

Mirroring a pattern that held in other states, New York became more hospitable to Catholics over the course of the Revolutionary War and early years of the Republic. The legislature quickly passed measures to guarantee religious liberty and to permit formation of religious societies and corporations. In 1784, an Irish Capuchin, Fr. Charles Whelan, arrived and devoted himself to the Catholics of Manhattan. New York was at the time the nation's capital, so there was support for the young Catholic community from the European diplomatic delegations. With assistance from the Spanish and French embassies and financial support from King Charles III of Spain, the Catholics of New York City laid the cornerstone for their first church in October of 1785. The small church with its square bell tower gradually arose at the corner of Barclay and Church Streets, which at the time lay just outside the city limits, on ground leased from the city's venerable Trinity Episcopal Church. On November 4 of the following year—the Feast of St. Charles Borromeo, patron of King Charles III—the church was dedicated to St. Peter, the Prince of the Apostles.

Fittingly, the first parish was populated by a diverse array of churchgoers, prefiguring the Catholic melting pot that New York would be in the centuries ahead. Merchants, soldiers, and diplomats worshipped alongside artisans, laborers, and servants. They were Irish, French, Spanish, Dutch, Portuguese, and Afro-Caribbean. The young St. Peter's Catholic Church was truly catholic.

A Controversy, a Convert, a Cardinal, and a Court Case

But diversity and unity are always in tension, and St. Peter's was also one of the earliest battlegrounds in a controversy that would tear apart Catholic parishes across the young country. Wherever laypeople had been the prime movers in the purchase of property and the erection of churches, they understandably sought to exercise some control over the temporal affairs of the Church. In many cases, lay Catholics formed parish corporations and installed themselves as trustees, with no reference to the diocesan authority (bishop) or his local representative (pastor). As the Church grew and the customary parochial and diocesan structures were put in place, the contrast between the existing reality of how lay trustees understood their right to govern and the ideal envisioned by canon law made the situation ripe for conflict.

Had lay trustees confined themselves to temporal affairs, it's possible that the delicate balance between lay and clerical control may have lasted for some time. As it happened, according to a historian of the affair, trustees often "intruded on spiritual affairs as well, even to the extent of assuming the right to hire or fire pastors and withhold their salaries should they displease them. All too frequently they interpreted their mandate to mean that they could administer the temporal possessions of the parish independently of, and frequently in opposition to, the spiritual authorities." In a series of disputes that have collectively become known as the "trustee controversy," laymen, priests, and bishops fought over control of parish property in a number of locales, including New York, Philadelphia, Baltimore, Norfolk, Charleston, Buffalo, and New Orleans.

At St. Peter's, one faction of the congregation rejected the duly appointed pastor, Fr. Charles Whelan, and invited another Franciscan Capuchin priest, Fr. Andrew Nugent, to serve as the head of the church. John Carroll presided over this and many such disputes, beginning even before he was installed as the nation's first bishop in 1789. (He had been appointed "Superior of the Mission" of the United States in 1784.) Carroll supported the rightful pastor but was forced to surrender when Whelan was driven from the city by hostile parishioners. (Whelan ended up in Kentucky; see chapter 9.) Nugent being the only minister in town, Carroll grudgingly validated his pastorate.

Unfortunately, the trouble with Fr. Nugent did not end there. The quarrelsome pastor alienated the parish's trustees with his exorbitant financial demands (an ironic source of conflict for a follower of St. Francis), and Carroll discovered that Nugent's priestly credentials had been revoked in Ireland. The matter came to a memorable head in 1787, when Carroll announced the end of Nugent's pastorate during a Sunday Mass at St. Peter's. The ejected pastor stormed the sanctuary and berated the bishop before the astounded assembly. When Carroll penned a vigorous denunciation of such subordination shortly thereafter, the trustees were at last shamed into submitting to proper episcopal authority regarding parochial assignments. The historic church got new locks, and Fr. Nugent was not given a key.

Under the new pastor, the Dominican Fr. William O'Brien, peace was restored. One of O'Brien's chief struggles was to keep the impoverished Catholic community afloat and to pay for the church building, modest as it was. When he returned from a successful fundraising trip to Cuba and Mexico, he brought with him some impressive furnishings, including a painting of the Crucifixion by the celebrated

Mexican artist José Maria Vallejo. It is the image that inspired Fr. Rutler's reflection on the 2001 death of Fr. Judge.

The painting also provided the backdrop for one of the American Church's most famous conversions. In 1805, Fr. Matthew O'Brien (brother of the pastor, William) received into the Church a young widow who had been raised Episcopalian but was persuaded of the truth of Catholicism during a journey to Italy undertaken in a vain attempt to improve her husband's health. Elizabeth Ann Seton described the moment she first dared cross the threshold of the city's Catholic church and beheld its famous painting: "'Here, my God, I go!' said I, 'heart all to you!' Entering, how that heart died away, as it were, in silence before the little Tabernacle, and the great Crucifixion over it."

When Seton professed the Catholic faith in the Manhattan church, she alienated a large and influential family who could not comprehend why a woman born into privilege should choose to join a marginal Church associated with foreigners and the downtrodden. Seton would not long remain in New York; in 1809 she moved to Maryland, where she inaugurated her marvelous career as foundress of the Sisters of Charity and pioneer in Catholic schooling. On September 14, 1975, St. Elizabeth Ann Seton was canonized by Pope St. Paul VI, making her the first American-born saint.

In 1810, a boy named John, the son of Irish Catholic immigrants, was baptized in St. Peter's. There was nothing remarkable in that, but the McCloskey baby would go on to become a priest, a bishop, and the archbishop of New York from 1864 to 1885. In 1875, Pope Pius IX bestowed on him the red hat, giving him the distinction of being the first American cardinal. When, in the 1880s, questions were raised about the possibility of dissolving the parish to accommodate the city's shifting pattern of residential and commercial districts, Cardinal McCloskey pledged, "St. Peter's Church will never be alienated." One hundred forty years later, his declaration remains true.

Three years after McCloskey's baptism, St. Peter's was the site of an incident that would lead to a landmark religious liberty case. One parishioner had stolen valuables from another and then confessed the deed to Fr. Antony Kohlmann, the Jesuit pastor. The priest insisted on restitution and the thief handed the contraband over to Kohlmann, who returned the items to the victim. The police, however, insisted that Kohlmann divulge the identity of the thief, which, citing the seal of confession, he refused to do.

The case was taken before a municipal court presided over by the mayor of the city: the former US senator and future governor of New York, DeWitt Clinton. Clinton was not Catholic, but he understood the issues at hand. In June 1813, assisted by Fr. Kohlmann's attorney, an Irish Protestant who had been exiled for defending Irish Catholics under British law, Clinton acquitted Kohlmann, observing, "It is essential to the free exercise of a religion, that its ordinances should be administered. . . . Secrecy is of the essence of penance. The sinner will not confess, nor will the priest receive his confession, if the veil of secrecy is removed." The principle of the seal of confession was later enshrined in New York law and became the norm across the United States.

The Saints of St. Peter's

In the late 1780s, revolution in the French colony of Saint-Domingue provoked an exodus of French-speaking Catholics, and the New York Catholic community was one beneficiary. Among the refugees were Jean-Jacques Bérard and his family, who brought with them their irreplaceable house servant, Pierre Toussaint.

Toussaint was born in Saint-Domingue (now Haiti) in 1766, the third child of Ursule Julien Toussaint, chambermaid to the mistress of a rich sugarcane plantation. Pierre was destined to be a "house slave"— good fortune of sorts in the world of Caribbean slavery. The plantation workers of Haiti were treated brutally by the French aristocrats who amassed immense wealth upon their backs, and it is no wonder that the slaves overthrew their masters by equally violent means in the Haitian Revolution of 1791. Bérard, discerning the storm clouds on the horizon, fled the increasingly unstable island with his family and a few slaves in 1787. Among them was Pierre, who arrived in New York unable to speak English, far from his parents, and bewildered at the bustling metropolis of a ten-year-old American nation. He would remain in the city for the rest of his long life.

Bérard died in 1801, and the firm holding his wealth failed, leaving his widow, Marie Elisabeth, destitute. By that time, Pierre was thriving in the highly competitive hairdressing profession, heavily in demand to manage the coiffures of the most elegant women of New York. His creativity and ability to adapt as quickly as the fashions assured him of success. His signature element was to weave flowers into the hair of his clients, a practice borrowed from the Haitian mulattoes he had observed as a child. He magnanimously took upon himself the financial support of the entire household.

One of the enslaved members of the household was his sister, Rosalie, whose release he purchased with his hard-earned savings. He also paid the way to freedom for a fellow Haitian he had met in New York, an attractive young woman named Juliette. On July 2, 1807, Pierre gained his own freedom when a dying Marie Elisabeth signed his liberation papers. Four years later, he and Juliette were married. Even though he was twenty years her senior, Pierre outlived his wife, who died of cancer in 1851.

Pierre had always been generous toward the many orphans of New York, and after his marriage, he and Juliette took children in off the street to feed and shelter them. As his means increased and his reputation for philanthropy grew, he became a major benefactor to an array of charitable causes, including aid to Haiti after a devastating earthquake in 1842.[1]

Pierre made his daily devotions at St. Peter's without fail for sixty years, stopping for morning Mass before continuing on to his appointments. In his eighties, Pierre could still be seen striding through the city, projecting an arresting dignity that caught the attention of onlookers. But after Juliette's death, Pierre's age finally caught up with him. Suddenly, one summer morning, he failed to appear at the church on Barclay Street. A brief illness was all that stood between Pierre and his God. A priest from St. Peter's was present when he crossed the threshold from this life to the next on June 30, 1853.

Glowing obituaries appeared in the city's papers. Toussaint's goodness, said one, "made his life a constant round of acts of kindness and sympathy." In 1989, the Archdiocese of New York formally opened his cause for canonization.

Another Catholic of extraordinary sanctity connected to St. Peter's was Teresa O'Sullivan, the daughter of an Irish Catholic father and an English Episcopalian mother. O'Sullivan was born in New York in 1817. The exact nature of the faith life of the family is unclear, but it seems that most of the children were baptized and raised in the Episcopalian church. There is an entry for Teresa in the records of St. Peter's Church, indicating that she was baptized there as an infant. In any case, she was determined to follow the practices of Catholicism from a young age, and in 1837 she entered the Visitation Convent in Georgetown, becoming Sr. Adelaide.

Sr. Adelaide transferred to the Carmelites of Havana, Cuba, in 1840, moved to a convent in Guatemala, and rose to the rank of prioress. After a brief return to New York, Mother Adelaide of St. Teresa went to Spain, where she died in 1893. Her cause for canonization has been opened, and she has been designated as Servant of God.

The New Old St. Peter's

Heavy Catholic immigration ensured that the minuscule Catholic congregation that raised the first St. Peter's Church would soon outgrow it. By the 1830s there were more than thirty thousand Catholics in New York City, and even with the addition of numerous new parishes, the original church for the city's first parish was no longer adequate. On October 26, 1836, the cornerstone was laid for a new St. Peter's, with Pierre Toussaint prominent among its donors. It was completed in 1840 in a classical design, Ionic columns framing a portico underneath a simple gable roof without dome or spire. More than double the size of the previous structure, the building, a contemporary parishioner declared, was "not only a great convenience to ourselves, but an ornament to the city."

It was this church that inspired a poet many decades later to reflect on the tableau presented by the religious edifice standing amid the din of New York's financial district. The sentiment is still apropos.

> Where the travel-tides' ebbing and flow never stops;
> 'Midst the clamor of mart and mill;
> Where each new steel-ribbed giant his neighbor o'ertops
> 'Midst the splendors of art and skill,
> Stands a temple of God, full a century old,
> That our forebears built stone on stone,
> When the faithful were few, and far-scattered the fold,
> And the pilgrimage long and lone.

From "St. Peter's Church," H. A. W.,
1906, in Ryan, Old St.Peter's.

Sources

Byron, Tim, SJ, et al. "14 June 1813—Fr. Kohlmann Acquitted in Landmark Trial in US." *Jesuit Restoration 1814* (blog), www.sj2014.net/blog/category/the-americas.

Duncan, Jason K. *Citizens or Papists? The Politics of Anti-Catholicism in New York, 1685–1821.* New York: Fordham University Press, 2005.

Feister, John. "No Greater Love: Chaplain Mychal Judge, OFM." *St. Anthony Messenger*, September 2003.

Golway, Terry, ed. *Catholics in New York: Society, Culture, and Politics, 1809–1946.* New York: Fordham University Press, 2008.

Jones, Arthur. *Pierre Toussaint.* New York: Doubleday, 2003.

Riforgiato, Leonard P. *The Life and Times of John Timon (1797–1867): The First Bishop of Buffalo, New York.* Edited by Dennis Castillo. Lewiston, NY: Edwin Mellen, 2006.

Rutler, George. "Infandum: 18 Years On." CrisisMagazine.com, September 11, 2019.

Ryan, Leo Raymond. *Old St. Peter's: The Mother Church of Catholic New York (1785–1935).* New York: United States Catholic Historical Society, 1935.

Shelley, Thomas J. *Empire State Catholics: A History of the Catholic Community in New York State.* Strasbourg: Editions du Signe, 2006.

Smith, John Talbot. *The Catholic Church in New York: A History of the New York Archdiocese from Its Establishment in 1808 to the Present Time.* Vol. 1. New York: Hall & Locke, 1905.

Starr, Kevin. *Continental Achievement: Roman Catholics in the United States: Revolution and Early Republic.* San Francisco: Ignatius Press, 2020.

Tarry, Ellen. *Pierre Toussaint: Apostle of Old New York.* 1981; 2nd ed., Boston: Pauline, 1998.

7.

The Prince of Pennsylvania

Basilica of St. Michael the Archangel
321 St. Mary Street
Loretto, Pennsylvania 15940

*Did you know that a Russian prince
served as a missionary in the
Pennsylvania wilderness?*

The name "Pennsylvania" is Latin for "Penn's Woodland," and even today, drivers traversing the state along the Turnpike (I-76) or Interstate 80 to the north can appreciate the density of the flora that greeted settlers in the seventeenth and eighteenth centuries. Combine the deciduous forests with the rivers and mountainous spines that slice from northeast to southwest across the state and it quickly becomes apparent how difficult it would have been to move west across the country from the Delaware River valley, where lay the nation's largest city at the time of independence, Philadelphia.

The remoteness of western Pennsylvania is precisely what recommended it to a young foreign priest who moved there in 1799 to serve a small and scattered flock of Catholic farmers. Fr. Demetrius Gallitzin hoped to build a truly Catholic culture from the ground up, upending what he viewed as a pernicious "democratic spirit" that had infiltrated the minds of many American Catholics. "There are few personages

connected with the history of the Church in this country," the great
Catholic intellectual and convert Orestes Brownson wrote of Gallitzin,
who are "more interesting, or more worthy to be remembered."

Signs of Catholic vitality, past and present, still dominate the landscape of this region east of Pittsburgh. They are the legacy of Gallitzin
and countless other religious and laypeople who built the communities
of Carrolltown, Latrobe, and Loretto. One of these monuments is the
Basilica of St. Michael the Archangel, whose sturdy, square, stone
tower leaves the impression that it has always been there and always
will be.

Sportsman's Hall

In 1785, several Catholic families from the colony of Conewago in
south-central Pennsylvania, and Goshenhoppen, a town north of
Philadelphia, moved deep into the western Pennsylvania wilderness.
For the most part, the Catholics from Conewago (mainly of Irish or
English heritage) settled in Cambria County, while the Goshenhoppen
group (mainly Germans) dispersed across Westmoreland County.
Among them were a Mr. and Mrs. Luther, about whom we know only
a few scintillating details. He, a descendant of the Protestant Reformation firebrand Martin Luther, came to America as a mercenary in
the Hessian forces employed by the British during the Revolution. He
converted to Catholicism after he deserted the army and was saved
from capture by his future wife, Elizabeth Smith.

A Dutch Capuchin, Theodore Brouwers, was sent by Bishop John
Carroll to serve these Catholic settlers. Fr. Brouwers bought a three-
hundred-acre tract and built a small log building that doubled as a residence and chapel. The land, formerly the hunting resort of a wealthy
Harrisburg gentleman, was known as Sportsman's Hall. The beloved
pastor died shortly afterward, but in his will, he left the property to the
"duly constituted pastor of the local Catholic community." Notwith-
standing a difficult period immediately following, when the mission
was troubled by the depredations of two successive scoundrel-priests,
Sportsman's Hall would serve as the foundation for one of the pillars
of the Catholic Church in western Pennsylvania.

The Prince

During those same years, a spiritual drama was unfolding in the life of one of the key figures in the erection of those Catholic pillars. Demetrius Gallitzin was the son of a Russian prince and a Prussian aristocrat. Russian empress Catherine the Great stood as godmother at the baby's baptism. In childhood, Demetrius was raised in an agnostic, nominally Orthodox household, but his mother Amalia's devotion to the upbringing of her children eventually led them both to Catholicism. Pursuing the best educational methods of the day, Amalia took her children to the center of avant-garde pedagogy in the German city of Münster. There she unwittingly rented a house recently occupied by members of the Society of Jesus, whose order had been suppressed by the pope five years earlier. Her circle of educational theorists included devout Catholics, and their virtuous behavior and intellectual prowess won Amalia's admiration. She returned to the faith of her infancy by receiving the Sacraments of Confession and Communion on the Feast of St. Monica Sacrament in 1786.

The young prince Demetrius—his parents called him "Mitri"—converted to Catholicism the next year at age seventeen. When his appointment to the Austrian army fell through five years later, he decided on a grand tour of America. This was a move approved by his father, who saw the venture as valuable experience for the military and diplomatic career he expected his son to pursue.

Mitri sailed from Rotterdam to Baltimore in the company of a priest, F. X. Brosius. By the time he reached the United States on October 28, 1792, the young aristocrat had decided to become a priest. He soon became acquainted with Bishop John Carroll and with the desperate need of the Church in the United States for capable ministers. Within a month, Gallitzin had entered Baltimore's St. Mary's Seminary. His father was strongly opposed, and even his mother questioned whether his decision was adequately informed. The rector of the seminary tried to reassure her. "I never brought to the altar a candidate for Holy Orders whose vocation I am so certain as I am of your son," he wrote. "This is also the opinion of Bishop Carroll, and of all who know him." On March 18, 1795, Demetrius "Mitri" Gallitzin became the second priest to be ordained in the United States. Soon he was working among the Catholics of western Pennsylvania.

St. Michael in Loretto

Fr. Gallitzin occasionally ministered to the Catholics already settled at Sportsman's Hall, but the Russian missionary was directly responsible for another pillar of the region's Catholicism: the settlement of Loretto. Like Sportsman's Hall, Loretto's terrestrial basis was the effect of a bequest. An Irish American army officer named Michael McGuire, originally from Maryland, was the first white man to settle in Cambria County, where he established a hunting camp in 1768. In recognition of his service during the Revolution, the Continental Congress awarded him two thousand acres of this region, and he built a homestead there in 1787. He sold parcels to other Catholic families, and soon there was a thriving Catholic community.

McGuire left four hundred acres to Bishop Carroll when he died in 1793. Carroll entrusted Gallitzin with this tract, known as McGuire's Settlement. Gallitzin, who enjoyed the monetary support of his well-to-do mother, bought another three hundred acres, much of which he distributed to poor Catholic families by way of mortgages on generous terms. Gallitzin named the blossoming new town after the place in Italy where pious tradition holds that the "Holy House" of the Virgin Mary at Nazareth was miraculously transported. He named his first parish for St. Michael, a much-honored figure in Russian Christianity and the patron saint of the benefactor, Captain McGuire.

In 1800, Gallitzin wrote to his superior, Bishop Carroll, to apprise him of the progress made in the development of McGuire's bequest:

> Our church, which was only begun in harvest, got finished fit for service the night before Christmas. It is about 44 feet long by 25, built of white pine logs with a very good shingle roof. I kept service in it at Christmas for the first time. There is also a house built for me, 16 feet by 14, besides a little kitchen and a stable.

From this modest headquarters, Fr. Gallitzin orchestrated the development of one of the country's most enduring Catholic enclaves.

Over the course of his career, Gallitzin purchased more than twenty thousand acres of western Pennsylvania, with the purpose of reselling to Catholic pioneers. Several other Catholic settlements sprang from Loretto, some during Gallitzin's lifetime and others during the tenure of his collaborator and successor, Peter Henry Lemcke. The towns of St. Benedict, Gallitzin, and Carrolltown, with their respective parishes, were progeny of Loretto Catholicism. The naming of Gallitzin and Carrolltown is a function of chronology. Fr. Lemcke proposed "Gallitzin" when he sited the settlement at Carrolltown, but the older priest strenuously protested and suggested naming it instead after the first bishop of Baltimore. When the town of Gallitzin was founded later, its namesake, being deceased, could no longer object.

Gallitzin's career was not without hardship and conflict. During one explosive dispute with his flock, he was physically assaulted and in mortal danger when another parishioner happened by. John Weakland, "the tallest and stoutest man within a hundred miles," took up a fence rail and drove off the attackers. Gallitzin predicted that one of Weakland's descendants would say Mass in the church that the Weakland family had helped to build, St. Joseph's in Hart's Sleeping Place—a prophecy that was fulfilled by Fr. Bernard Weakland more than a century later.

During the War of 1812, Gallitzin actively supported the raising of the local militia, organized under the leadership of Captain Richard McGuire, the son of the Loretto founding father. When the company was ready, they celebrated Mass together in St. Michael's Church, Gallitzin solemnly blessed their banner, and then off they marched to battle the British.

By 1840, there were five thousand Catholic families in Cambria County. Shortly after Easter of that year, Gallitzin took to bed. Frs. Lemke and Heyden accompanied him during his final two days. On May 6, in his rectory at Loretto, Demetrius Gallitzin passed away. For four days, mourners filed past his body as it lay in state. He was buried on the grounds of St. Michael's. The property on which the church stands was still his, and in his will, he left it to the Catholic bishop of the region and his successors. His name is preserved, among other places, at nearby Prince Gallitzin State Park.

Fr. Lemke Takes Up the Charge

Gallitzin's legacy was in good hands. Fr. Thomas Heyden, a native of Ireland, was a youngster living in Bedford, Pennsylvania, when Fr. Gallitzin visited his family. Ordained in 1821, Heyden was sent to assist Gallitzin in the Loretto area and then became pastor of St. Thomas, Bedford, where he served until his death in 1870. A year earlier, he had completed *A Memoir on the Life and Character of the Rev. Prince Demetrius A. de Gallitzin*.

Gallitzin's other clerical companion and biographer followed a more circuitous route in finding his way to western Pennsylvania. Peter Lemke was born in northeastern Germany, solid Lutheran country, in 1796. While attending school in the town of Schwerin, he first encountered Catholicism through a friendly family who invited him to attend Mass. After a stint in the army, he entered the Lutheran seminary at Rostock. During this period Lemke was drawn a bit closer to Catholicism by a fellow student who returned to the Catholicism of his youth during his studies in the Lutheran university. Then, during his pastoral apprenticeship, Lemke read a set of the original works of Luther and was repelled by what he found. He resigned from the seminary and floundered for a time as he searched for a spiritual home. He finally found it in Ratisbon (located in what is today southeastern Germany), where he befriended the future cardinal, Melchior von Diepenbrock. He was ordained a Catholic priest in 1826.

A few years later, a priest-friend shared with him a letter from Fr. (future bishop) Francis Kenrick of Philadelphia, imploring Germany to send priests for the immigrants of America. Lemke decided to answer the call. He arrived in New York in 1834. Kenrick, by that time coadjutor bishop of Philadelphia, gave him his first American assignment as assistant pastor at the German parish of Holy Trinity. Here Lemke's anti-Lutheran passion got him into hot water. On the occasion of a commemoration of the Protestant Reformation in

Philadelphia, Lemke preached a sermon on the topic at Holy Trinity. The trustees of the church paid him a visit afterward, explaining that "as we wish to live in peace with our Protestant neighbors, we have come in to tell you that you must not preach any more sermons like that in this church." The priest erupted in a fit of anger and threatened the startled parishioners. He went to Kenrick the next day and asked to be reassigned. He was granted permission to go on a missionary tour of Pennsylvania, ministering to the widely scattered German-speaking Catholics of the state.

Lemke soon fell in love with the wilderness and the Catholics of Penn's Woodlands. At one settlement along the Susquehanna River, he spent a few days with Swiss settlers. He witnessed his hosts dispatch a black bear with axes, followed by a feast of bear meat. He received a mother, four weeks postpartum, who trotted in on a horse with her newborn to have the baby baptized by a priest. Catechism classes and baptisms had been handled for years by an elderly man, sire of many of the area's Catholics. Lemke was "filled with wonder at the healthy and correct religious views of these people, who had grown up in the woods, as also at the simplicity and purity of their lives. Here one sees the power of the Catholic faith; here one for the first time fully realizes what is meant by tradition."

Three hundred miles west of Philadelphia, at the "top of the Allegheny Mountains," Lemke arrived in Munster, the heart of Catholic territory. His host assured him that "in the entire neighborhood and for many miles around there is not an un-Catholic bone to be found." There he met one of the area's most respected residents, who arrived in a horse-drawn sled. "Before me I saw an old reverend gentleman with snow-white hair, wide-brimmed, badly-worn hat, and a coat of homespun twill, but noble in bearing and mien—it was Prince Gallitzin." Lemke's pencil sketch of this encounter remains the only likeness of Gallitzin that survives.

The First American Monastery

After a brief return to Philadelphia, Fr. Lemke was granted a permanent assignment in the west and became Fr. Gallitzin's assistant.

When the prince-priest died, Lemke replaced him in Loretto, and for the next year, as Gallitzin had been, he was the only priest serving Cambria County. After the Diocese of Pittsburgh was established in 1843, Lemke returned to Germany to raise funds for the support of his penurious parishes. In Munich, he met a Benedictine monk, Boniface Wimmer, who was considering joining the American missions. Lemke encouraged him to think bigger: Why not establish a Benedictine abbey in the United States? Pennsylvania would be the perfect spot. Less than two years later, Lemke welcomed Wimmer to Pennsylvania, where he founded the nation's first Benedictine monastery. The former Sportsman's Hall settlement had become St. Vincent's parish, with a thriving Catholic community and new brick church (1835). The pastor of St. Vincent's, Michael Gallagher, turned the parish and its property over to Wimmer and his monks. They built what would become St. Vincent's Archabbey, from which sprang other Benedictine monasteries in New Jersey, North Carolina, Kansas, Alabama, Illinois, and Minnesota.

Lemke decided to join the Benedictines at St. Vincent's and was received into the order in 1852. His tenure there was sadly shortened, as he became embroiled in a series of legal problems, the result of both unfortunate circumstances and financial mismanagement of the properties that he held. Lemke fled to Kansas, where he joined his friend, Bishop John Baptist Miège. He gradually reconciled with Abbot Wimmer, and in the process served as the catalyst for the founding of a Benedictine monastery in Atchison, Kansas. Lemke lived out his final years at Carrolltown, where he died on November 28, 1882.

The Catholic community continued to thrive after Gallitzin, Heyden, and Lemke passed from the scene. Gallitzin's humble log church in Loretto was replaced in 1817 by a frame building. In 1854, a larger brick church was built to meet the needs of the growing congregation. Then, in 1900, the brick church was razed and a grand Romanesque edifice faced with Ohio sandstone was constructed. The enormous cost of what was to become the Basilica of St. Michael was borne by the president of America's largest corporation, US Steel.

The Steel Titan from Loretto

Charles Schwab (1862–1939) was born in Williamsburg, Pennsylvania. His grandparents were among the contingent of German Catholic immigrants who had populated the Loretto area. In 1874, the Schwab family moved back to Loretto, where Charles spent most of his childhood. Schwab's early education was provided by the Sisters of Mercy, and the boy also benefited from the tutelage of Fr. Horace Brown. Fr. Brown had been a pupil of the celebrated Hungarian composer and pianist Franz Liszt before coming to the United States and taking a chaplaincy with the Sisters of Mercy. Brown gave young Schwab singing lessons for several years, nurturing what was to be a lifelong love of music.

Schwab completed his education—the equivalent of today's high school curriculum—at Loretto's St. Francis College. Beginning as a day laborer in the steel industry, Schwab was, within ten years, the "foremost production expert" in the United States. At age thirty-five, he became president of the Carnegie Steel Company. When Carnegie and J. P. Morgan merged their concerns into U.S. Steel, Schwab became president of the first billion-dollar company in America.

Like others, Schwab suffered financially in the thirties, even attempting to sell his New York mansion. In Loretto, however, he kept operating his vast estate with no reduction in staff. Instead, he hired more employees, helping to keep the town's economy afloat.

Throughout most of his life, Schwab kept his distance from both the moral code and the institutions of the Catholic faith in which he had been raised—but he never abandoned Catholicism entirely. In 1928, his sister, Mary Jane, who was a talented singer, recovered from a throat ailment and determined in return to fulfill a vow to God to become a cloistered nun. Charles contributed $200,000 to build a new monastery in Loretto for her congregation, the Discalced Carmelites.

As a tribute to his deeply Catholic mother, Pauline, in 1903 Schwab arranged an audience for her with the pope. But Pauline remained disappointed that Charles would not go to church. After her husband's death, she obtained from Charles an agreement to attend Mass with her during the four months out of each year that he spent at his Loretto estate.

The religious communities of Loretto, who had educated Schwab but whose principles he had mostly disdained, nonetheless received recompense in the end. When the Schwab estate was auctioned in 1942, the only bid came from the trustees of St. Francis College, a school established by Franciscan teaching brothers in 1847. The estate is now a friary. High on a hill overlooking the town of Loretto, Franciscan priests inhabit the spacious rooms of the manor house built as a showpiece for one of the country's most famous capitalists.

Nearby is the church, funded by Schwab, that serves the parish founded by Demetrius Gallitzin. In 1996, the historical significance of St. Michael's was recognized by the Vatican when it was designated a basilica. In the midst of a green lawn outside the church is a rectangular enclosure surrounded by a black wrought iron fence. Here lies Gallitzin's tomb, surmounted by a statue of this first pastor of St. Michael's parish. It is, one might say, a burial place fit for a prince.

Sources

Brownson, Sarah M. *Life of Demetrius Gallitzin, Prince and Priest.* New York: Fr. Pustet, 1873.

Bunson, Margaret, and Matthew Bunson. *Apostle of the Alleghenies: Reverend Demetrius Augustine Gallitzin.* Hollidaysburg, PA: Diocese of Altoona-Johnstown, 1999.

Dichtl, John R. *Frontiers of Faith: Bringing Catholicism to the West in the Early Republic.* Lexington: University Press of Kentucky, 2008.

Flick, Lawrence F. "Biographical Sketch of Rev. Peter Henry Lemke, O.S.B., 1796–1882." *Records of the American Catholic Historical Society* 9, no. 2 (1898): 129–92.

Hessen, Robert. *Steel Titan: The Life of Charles M. Schwab.* Pittsburgh: University of Pittsburgh Press, 1990.

Lemcke, Peter Henry, OSB. *Life and Work of Prince Demetrius Augustine Gallitzin.* Translated by Joseph C. Plumpe. London: Longmans, Green, 1941. (First German ed., 1861.)

Oetgen, Jerome. *Mission to America: A History of Saint Vincent Archabbey, the First Benedictine Monastery in the United States.* Washington, DC: Catholic University of America Press, 2000.

Schlafly, Daniel L., Jr. "Father Demetrius A. Gallitzin: Son of the Russian Enlightenment." *Catholic Historical Review* 83 (October 1997): 716–25.

Wirtner, Modestus, OSB. *The Benedictine Fathers in Cambria County Pennsylvania (1925).* USGenWeb Archives, www.usgwarchives.net/pa/cambria/chur-benedict-01.html.

8.

Prompt Succor for Andrew Jackson

The Ursuline Convent, New Orleans
1100 Chartres Street
New Orleans, Louisiana 70116

*Did you know that Catholic nuns held
vigil in prayer for an American victory
at the Battle of New Orleans?*

The Battle of New Orleans is an iconic episode in American history. It launched General Andrew Jackson into a national notoriety that would ultimately lead him to the White House. Country music star Johnny Horton sang about it in his 1959 chart-topper that boasted about the Americans sending the British running back to the Gulf of Mexico.

The final battle of the War of 1812, it has often been said, took place after the War of 1812 was over. The peace treaty ending hostilities between the United States and Great Britain had been signed in Ghent, Belgium, on December 24, 1814, but word hadn't yet reached the opposing armies facing off along the Mississippi River in January of 1815. Technically, however, the war had not ended; the terms of the treaty specified that the state of war ceased when both countries ratified the treaty, which was only accomplished on February 16, 1815.

In any case, the decisive victory was a morale booster for the American nation. The triumph of the out-trained and outnumbered Americans over a seemingly superior force was a satisfying conclusion to a war that had seen British troops ransack and burn the capital city, putting Congress and President James Madison to flight.

It's no surprise, then, that many Americans, led by Andrew Jackson himself, attributed the victory to divine intervention. The epigraph in radio personality Brian Kilmeade's book on the subject—whose title uses the phrase "the miracle of New Orleans"—is a passage from a memoir by one of the American officers who was present. "Our situation seemed desperate," he wrote, and "we could hope to be saved only by a miracle."

It is more surprising, however, that the intervention on behalf of what was at the time an overwhelmingly Protestant and often anti-Catholic country appears to have come through the intercession of the Blessed Virgin Mary, invoked by a group of Catholic nuns. They had already been part of the Crescent City community for more than ninety years.

The Ursulines of New Orleans

St. Angela Merici founded the Ursuline order in Italy in 1535 with the express purpose of educating girls. It was the first Catholic religious institute dedicated to that aim, and nearly five hundred years later the Ursulines remain true to that original purpose. The Ursulines thrived especially in France, and by the early eighteenth century there were three hundred convents there.

But they were also in conflict with the French government of Louis XIV. Ironically, it was a situation in Louisiana that was partly to blame. John Law, the king's finance minister, organized a scheme for raising funds by selling shares in the government-controlled company that exploited the resources of France's holdings in North America. All of Europe enthused over the latest get-rich-quick scheme as share prices rose. But the "Mississippi Bubble" burst in 1720, destroying the finances of many investors, including Catholic religious orders that Louis had forced to buy shares.

In response, the French government instituted a commission to oversee religious congregations' finances, allegedly for the purpose of preventing them from becoming burdens on the state. But this mechanism also gave the Crown a lever to exert control over the orders' activities. The Ursulines resisted this abridgement of their independence and found themselves at odds with the king.

Louisiana, initially the source of distress, now became the means of liberation and revival. In 1727, the Ursulines signed a contract with the Company of the Indies—the French firm charged with managing the Louisiana colony—that spelled out the terms of the order's settlement in New Orleans. In essence, the company agreed to provide the nuns with the material means necessary for their maintenance, and in return, the Ursulines would staff a hospital to serve the healthcare needs of the colony—soldiers and company employees first and foremost.[1]

Not for the first time, the European passengers found the Atlantic crossing a harrowing experience. Surviving pirates, storms, and shortage of provisions, the twelve sisters led by Mother St. Augustin arrived at New Orleans in August of 1727. By the end of the eighteenth century, the Ursulines were a thriving community of French Creole and Spanish Cuban sisters providing much-needed educational services to a multiethnic clientele. One of their early convents, completed in 1751, still stands in the French Quarter as a national landmark, and their earliest apostolate, a school for girls, remains in operation as Ursuline Academy.

Becoming American

When the Ursulines' property, along with the rest of New Orleans, became part of the United States through the 1803 Louisiana Purchase, the nuns were at first wary of their new government. "They had heard about the inhospitable climate that Catholics endured in many of the British colonies and were uncertain about their place in the largely Protestant new republic. Convents of women religious—"nunneries" in the populist patois—were frequently targets of harsh criticism from Protestants on both sides of the Atlantic.

The secrecy surrounding the cloister at once titillated and troubled anti-Catholic critics.

The superior of the New Orleans convent, Mother Therese de St. Xavier, wrote to President Thomas Jefferson seeking assurance that their educational work and religious practice might proceed unimpeded. The president replied with what has become a classic document in the history of religious liberty in the United States. "The principles of the constitution and government of the United states," he began, "are a sure guarantee to you that [your property] will be preserved to you sacred and inviolate, and that your institution will be permitted to govern itself according to its own voluntary rules, without interference from the civil authority. . . . Be assured it will meet all the protection which my office can give it." Jefferson's solicitude sealed the Ursulines' allegiance to their new country, which they had opportunity to demonstrate when war with Britain erupted a few years later.

In 1815, the nuns were located on Chartres Street. The sisters used their classrooms as a hospital for the wounded of both British and American armies, but there was no doubt where their loyalties lay. On the night of January 7, as British troops prepared to invade the city with nothing but Jackson's unintimidating band of Americans standing in their way, the Ursulines began praying. Specifically, they prayed to Our Lady of Prompt Succor.

The statue of Our Lady under this title features Mary holding Jesus, both of them topped with tall, intricate crowns. The child is mostly naked, but the skin tones of his body and the mother's face are overshadowed by the gleaming golden veneer of Mary's veil and flowing garments. The representation is a tribute to the faith of one of the Ursuline superiors.

As the nineteenth century opened, the convent in America was struggling and needed reinforcements. Mother St. Michel wanted to go to New Orleans, but she needed permission from the pope to leave France. She prayed for Our Lady's intercession and permission was quickly granted. The speedy assistance spurred Mother St. Michel to promise to promote devotion to the Blessed Mother under the title

"Our Lady of Prompt Succor." She commissioned a statue that would serve as the image of Mary under that title, and it arrived with her at the Ursulines' Chartres Street convent in 1810. In 1812, the sisters prayed to Our Lady of Prompt Succor to protect the convent from a fire that was ravaging the city. The wind promptly changed direction, sparing the sisters and their shrine.

The Battle of New Orleans

Jackson's Americans would likewise need a miracle, it seemed. He was attempting to hold New Orleans with a motley force of 4,700 men, which included a few regular army and navy soldiers but was mostly militia and volunteers from Louisiana and neighboring states. Against them came eight thousand experienced British regulars, supported by King George III's Royal Navy. When the fleet set sail from Jamaica in November, it was the largest naval force that had ever been assembled in the Western Hemisphere.

New Orleans and its environs housed a population of twenty-five thousand, making it the largest city in the American West. It also controlled access to the transportation artery that carried the economic lifeblood of the Midwest, the mighty Mississippi. Jackson had been boxing with the British along the Gulf Coast for several months, trying to keep them out of the vital port city. A British victory at the Battle of Lake Borgne in December 1814 put them on the doorstep of New Orleans and alarmed both the city and the American military command. Jackson declared martial law in New Orleans so as to organize its defenses and confiscate any necessary materiel of war. So desperate was his plight that he flouted convention by enlisting the help of two battalions of free Black men as well as the Baratarian pirates who operated a local smuggling enterprise and whom he had earlier denounced as "hellish banditti."[2]

The first skirmish occurred on December 23, when Jackson launched a nighttime raid on the British camp. He then constructed a defensive line made of earthworks (not cotton bales, as the legend has it) and awaited the British advance. At dawn on January 8, a barrage of artillery signaled the beginning of the Battle of New Orleans.

In thirty minutes, it was over. The British had stumbled into a shooting gallery, and when they staggered out, they had lost two thousand men, including their chief officers. The Americans lost fewer than a hundred, and their commanding officer had taken his first step toward the White House. Jackson marched triumphantly into New Orleans to public celebration. On February 4, news reached the East Coast, where newspaper headlines declared, "Glorious Victory!"

Back in the Ursuline chapel, the sisters and some lay collaborators finished their all-night vigil and prepared to join Bishop Louis DuBourg, apostolic administrator of the Diocese of Louisiana, for Sunday morning Mass on January 8. The service was nearing its completion when someone burst into the chapel shouting, "Victory is ours!" DuBourg ended the Mass with a *Te Deum*, the celebratory hymn traditionally sung on major feast days. On January 23, the bishop presided over a thanksgiving service at St. Louis Cathedral, where ten thousand Americans joined Jackson and DuBourg in offering gratitude for the providential course of events.

When General Jackson learned of the sisters' prayers, he publicly thanked them and sent a letter expressing his gratitude for the "heavenly intercession" that ensured victory. Later, as president, Jackson's travels brought him back to New Orleans, and his schedule included a visit to the Ursuline Convent.

For their part, the Ursulines pledged to offer a Mass of thanksgiving every year, in perpetuity, on January 8, the anniversary of the Battle of New Orleans. That custom has continued to the present, and it is often the archbishop himself who celebrates the liturgy.

The sisters have moved twice since 1815, and in 1910 they settled at their current location on State Street. There they built a new academy as well as a chapel for their venerable statue. That chapel is today the National Shrine of Our Lady of Prompt Succor.

Sources

Clark, Emily. *Masterless Mistresses: The New Orleans Ursulines and the Development of a New World Society, 1727–1834*. Williamsburg and Chapel Hill: Omohundro Institute of Early American Culture and University of North Carolina Press, 2007.

Cruzat, Heloise Hulse. "The Ursulines of Louisiana." *Louisiana Historical Quarterly* 2 (January 1919), www2.latech.edu/~bmagee/louisiana_anthology/texts/cruzat/cruzat--ursulines.html.

Donze, Beth. "'Our Lady of Prompt Succor' Title Dates from 1810." *New Orleans Clarion Herald*, January 6, 2018.

Hickey, Donald R. *Glorious Victory: Andrew Jackson and the Battle of New Orleans.* Baltimore: Johns Hopkins University Press, 2015.

Kilmeade, Brian, and Don Yaeger. *Andrew Jackson and the Miracle of New Orleans: The Battle That Shaped America's Destiny.* New York: Sentinel, 2017.

Peschier, Diana. *Nineteenth-Century Anti-Catholic Discourses: The Case of Charlotte Brontë.* New York: Palgrave Macmillan, 2005.

Woods, James M. *A History of the Catholic Church in the American South, 1513–1900.* Gainesville: University Press of Florida, 2011.

9.

Catholicism on the Bourbon Trail

Church of St. Thomas
870 St. Thomas Lane
Bardstown, Kentucky 40004

Did you know that one of the earliest American dioceses was on the Kentucky frontier, at the settlement of Bardstown?

Just off the Bluegrass Parkway in north-central Kentucky, less than a mile east of US 31-E at the end of St. Thomas Lane, stands a brick church fronted by a square façade featuring statues of Jesus and Mary in niches on either side of the entry door. Close beside is a two-story log cabin with weathered gray siding, which is now a historical museum. The parish boasts of being the "cradle of Catholicism in Kentucky," and for good reason. From this modest patch of real estate sprouted Kentucky's first Catholic seminary, the home of Kentucky's first bishop, and the motherhouse of a new American religious order. To appreciate this region, you need to appreciate what stands at the heart of it: Catholicism.

Well, that and whiskey. A few miles from St. Thomas Church is another museum that highlights the other major influence in the region's history and culture: the Bourbon Heritage Center.

Through the Cumberland Gap

In the aftermath of independence, American pioneers, many from Maryland and Virginia, quickly availed themselves of western lands that had been successfully claimed by the new nation. They crossed the great barrier of the Appalachians in western Maryland by funneling through the Cumberland Gap on the Wilderness Road, a trail blazed by Daniel Boone. For a few years, these settlers remained part of the state of Virginia, but the natural barrier of the mountains made that arrangement impractical, and there was soon clamor for a new state. In 1792, Kentucky became the first state west of the Appalachians.

Settlers in the Bardstown area encountered several unusual natural features that became valuable assets for resourceful Kentuckians. White-oak trees populating the woods could be made into flavorful casks, which are assisted in maturation by the local climate of alternating hot summers and cold winters. The land is undergirded by a shelf of blue limestone, which serves as a filter for groundwater, taking iron out and putting magnesium and calcium in.[1] And the rich soil supported the growing of corn rather than the rye that was favored in Virginia. All of these provided the ingredients for "America's native spirit," Kentucky bourbon.

Bourbon County was one of the earliest organized jurisdictions in Kentucky. Formed immediately after the Revolution, it was named in honor of King Louis XVI of France, who had so critically provided assistance during the conflict with Britain. The House of Bourbon's rule would come to a violent end a few years later, when French revolutionaries executed the king by guillotine. In America, meanwhile, the county of Bourbon was thriving.

Initially, Bourbon County encompassed most of the bluegrass region. As Daniel Boone and other pioneers showed the way, white settlers began streaming into the fertile meadows and forests. The corn-based whiskey took its name from the county in which it was created.

Liquor was a hot political issue in the early days of the United States. Consumption of alcoholic beverages was building to its apex in the early 1800s. Taverns were centers of social life, and drink was a marker of regional, class, and ethnic identity. In some places, liquor was a medium of exchange. Thus, the federal government's imposition of a tax on distilled spirits met stiff resistance, especially in western Pennsylvania, where farmers took up arms against the government in 1794. This "Whiskey Rebellion" was suppressed by order of President George Washington, but a new political issue was born—one that Thomas Jefferson's Republican Party exploited in the course of its victory over John Adams's Federalists in 1800. The Jefferson administration abolished the liquor tax, and whiskey consumption soared. Bourbon County became bourbon country, and it remains so to this day. Ninety-five percent of the world's bourbon is produced in the state of Kentucky.

On the western edge of the bluegrass region is the city of Bardstown, seat of Nelson County. Among the early settlers lured into the west by the promise of bountiful and productive land were Catholics, many of them from old Maryland families. "Maryland was, in every respect," the priest-historian Martin Spalding wrote, "the great alma mater of the Catholics of Kentucky. She supplied them with people from her superabundant population; and she too sent out the first missionaries who broke to them the bread of life."[2]

The Howard Estate

There were only thirty Catholic churches in the entire nation when Catholics began moving to the Kentucky frontier. The Marylanders who settled in Nelson County were not the first Catholics in Kentucky, but they would create the institutional infrastructure for the state's Catholic community. In 1787, one of them, Edward Howard, made his home near Bardstown at a place called Poplar Neck; it likely served as the headquarters for one of Kentucky's earliest missionaries, the Irish Capuchin Charles Whelan (who had been ejected from St. Peter's

Church in New York during the trustee dispute; chapter 6). Edward's son Thomas inherited the estate and lived there with his family for the rest of his life. Thomas died shortly after the establishment of the diocese, and the region's stalwart missionary, Fr. Stephen Badin, wrote to Archbishop Carroll to report that his "good old friend" (Thomas) had bequeathed to Badin "a good plantation."

By the terms of the will, the Howard estate, a tract of nearly 370 acres, was to remain in the possession of the Catholic Church in perpetuity. It was property that would be put to good use.

Fr. Benedict Flaget had been among the exile-priests who shifted their ministries to the New World after the French Revolution. When Bishop Carroll persuaded Pope Pius VII to lighten his burden by creating four new dioceses in 1808, the pope selected Flaget to fill the bishop's office in the Diocese of Bardstown.[3] The new diocese not only encompassed all of Kentucky and Tennessee but also carried with it pastoral responsibility over the territory that is now occupied by the states of Michigan, Ohio, Indiana, Illinois, Missouri, Iowa, and Wisconsin.

This was the endless wilderness through which Badin and other missionaries traveled tirelessly. Of those early ministers one historian wrote, "They virtually lived in the saddle, and almost performed the miracle of multi-location, so rapid were their movements." It is not surprising, then, that Flaget was at first overwhelmed by the task set before him. "Without money, without a house, without property, almost without acquaintance," he reflected in a later letter, "I found myself in the midst of a diocese larger than France . . . and myself speaking the language, too, very imperfectly." There were by this time perhaps a thousand Catholic families in all of Kentucky.

By the time Bishop Flaget arrived at his diocese in 1811, Thomas Howard had died and the Church was the beneficiary of his bequest. The Howard farm would be the terrestrial nucleus of the Bardstown diocese, but it would also be the source of conflict among the religious leaders of the local church: Bishop Flaget, Fr. (later bishop) Jean-Baptist David, and Mother Catherine Spalding.

The itinerant missionary Stephen Badin, whose land purchases included the future site of the University of Notre Dame (see chapter 11), also held extensive property in Kentucky. Badin was "by no means unique" in his acquisition of property, says historian Marvin O'Connell, but "the zest with which he entered into buying, selling, and transferring real-estate, and his failure to distinguish carefully enough between what belonged to him and what belonged to the Catholic community . . . to some extent set him apart." This legal sloppiness sometimes gave rise to conflict.

Prior to Flaget's appointment, Badin was Bishop Carroll's vicar general in Kentucky. In that capacity, Badin purchased land that was "held in his own name, but in trust for the Church." Badin promised Carroll that he would furnish adequate property for Flaget to take up his role as bishop in 1811, but Flaget later reported that Badin refused to do so.

Soon after Thomas Howard's death, his widow moved into smaller quarters so that the Howards' house could be occupied by Bishop Flaget. Flaget moved from his log cabin a few miles away into the Howards' former homestead, a similarly humble log cabin. A new, larger log house was built shortly thereafter. The bishop's residence would double as the diocesan seminary. Six young men moved in, and the place was soon bustling with spiritual and material activities.

Fr. William Howlett, who studied at St. Thomas Seminary in the nineteenth century, describes the spot:

> Far enough from town and highway to be beyond the sound of the tramp of the world's parade, it offered an opportunity for study and meditation that a St. Jerome might have envied. The surrounding farms, studded with groves, showed the hand of man without blotting out nature's work, and the general view was of an undulating surface gradually rising to the distant hills. . . . To its own doors came forests of giant beech and stately elm, of waving oak and trembling poplar, and from many ravines almost hidden by thicket of vine and shrub, there flowed out rills of crystal water. . . . Skirting the grounds, concealed by trees but within easy walk, the Beech Fork, gently laving its sloping banks or

dashing between confining cliffs, wound its way to meet its sister stream. . . . The presence of God could be felt and seen in everything.

In this pastoral paradise the clerics lived like the Kentucky backwoodsmen they were—wearing homespun, eating and drinking from tin vessels, subsisting on bacon and cornbread. Fr. Badin recounted these early days, when "the poverty of our infant establishments compelled [the seminarians] to spend their recreations in labor. Each day they devoted three hours to work in the garden, in the fields, or in the woods." This monastic lifestyle extended to other matters as well: "Nothing could be more frugal than their table . . . in which water is their ordinary drink; nothing, at the same time, could be more simple than their dress."

Among the students' more remarkable labors was the building of a church, designed by Maximilian Godefroy in the rococo-Gothic style, without spire or bell tower. The French-born Godefroy had immigrated to Baltimore in 1805 and promptly found work as an architect and professor at St. Mary's Seminary.

At thirty-five by seventy feet, the Bardstown chapel would be dwarfed by the Gothic behemoths built across Catholic America later in the century, but on the Kentucky frontier, where log huts were the norm, it was impressive enough. Completed in 1816, the church was dedicated to the patron saint of the benefactor who donated the land on which it stood. The seminarians made the bricks, mixed the mortar, and cut the lumber needed for the project; then they did the same for a new brick seminary building. The St. Thomas campus was expanding by leaps and bounds.

The Sisters of Charity of Nazareth

Bishop Flaget and his seminary director, Fr. Jean-Baptist David, before their postings to the frontier, had served in Emmitsburg, Maryland. There they had been involved in the formation of the Sisters of Charity by Mother Elizabeth Ann Seton. Knowing that the development of the Bardstown diocese could not continue without the assistance of consecrated women religious, and knowing at the same time that existing congregations were reluctant to expend their precious personnel on risky frontier endeavors, the two priests conspired to create a new, native Kentucky sisterhood.

On December 1, 1812, two young local women, in response to the invitation of Fr. David, dedicated themselves to the service of God. Less than a month later, a third woman joined; only nineteen years of age, she nonetheless quickly emerged as the leader of the group. Catherine Spalding was a Maryland native whose ancestors had helped to settle the colony 150 years earlier. The sisters at first occupied quarters in a corner of the bishop's residence next to St. Thomas Church, but they soon moved to a nearby cabin. They named this first motherhouse "Nazareth." Combined with their use of the rule derived from Elizabeth Seton's new congregation in Emmitsburg, it supplied the group's enduring name: Sisters of Charity of Nazareth.

The poverty of the sisters' early days is captured in the recorded account of their inaugural elections of offices: "They elected no treasurer, for they had no money to keep." Nonetheless, the sisters' numbers and apostolate grew rapidly, and they expended what few financial resources they acquired in building additions to their convent and school. Only after investing heavily in these structures did they learn that "the ground on which they had built was not their own, and never could be theirs." This was a shock not only to the sisters' material well-being but also to their morale—the violation of trust struck Mother Catherine as "the most dire calamity she had ever known."

It's difficult to sort out, but at least part of the problem was the language of Thomas Howard's will, which bequeathed the farm to Stephen Badin and Charles Nerinckx (the two priests working in the area) and "the then Roman Catholic Bishop of Kentucky" (Flaget) and to the "lawful heirs of the last survivor forever." Flaget seems to have discovered, too late, that this stipulation would prevent his transferring the land's title to the Sisters of Charity.

Flaget finally prevailed on Badin to deed the property of St. Thomas Church, but Flaget afterward discovered that only half the property had been legally conveyed and "the very house in which I am now living with my seminarians was not included in the document."

Archbishop Carroll himself was eventually compelled to intervene in the dispute. Badin retired to France in 1819, after which time the title was apparently settled in favor of Flaget.

Catherine Spalding and her sisters recovered quickly. A Presbyterian minister offered for sale a well-situated 237-acre plot. Meanwhile, from Baltimore came a new sister, Ann O'Connor, a convert and a wealthy widow, who immediately placed her resources at the disposal of the congregation. This transaction was not straightforward either: with O'Connor drawing funds from depleted land values in the yellow-fever-stricken East Coast, payment was delayed and the title was in limbo for three years. Finally, in 1825, the Sisters of Charity of Nazareth received the deed to their property. Today, the impressive motherhouse of the congregation stands on this same land, the "new" Nazareth to which the sisters moved in 1822.

During the previous year, the inevitable dispossession of the Diocese of Bardstown had begun, as the creation of the Diocese of Cincinnati detached a giant territory from its northern reaches. Eventually, some thirty diocesan sees would be formed out of what had once been the great western diocese. But Catholicism had sunk deep roots in Bardstown, and its branches continued to spread. In the same year that the Sisters of Nazareth were founded, the Sisters of Loretto had their start nearby, and the first Trappist monastery in the United States, Our Lady of Gethsemani, set up on some of the sisters' land in 1848. Nazareth, Loretto, and Gethsemani are some of the place names that gave the area its sobriquet, the "Holy Land of Kentucky."

As for St. Thomas, its status as the bishop's home was shortly relinquished when St. Joseph Cathedral was built in the city of Bardstown in 1819. The St. Thomas campus continued as home to a seminary and various other educational institutions through the 1860s, but afterward it fell into disrepair. St. Joseph's subsequently lost its rank when the diocese itself was transferred to the thriving Ohio River port city of Louisville in 1841.

Thus the church on Thomas Howard's farm now lies far from the seat of ecclesiastical power. St. Thomas is a humble country church, but it remains the hub of a parish community and, as dictated by Howard's will, the property of the Catholic Church. It also retains its status as the cradle of Kentucky Catholicism.

Sources

Crews, Clyde F. *An American Holy Land: A History of the Archdiocese of Louisville.* Wilmington, DE: Michael Glazier, 1987.

Doyle, Mary Ellen, SCN. *Pioneer Spirit: Catherine Spalding, Sister of Charity of Nazareth.* Lexington: University Press of Kentucky, 2006.

Fox, Columba, SCN. *The Life of the Right Reverend John Baptist Mary David (1761–1841).* New York: U.S. Catholic Historical Society, 1925.

Fulkerson, Norman J. "America's Native Spirit." *ReturnToOrder.org,* www.returntoorder.org/2015/10/americas-native-spirit.

Guilday, Peter. *The Life and Times of John Carroll, Archbishop of Baltimore (1735–1815).* New York: Encyclopedia Press, 1922.

Howlett, William J. *Historical Tribute to St. Thomas' Seminary at Poplar Neck Near Bardstown, Kentucky.* St. Louis: B. Herder, 1906.

Klein, Christopher. "How Kentucky Became the World's Bourbon Capital." History.com, www.history.com/news/how-kentucky-became-the-worlds-bourbon-capital.

Lancaster, Clay. *Antebellum Architecture of Kentucky.* Lexington: University Press of Kentucky, 1991.

Mattingly, Mary Ramona. *The Catholic Church on the Kentucky Frontier (1785–1812).* Washington, DC: Catholic University of America, 1936.

O'Connell, Marvin R. *Edward Sorin.* Notre Dame, IN: University of Notre Dame Press, 2001.

Peter, Robert. *History of Bourbon, Scott, Harrison and Nicholas Counties, Kentucky.* Edited by William Henry Perrin. Chicago: O. L. Baskin, 1882.

Spalding, Martin J. *Sketches of the Early Catholic Missions of Kentucky from Their Commencement in 1787 to the Jubilee of 1826–7. 1844;* rpr. New York: Arno, 1972.

10.

A Hurricane Survivor on the Gulf Coast

St. Mary's Cathedral Basilica
2011 Church Street
Galveston, Texas 77550

*Did you know that the deadliest
hurricane in American history hit
Galveston in 1900?*

Three spires of stone rise from the streets of historic downtown Galveston, an island city just off the Texas mainland. Atop one stands a fifteen-foot statue of the Blessed Virgin Mary. "Mary, Star of the Sea" was erected in 1878, and her illuminated crown was a beacon to seafarers in the Gulf of Mexico. Her arms are extended over the roof of the nave, as though in protection of the building itself. Some local Catholics say that she has helped the church remain standing through two devastating hurricanes.

Galveston's Catholic Roots

The Spanish heritage of Texas is obvious even today, but Catholicism there also owes much to France. The French Revolution of 1789 was a painful chapter in the history of the Church in France, but France's pain was America's gain: persecution drove many clergy out of the country and, often enough, into the mission territory of the United States. With the link established, a pipeline of priests, brothers, and sisters continued to deliver Church personnel from the Old World to the New throughout the nineteenth century.

The Archdiocese of Lyon in southern France is the oldest of Catholic centers in an ancient Catholic country. In the early nineteenth century, it was a training ground for priests who would later collaborate in building the Catholic Church in America. As a seminarian in Lyon, the future bishop of Galveston, Jean-Marie Odin, met the newly ordained Antoine Blanc, who would preside over Galveston's next-door neighbor, the Archdiocese of New Orleans. Another product of Lyon, Michel Portier, would lead the diocese east of New Orleans at Mobile, Alabama.

In 1816, New Orleans's bishop was another Frenchman and an exile from the Revolution, Louis DuBourg. Traveling in Europe to recruit priests and religious, he took the opportunity to ordain Odin, who had already been persuaded to join the American mission by one of DuBourg's representatives.

Odin arrived in New Orleans in 1822. There he was introduced to slavery, an appalling institution that had no presence in France. Odin would remain mostly quiet on the topic throughout his years of ministry, but his initial reaction revealed his views of the matter. He wrote to his sister of "one spectacle very deserving of pity; it is that of the Negroes. . . . They are treated as one would treat a beast of burden in France." He described the slavery he encountered as "the greatest cause of sadness" and lamented the fact that many slave owners would not educate their laborers, permit them to marry, or even allow them to attend church services.

In the South, however, many Catholics—including religious orders such as Jesuits and Vincentians—owned slaves. Odin himself would later possess some slaves for a time in Galveston. They were bestowed as a gift, and he agonized over what to do with them.

Galveston, however, lay in the future. Odin's American adventure began in earnest not in Texas but in Missouri.

Connections between Barrens Colony, Missouri, and Texas

It was old Maryland Catholic families, who had settled in Kentucky and then moved farther west across the Mississippi River, who created the Barrens Colony in southeastern Missouri. The Congregation of the Mission—Vincentians—served the spiritual needs of this settlement. Led by Fr. Joseph Rosati, they founded a seminary at the Barrens in 1818. In a letter back to Bardstown, Rosati paid tribute to the Maryland/Kentucky heritage in his description of one of the buildings. The planned residence, he wrote, would be "much like the brick house of St. Thomas in Kentucky" (see chapter 9).

Odin joined the Vincentians at the Barrens, trained in the seminary there, and met John Timon, who would become his lifelong friend. After ordination, Odin worked for a time as a missionary in Missouri and Arkansas. When the Second Provincial Council of Baltimore was called in 1833, Odin traveled to the historic center of American Catholicism as a theologian for now-Bishop Rosati, meeting the great Western missionary Pierre De Smet, SJ, along the way.

Although he didn't know it yet, Odin's life would be changed by political events in the region that had been New Spain. Spain had laid claim to Texas with the explorations of Alonso Álvarez de Pineda in 1519. Franciscan and Jesuit missionaries were active on the north side of the Rio Grande by the early 1600s, a result of the region's proximity to the capital of New Spain at Mexico City. The first Franciscan mission in Texas was established in 1632 near what is now San Angelo. By the end of the 1700s, some three dozen more missions were founded. The most famous of those early missions is undoubtedly San Antonio de Valero (1718), on whose grounds was fought a renowned battle of American history. Mission San Antonio is better known as the Alamo.

During the nineteenth century, immigrants to Texas—notably Irish settling at San Patricio de Hibernia (1830)—added another dimension to Hispanic Catholicism. Thus there was a large Catholic presence in Texas when the territory declared independence from Mexico in 1836. The ensuing conflict, during which Davy Crockett, Jim Bowie, and others famously defended the Alamo mission compound, culminated in the short-lived Lone Star Republic. In 1845, the United States annexed Texas, which became the twenty-eighth state.

Meanwhile, in 1838, the Vincentians had been assigned to the district of Texas. When Texas declared its independence from Mexico, Pope Gregory XVI formed the Prefecture Apostolic of Texas in 1839. (A prefecture apostolic precedes the formation of a diocese.) Odin's friend Bishop John Timon was named prefect apostolic, and Odin was appointed his vice prefect. Given the difficulties of travel and his later appointment to head the Diocese of Buffalo, Timon would never spend much time in Texas, and Odin effectively functioned as the spiritual head of the region. In 1840, Odin and three other Vincentians floated down the Mississippi River from Missouri to New Orleans and then traveled on to Texas. Odin's travels had just begun. He undertook a thorough visitation of his new pastorate, ranging from San Antonio to Galveston, where he arrived in early 1841.

Arrival in Galveston

Odin's confrere Bishop Timon had scouted the island city in late 1838. Texas was, like most of the nation, rural. Only 4 percent of its population lived in urban areas, and it boasted none of the metropolises—Houston, Dallas, San Antonio—that would later arise. Galveston was incorporated in 1839. Possessing the region's best harbor, the city grew rapidly, and by 1860 it contained seven thousand residents. Timon found a diverse Catholic population among the residents of the busy port. French Canadians, Louisiana Creoles, Italians, Germans, Spanish, and Irish were all represented in the nucleus of the Texas Church. On December 28, 1838, in a house newly built to accommodate the growing number of American newcomers, Timon celebrated Galveston's first Mass.

There was still no church building in the city when Odin arrived in 1841. On July 16 of that year, Texas was raised to a vicariate apostolic and Odin was given charge of the area. On February 6, 1842, there was a Mass to celebrate the appointment—the first Mass said in the new Church of St. Mary. With his flock composed mostly of humble people of modest means, Odin himself had contributed more than half of the nine hundred dollars required for construction of the small, wood-frame structure. It was the first step toward the three-towered bastion that now anchors the city and defies hurricanes.

As vicar, Odin would be raised to the rank of bishop. Odin's episcopal consecration was held at the ornate Cathedral of St. Louis in New Orleans. Bishops Blanc of New Orleans and Portier of Mobile (Odin's friends from the Lyon seminary days) and Bishop John Chanche of Natchez presided over the magnificent ceremony. It was a display not only of the growing demographic and institutional clout of Catholicism along the Gulf Coast but also of the domination of the region's leadership by French clerics—most of them from the Archdiocese of Lyon.

Odin had prepared for his consecration by going on retreat at the Ursuline Convent. His spiritual grounding ensured that he would suffer no delusions of grandeur. To his mother he wrote, "Don't go imagining that with this title your poor son will be obliged to live in an episcopal palace, to go out in a carriage, etc. A bishop of Texas must always lead the life of a missionary." This meant, among other things, that Odin would at times lead the life of a beggar. Here, his French roots provided more than episcopal camaraderie. An 1845 visit to France included a meeting with the Society of the Propagation of the Faith in Paris. This lay-initiated society was a boon for many fledgling American dioceses in the nineteenth century. From 1850 to 1900, the Diocese of Galveston received $250,000, making it the largest single beneficiary of the society's funds.

The New St. Mary's

By the time Odin returned to Galveston in the summer of 1846, it was clear that a grander church would be necessary to serve the city properly. Odin once again drew on his ethnic contacts, hiring the French émigré architect Theodore Giraud to design and oversee construction of the structure. Gothic in style and cruciform in shape, it was to be 120 by 60 feet, with an 80-foot transept.

The cornerstone for the new St. Mary's was laid on March 14, 1847. Less than two months later, Galveston was elevated to a diocese. In an unusual twist, the exact boundaries of the new diocese remained indeterminate due to the turmoil of the Mexican-American War. The papal bull from Pope Pius IX decreed that the diocese would encompass "all of Texas such as its limits may be after the difficulties with Mexico have been settled." What was certain was that the new church would be a cathedral, the mother church of a new diocese.

Odin had been promised a donation of five hundred thousand bricks by a Belgian brick merchant, but the donation never materialized. So the bricks were made locally, adding greatly to the expense. Another challenge was the weather. Life on the Gulf of Mexico means the annual summer threat of hurricanes. An 1847 storm damaged the roof of the new building, but construction soon resumed, and the Cathedral of St. Mary's was consecrated on August 25, 1848. Odin's old friends Bishop Blanc of New Orleans and John Timon, now bishop of Buffalo, were there. Ursuline sisters from New Orleans, whom Odin had managed to recruit for his diocese the previous year, joined the priests and dignitaries in a quarter-mile procession from the episcopal residence to the cathedral.

The event was a triumph for Odin. He confessed in a letter afterward that he had been worried there would be only a small crowd for his huge church, but as it turned out the space was "sufficiently full." As always, his purpose was not personal glory but the welfare of his people and the Church. "This building," he wrote, "which gave me so much anxiety, will, I hope, contribute to the strengthening and the propagation of the Faith."

The cathedral quickly became a center of activity for the Catholic Church in Texas. On Sunday, June 13, 1858, the first diocesan synod was opened with a Solemn Pontifical High Mass. The synod set rules for the diocese regarding matters such as parish life, education, and financial affairs. Another Pontifical High Mass closed the proceedings a week later.

By that time, the storm clouds of sectional strife were on the horizon. Texas would soon join other southern states in separating itself from the Union. On April 12, 1861, Confederate troops under the command of P. G. T. Beauregard—a Catholic from New Orleans—fired on Fort Sumter, South Carolina, and the Civil War began. A few days later, word reached Galveston that a successor for Archbishop Blanc, who died in June 1860, had been chosen for New Orleans. Bishop Odin would have to leave behind his beloved Texas diocese, including the cathedral he had built, to return to New Orleans.

As archbishop of New Orleans, Odin was attending the First Vatican Council when he took ill. He returned to his hometown in France, where he died in May of 1870.

Weathering the Storms

The Diocese of Galveston continued to prosper in the post–Civil War years. During the late nineteenth century, Galveston served as a kind of Texan Ellis Island, as immigrants streamed in from ships docking at its port. Newcomers helped to swell the Catholic population of the state, home to more than three million people by the turn of the twentieth century. From its infancy as a Franciscan mission system through its humble early growth under the leadership of Bishop Odin, the Catholic Church in Texas had reached maturity, its presence firmly established in the Lone Star State.

The natural climate, however, remained as volatile as ever. On September 8, 1900, the deadliest hurricane in American history slammed into Galveston Island. The storm surge inundated the city, taking eight thousand lives.[1] Among the few buildings left standing was the Cathedral of St. Mary.

The hurricane squelched the hopes of Galveston's business boosters. Industrialists—oil executives, in particular—began to doubt the wisdom of investing heavily in the Galveston area, and economic momentum shifted elsewhere. By the 1950s, it was clear that the nearby inland city of Houston had outpaced Galveston as a commercial and population center. The Church changed the name of the diocese to "Galveston-Houston," and a co-cathedral was designated in the larger city. The population of the state continued to rocket upward, fueled by oil booms, Mexican immigration, and new industries in defense and transportation. By 2000, Texas's twenty million people made it the second most populous state in the Union. The continued growth of the Church in Texas prompted the Vatican to raise the diocese to the rank of archdiocese in 2004.

Four years later, the durability of St. Mary's was once again tested, when category 4 Hurricane Ike struck Galveston, battering the cathedral with 110-mile-per-hour winds. The roof was severely damaged and water filled the first story, destroying pews, furnishings, and HVAC equipment. The survivor of the Great Storm of 1900 was temporarily put out of commission.

But the hardy St. Mary's survived. Following a costly repair process, the cathedral was ready to host Mass for Easter of 2014. "Easter is a time of rebirth," said the archbishop of Galveston-Houston, Cardinal Daniel DiNardo, "and this is the rebirth of our first church." Looking out over the church, the city, and the gulf stands Mary, Star of the Sea, beckoning and protecting, watching over a Catholic community in Texas that stretches back nearly half a millennium.

Sources

Bayard, Ralph, CM. *Lone-Star Vanguard: The Catholic Re-Occupation of Texas (1838–1848)*. St. Louis: Vincentian Press, 1945.

Calvert, Robert A. "Texas Post World War II." Reviewed by Sean P. Cunningham (2010/2019), Handbook of Texas Online, www.tshaonline.org/handbook/online/articles/npt02.

Foley, Patrick. *Missionary Bishop: Jean-Marie Odin in Galveston and New Orleans*. College Station: Texas A&M University Press, 2013.

McComb, David G. *The City in Texas: A History*. Austin: University of Texas Press, 2015.

Turner, Allan. "After Almost Six-Year Closure, Ike-Devastated Galveston Cathedral to Reopen with Easter Mass." *Houston Chronicle*, April 18, 2014.

Vara, Richard, and Tara Dooley. "St. Mary Cathedral Basilica Is the Cradle of Texas' Catholicism." *Houston Chronicle*, March 29, 2008.

11.

Faith and Football at Our Lady's Lakes

University of Notre Dame
Notre Dame, Indiana 46556

*Did you know that the University
of Notre Dame started as an Indian
mission?*

The Golden Dome is an impressive sight. As you pull into Notre Dame Avenue from the south, it looms ahead, sparkling in the blue Indiana sky. To the right is a massive football stadium, and directly to its north, the thirteen-story wall of the Hesburgh Library. That wall features an image of Christ with his hands raised. It's not an unusual pose in the history of Christian iconography, but the fact that it can be conveniently viewed out the north end of Notre Dame Stadium has given rise to a somewhat irreverent moniker, "Touchdown Jesus."

The spiritual heart of the campus is Sacred Heart Basilica and the Lourdes Grotto nearby. The grotto looks out over the two lakes that gave the school its name. It was a priest, Stephen Badin, who first called this parcel of land "Sainte-Marie-des-Lacs"—St. Mary of the Lakes—and devotion to the Blessed Mother has been a central feature of the place ever since. Catholicism, football, and Mary are the themes at play throughout the history of the most prominent Catholic university in America, Notre Dame.

Fr. Badin, Land Baron

Stephen Badin was one of the itinerant priests who served the scattered Catholics of the American frontier in the early nineteenth century. He became the first priest ordained in the United States when Bishop John Carroll laid hands on him in Baltimore's Cathedral of the Assumption in 1793. There was a desperate need for priests on the frontier beyond the Appalachian range, so the first American ordinand was immediately sent west. He's been called a "circuit-rider par excellence," and it's estimated that over the course of his long career he traveled more than one hundred thousand miles on horseback.

Badin was also a land speculator. Because the Church as an institution could not hold property in the early 1800s, individual priests and laymen would acquire property in their own names and build churches on them for the benefit of the Catholic community. Like other visionary American missionaries, Badin anticipated that American Catholicism would grow by leaps and bounds. Though Catholics on the frontier in 1819 were scattered here and there, worshipping in one-room log churches, the future was bright, Badin believed. Someday, the large plots of land would be used to build the brick churches, convents, and schools that would serve the exploding Catholic population of an expanding nation.

To that end, Badin purchased parcels of land all over the Northwest Territory. As Native Americans were expelled from their ancestral homes by the federal government, speculators stood by ready to scoop up the cheap land, in anticipation of the families of farmers and merchants who would pour into the region from the crowded East. Badin was among them. He bought 250 acres in northwest Indiana directly from the government and acquired an adjacent 250 from two private owners. The defining feature of the tract was a pair of lakes, which would be named after the parents of Jesus.[1] Those five hundred acres are today the campus of the University of Notre Dame.

Most Indigenous people had been chased from the area by the time Badin arrived in 1828, but there remained a small number of Potawatomis, one band of which was led by a chieftain named Pokagon. This group had been evangelized by Jesuit "black robes" and had received missionary attention periodically over the decades since. Badin built a log chapel on his lakeside property with a view to solidifying this native Catholic community.

When the Diocese of Vincennes was created in 1834, Badin transferred the property to its bishop, Simon Bruté, with the stipulation that it would be used for a Catholic charitable institution. The initial vision for a hub of Native American Catholicism was dispelled in 1838, when the remaining Potawatomis were forcibly moved west—excepting only Pokagon's clan.

Bruté's successor, Bishop Célestine Hailandière, appealed to his countryman Fr. Basil Moreau, who had recently formed the Congregation of Holy Cross, for religious to staff his frontier diocese. Fr. Edward Sorin and six Holy Cross brothers arrived in Indiana in 1841. Hailandière offered St. Mary of the Lakes to the Holy Cross men as a location for the college they envisioned. Badin's log chapel served as an incommodious worship space until a new log church was inaugurated in 1843. The second building was made of brick and formed the nucleus for the new school. It still exists and is known as Old College, the undergraduate house of formation for the Congregation of Holy Cross seminary.

When Sorin and his confreres arrived, there had been some question about whether the lakes, connected by a stretch of marshy land, were in fact separate bodies of water. Possibly because their initial view of the topography was obscured by snow, they began referring to the place in the singular as "Notre Dame du Lac." Later, the two lakes each acquired its own name: St. Mary and St. Joseph. On January 15, 1844, the College of Notre Dame du Lac was chartered by the state of Indiana. It would gradually grow into one of the largest, wealthiest, and most prestigious Catholic institutions in America.

This growth owed much to Notre Dame's reputation as a football powerhouse. A Catholic football powerhouse.

God, Football, and Notre Dame

President Dwight Eisenhower once said that the definition of an athe-ist is someone who watches a football game between Notre Dame and Southern Methodist University (SMU) and doesn't care who wins. Like most jokes, there was some truth behind Ike's quip. For many Ameri-can Catholics in the mid-twentieth century, Notre Dame football and the faith went hand in hand.

Notre Dame's athletic prowess evolved in the face of anti-Catho-lic sentiment. Like the 1850s, the 1920s saw an outbreak of anti-Ca-tholicism in the United States. Anti-Catholicism was one important element in the toxic compound of nativism, which in that decade achieved one of its chief political objectives: the restriction of immigra-tion, with new quotas based on the goal of keeping the United States predominantly white and Protestant.

In the same decade, the Ku Klux Klan—originally founded to combat Reconstruction—was resurrected as an anti-Black and anti-Catholic organization with considerable strength in the North. The Klan targeted Catholic education in particular, as its efforts to outlaw parochial schools in Oregon attest. (The Supreme Court settled the matter in favor of the right to private education in the *Pierce v. Society of Sisters* decision of 1925.) One of the hotbeds of Klan activity was Indiana. A young priest there, Fr. John Noll, started a Catholic newspaper for the purpose of countering anti-Catholic literature. It developed into Our Sunday Visitor Press, one of the largest religious publishing houses in the world. Noll went on to become the bishop of the Diocese of Fort Wayne, whose territory included South Bend.

Meanwhile, in South Bend, a Lutheran immigrant from Norway was molding young men into a formidable football team. Football was gaining traction as an intercollegiate sport, and Coach Knute Rockne's teams arrived just in time to capitalize on both the growing popularity of collegiate athletics and the longing of a growing Catholic communi-ty for achievement and respect from their non-Catholic fellow citizens.

The Fighting Irish won their first national championship in 1924.[2] When Al Smith went down to defeat in 1928 as the first major-party

Catholic candidate for president, the Paulist priest James Gillis captured the feisty spirit of the Catholic working class in his defiant commentary in the *Catholic World*: "We shall not wither up and blow away!" Notre Dame football was the embodiment of that spirit, no matter that the team was coached by a Protestant and included non-Catholic players. Rockne's squads proceeded to win national championships in 1929 and 1930. "The national prominence of Knute Rockne's teams from an obscure and penurious Catholic school in one of the most Protestant states of the Union," writes the historian Mark Massa, "became a source of both pride and group esteem for millions of American Catholics who never set foot on the campus."

Ethnic pride played an important role in the Notre Dame mix as well. As nativist groups such as the Ku Klux Klan recognized, ethnicity and religion were bound together for many Americans, including recent immigrants. The education provided by Catholic colleges such as Notre Dame was a ladder out of the socioeconomic basement for working-class Catholic ethnics. For this downtrodden but optimistic group, the success of the football team was the exclamation mark that punctuated the cry, "We will not wither up and blow away!" This view of Notre Dame and its gridiron magic as the stuff of American dreams endured until at least the 1970s. In that decade, Daniel "Rudy" Ruettiger, against all odds, scrambled out of the shadow of the steel mills of Joliet, Illinois, and walked on to the varsity football team, providing the plot for the 1993 motion picture *Rudy*.

Rudy was the second movie filmed on campus. The first, *Knute Rockne, All American* (1940), captured the legend of George Gipp, the multitalented star player who died tragically of pneumonia during the 1920 season. *Rockne* related the story of a moving conversation with Gipp to motivate his 1928 team during a stunning victory over Army. Future president Ronald Reagan portrayed Gipp in the 1940 film, and later invoked the catchphrase "Win one for the Gipper" as a slogan for his political campaigns.

Notre Dame officials encouraged the link between Catholicism and Fighting Irish football. In a campus newsletter in 1930, the college's prefect, Fr. John O'Hara, CSC, explained that it was a "pious

tradition at Notre Dame" to remember the football team during reception of Communion on game days. O'Hara urged football players to
go to Mass in the morning before games.

And what could be more Catholic than devotion to Our Lady?
Sometime during the Rockne era, Fighting Irish players introduced
the term "Hail Mary" into the American football lexicon to describe
a desperation pass play. The first Lourdes grotto at Notre Dame was
constructed in 1877, just nineteen years after Mary appeared to St.
Bernadette in Lourdes, France. The current grotto was completed in
1896, and fans light thousands of candles there during home-game
weekends. "No football weekend would be complete," says the sacris-
tan of the adjacent Basilica of the Sacred Heart, "without a visit to this
peaceful shrine that sits in the shadow of the Golden Dome."

From the beginning, the Notre Dame football bandwagon had its
detractors. Some criticism came from within. George Shuster, who
headed the school's English Department from 1920 to 1924, frequently
deplored the low academic status of Catholic colleges and urged Catholics to devote more money and energy to cultivating the American
Catholic mind. In a 1925 article, he took a swipe at his former employ-
er, complaining that, instead of Catholic colleges pulling students into
the higher echelons of the nation's intellectual life, "we have superim-
posed upon a splendid system of elementary training little more than
excellence in football." Critiques of the deployment of resources to
athletics would echo through the university's academic departments
over the ensuing decades.

That criticism was blunted in the 1950s when thirty-five-year-old
Holy Cross priest Theodore Hesburgh began a thirty-two-year administration as the school's president. Hesburgh wanted Notre Dame to be
thought of as a "Catholic Harvard," a great Catholic research university.
To a remarkable degree, he accomplished that aim. In recent decades,
Notre Dame has been consistently ranked in the top twenty in the *U.S.
News* report of top academic institutions, and in 2020 it enjoyed the
highest athletic graduation rate of all NCAA Division I schools for the
fourteenth consecutive year.

A different, more existential charge was leveled in the early twenty-first century. Might the success and tradition of Notre Dame be built on an unstable foundation? The unjust treatment of Native Americans had long been known and conceded, but new questions were raised about whether land takings might be compensated by restoration of the property itself. In 2000, longtime Notre Dame philosophy professor and mystery novelist Ralph McInerny used the questionable basis of the university's original land grant as the background of one of his Notre Dame series mysteries. Four years later, fact following fiction, a Potawatomi tribe in Michigan filed suit, contending that the University of Notre Dame stood on earth unjustly taken from Native Americans in the early nineteenth century. "We are fully confident that we have proper title to our land," said the university's spokesman. The university still enjoys title to its land and shows no signs of letting go.

Sources

Cohen, Ed. "One Lake or Two?" *Notre Dame Magazine*, Autumn 2004, magazine.nd.edu/stories/one-lake-or-two/.

"Edward Sorin & the Founding of Notre Dame." Notre Dame Archives, February 6, 2014, www.archives.nd.edu/about/news/index.php/2014/edward-sorin-the-founding-of-notre-dame/.

Gordon, Linda. *The Second Coming of the KKK: The Ku Klux Klan of the 1920s and the American Political Tradition*. New York: Liveright, 2017.

Massa, Mark. *Catholics and American Culture: Fulton Sheen, Dorothy Day, and the Notre Dame Football Team*. New York: Crossroad, 1999.

McInerny, Ralph. *The Book of Kills*. New York: St. Martin's, 2000.

O'Connell, Marvin. *Edward Sorin*. Notre Dame, IN: University of Notre Dame Press, 2001.

[Shuster, George N.] "Insulated Catholics." *Commonweal* 2 (August 19, 1925): 337–38.

Tiberio, Tom. "Tribe Sues over Piece of Campus." *Notre Dame Magazine*, Spring 2004.

12.

"No Holier Place in the New World"

Maria Stein Shrine of the Holy Relics
2291 St. John's Road
Maria Stein, Ohio 45860

Did you know that one of the largest collections of relics in the world is located in rural Ohio?

Rising from the fertile farm ground of west-central Ohio are church spires—lots of them. "It is a close call whether churches outnumber grain elevators here," a *New York Times* reporter wrote in 2019. "Both stand sentinel over the browns, greens and golds of the soybean fields and cornfields rolled out on the flatlands like a handcrafted rug."

The church spires are the landmarks that give this area its name, the "Land of the Cross-Tipped Churches," so designated by the Ohio Scenic Byways Program. Almost all of these towers belong to Catholic churches, and most of them were built by German immigrants during the nineteenth century. In the town of Maria Stein, far from any major highway, there are two steeples. One belongs to the parish church of St. John the Baptist, the other to the relic shrine less than a mile away. This rural outpost houses more than one thousand relics—the second largest collection in the United States.[1]

A Fertile Soil

The story begins in the 1840s, when German Catholics were settling Auglaize, Mercer, and Shelby Counties. The clever Germans staked claim to some of the finest farmland in the country. Ohio had been part of the vast territory organized by the 1787 Northwest Ordinance and then opened up to white settlement by a series of conflicts and treaties between the US government and Native Americans. Twenty miles west of Maria Stein is Fort Recovery, a stronghold built by General "Mad" Anthony Wayne and a reminder of the Indigenous peoples forced to make way for the newcomers.

In 1803, Ohio became the seventeenth state in the Union, and in 1820 a number of counties in the northwest quadrant of the state were formed, including Mercer, which was named after the Revolutionary War general Hugh Mercer. In the 1840s, the construction of the Miami-Erie Canal furnished an aquatic highway into the region. "The soil of Mercer County," a 1907 history stated, "will always be the source of its greatest material wealth." Germans snatched up much of that land, planting crops and churches in abundance.

In a situation common among immigrant groups in American history, there was a shortage of priests to serve this German-speaking population. The new congregation of the Missionaries of the Precious Blood, founded by St. Gaspar del Bufalo in Rome in 1815, stepped into the gap. A former Benedictine-turned-Precious Blood father, Francis de Sales Brunner, would come to the United States and help to build the Catholic communities of this newly settled region.

Mary of the Rock

A legend from the late Middle Ages tells of a shepherd boy who fell off a cliff in northern Switzerland, surviving through the intercession of the Blessed Virgin Mary. Devotion to Maria Stein, "Mary of the Rock," gradually increased. The Swiss shrine of Mariastein was built and given to the care of the Benedictine order, which added an abbey there in 1645. It was destroyed during the Napoleonic wars but had recently been reestablished when Nicholas Brunner entered in 1812, taking the name Francis de Sales.

Francis de Sales Brunner was ordained in 1819, but by that time he had already experienced serious doubts about the Benedictine abbey remaining his permanent home. Manifesting a restlessness that would run through much of his life, Brunner found fault with both the monastery and his own lack of spiritual rigor. Thinking that a more severe rule might be the solution, he left Mariastein and Switzerland in 1829 for France and a stricter branch of the Benedictine family tree, the Trappists. A year later, revolution caused the non-French members of the monastery to be expelled. Brunner tried to continue his religious life in Switzerland, but he also formed a plan to venture into the New World. Although his former abbot wrote to Bishop Edward Fenwick of Cincinnati and received a favorable reply, complications prevented any immediate action on that front. The American plan was delayed but not forever. "The more numerous the obstacles that daily sought to prevent his going to America," his biographer writes, "the more his heart was inflamed with the desire to enter that land of promise."

During an extended visit to Rome, Francis and his widowed mother, Maria Anna Brunner, met St. Gaspar del Bufalo and embraced his special devotion to the Most Precious Blood of Christ. At the same time, Francis, hearing a call to the mission field, prepared to preach the Gospel in Africa. He would once again be knocked off his planned course. In 1834, back in Switzerland, Maria Brunner founded the Sisters of the Precious Blood, and Francis was obliged to take responsibility for the spiritual direction of the new congregation.

Maria died in 1836, and Francis joined the Fathers of the Precious Blood shortly thereafter—the first non-Italian member of the society. While he was in Rome sorting out his canonical status,[2] Brunner received from Pope Gregory XVI the recently discovered remains of an early martyr, one of the first contributions to the great collection of Maria Stein.[3]

Having returned to Switzerland, Brunner gathered about him a group of young men who would serve as the nucleus of the American province. In 1842, he resumed communication with the Diocese of Cincinnati. Bishop John Purcell formally invited the Precious Blood Fathers to his diocese the following year, affirming his personal support for the society's move to Ohio. "Rest assured," he wrote to Brunner, "they will find in me a devoted brother."

Later that year, Bishop Purcell himself went to Europe in his quest for priests, and his firsthand view of the situation initially cast doubt on his earlier assurance. After hearing rumors about the instability of the Precious Blood congregation, he by chance encountered the group themselves in Le Havre, France, as they awaited passage to the United States. Brunner, along with the seven priests and seven seminarians selected to inaugurate the American project, failed to impress their new bishop. Among other eccentricities, their extreme poverty was reflected in their mode of dress, which Purcell found shocking. But the bishop was quickly and completely won over by their charm. The humble attire became a laughing matter to the group. "Yesterday he suggested that we give our old clothes to beggars, since they were not worth dragging along to America," Brunner wrote to his confreres in Switzerland. "He told me to throw my cassock into the ocean." As for Brunner's opinion of Purcell, he concluded that "he is a saintly man."

Bishop Purcell accompanied the Precious Blood group for part of their journey. While crossing the English Channel, the ship was threatened by a storm. Brunner had among his belongings a painting of Our Lady of the Rock, which had been given to him by the Benedictines of his former abbey. He displayed the image on board and asked for the intercession of Our Lady of the Rock, and the weather calmed. He and Purcell attributed their safe arrival in America to Our Lady, Maria Stein, and Brunner would name the Mercer County town after their intercessor. (The painting now hangs in the relic chapel at the shrine, and other miracles have also been reported by pilgrims praying for the intercession of the Lady pictured in it.)

In late December of 1843, Brunner's band arrived in Cincinnati. The first Precious Blood sisters arrived in the United States in 1844 and established their first house at New Riegel. The Society of the Precious Blood grew with the Catholic Church of western Ohio, gradually assuming responsibility for more than twenty rural parishes. This spate of parish founding and church construction in western Ohio was but part of a national boom. Between 1820 and 1850, more than a thousand Catholic churches were built in the United States, and another thousand in the following decade.

One of the Precious Blood parishes was St. John's, which anchored a town of the same name (along with the biblical saint, it was also named after the three men called John who had first settled the place). The town was gradually subsumed by the town of Maria Stein a half mile west. In 1845, Francis Brunner set his sights on some land near the church for the purpose of constructing a convent. This sixty-acre parcel was owned by a "bigoted non-Catholic" who, Brunner was informed, would never sell to a priest. A St. John's parishioner instead made the offer to the owner, on behalf of "a friend of his, a man of slender means." It was the truth, so far as it went. When the erstwhile owner discovered the identity of the buyer, he was livid and sought to void the deal, to no avail. When the cornerstone of the new Precious Blood house was laid later that year, he reportedly "wept bitterly" at the fate of his former estate.

Saving the Relics

The priests, sisters, and laypeople of the Mercer County area were thriving in the 1860s when trouble came to Rome, the center of the Church. Italy's assemblage of city-states and principalities, under the leadership of Antonio Garibaldi and Giuseppe Mazzini, had joined the European push toward modern statehood. In Italy, that meant divesting the pope of his millennium-old temporal authority as head of the Papal States. As a beleaguered Pope Pius IX fought to retain his power in central Italy, the conflict was perceived as a battle between secular modernity and reactionary Catholicism. The Catholic churches of Rome became targets for anticlerical zealots and avaricious looters.

Among the many valuables held in Roman churches were thousands of relics of the saints. Nearly two millennia of Christian history were reflected in the pieces of bone, cloth, and other material connected to the bodies and lives of the men and women who had been recognized by the Church as exemplars of holiness. There were the apostles and early Christian martyrs: Peter and John, Stephen and Cecilia. There were medieval holy men and women: Francis and Clare of Assisi, Thomas Aquinas, and Catherine of Siena. There were saints of the Catholic Reformation: Teresa of Ávila and Charles Borromeo. From St. Abdon to St. Zosimus, the collection was a veritable catalog of Christian holiness through the ages.

Fr. J. M. Gartner was a priest from Bohemia who had worked among Polish, Czech, and Slav immigrants in the Great Lakes region. He was vicar general of the Diocese of Milwaukee (under Bishop John Martin Henni, the recruiter of Francis Brunner) when he visited Rome in 1872 and observed with dismay the treatment of the city's holy places. Taking upon himself the task of keeping these cultural and spiritual treasures intact, he scoured Rome, purchasing relics from the city's pawnshops and collecting others from priests and Vatican officials who supported his safekeeping crusade. By 1875, he had 175 relics. Now, what to do with them?

Their historical home in Europe had proved unsafe. If Italy was unstable and prone to bouts of anticlericalism, Britain, Germany, and France weren't much better. In the United States, however, there was political stability as well as strong principles of property rights and religious liberty. The Church there was growing by leaps and bounds.

Gartner approached the archbishop of New York, Cardinal John McCloskey, who urged him to keep the collection together in one place. Gartner learned that Fr. Francis Brunner already possessed a sizable collection of relics, housed respectfully in a chapel of the motherhouse of the Sisters of the Precious Blood. At that remote location, deep in the Catholic territory of Ohio, they would be safe both from the marauding anti-Catholics of Europe and the Catholic-Protestant strife that occasionally plagued American cities (see chapter 14).

A couple of weeks after Easter in 1875, Fr. Gartner arrived at Maria Stein with his collection. There was initially no publicity for their arrival; the point was to keep them safe, not to arouse attention. Yet news quickly spread through the Catholic countryside, and the laity expressed their desire to honor this extraordinary spiritual treasure. On May 2, the sisters led a solemn procession of parishioners from St. John's Church down the road to the convent chapel. At the High Mass that followed, Fr. Gartner preached on the importance and proper veneration of relics. Less than two years after placing the relics with the sisters, he died.

A New Shrine

The collection of Roman relics has remained at Maria Stein ever since. In the 1890s, the sisters built a new motherhouse chapel designed specifically for the relics. Exquisite wood-carved, glass-faced reredoses housing dozens of brass reliquaries rise twenty feet above the chapel floor and are set off from the pews below by a matching, carved wooden railing. Prayers and scriptures in German appear on the railing and above the sanctuary of the adjacent adoration chapel, bespeaking the shrine's origin and heritage. In the east wall of the relic chapel are two stained glass windows that commemorate the visionary donors, Frs. Gartner and Brunner. Above the entrance to the chapel, the visitor is greeted with the words, "Enter devoutly, O Pilgrim, for there is no holier place in the New World than this."[4]

On November 22, 1892, the new chapel was dedicated by Archbishop Henry Elder in a dazzling ceremony that reflected the community's dedication to the vision of Fr. Gartner. The vanguard of the procession was

> a hundred girls clad in white. These were followed by members of the various societies and sodalities of St. John's parish. Four priests supported a bier covered with red velvet and decorated with gold studdings, on which rested several major relics; four more carried the body of St. Victoria encased in glass. Then came thirty priests bearing ostensoria [vessels for display] containing smaller relics, while Archbishop Elder, holding aloft the precious relic of the true cross, brought up the rear of the triumphal procession.

The character of the region has remained remarkably stable since the time of Fr. Brunner. Although industry has taken its place in the economy, agriculture still sets the tone. Even the high school sports are old school: there's no soccer team, and half the boys in the school play football. The public high-school Flyer football team gathers at morning Mass at St. John's Church on football Fridays in the fall, and afterward the parish's Precious Blood pastor provides doughnuts.

One contemporary trend that has not bypassed Mercer County is falling numbers of Catholic consecrated religious. By the twenty-first century, there were no longer enough Precious Blood women to serve the shrine, and the sisters passed responsibility for the old motherhouse complex, including the relic chapel, to a board of trustees, a majority of whom are local laity.

The lay board now strives to preserve the legacy of the Precious Blood missionaries by securing the financial and spiritual future of the shrine for generations to come. The shrine, despite its out-of-the-way location, remains a popular attraction for Catholics and others from near and far. The tranquil country is an appropriate setting for meditating on the role of the saints in building and guiding the Catholic Church—and in continuing to intercede for those who are still earthbound, struggling to emulate their holiness.

Sources

Brown, Mary Ann, and Mary Niekamp. National Register of Historic Places Inventory Nomination Form, npgallery.nps.gov/NRHP/GetAsset/NRHP/64000616_text.

Knapke, Paul J., CPPS. *American Province C.PP.S.* 2 vols. Carthagena, OH: Messenger Press, 1958.

Maria Stein Shrine of the Holy Relics. Www.mariasteinshrine.org.

Rose, Michael S. "A Harvest of Relics amid Cornfields." *National Catholic Register*, July 11, 1999.

A Sister of the Precious Blood [Mildred (M. Octavia) Gutman]. *Not with Silver or Gold: A History of the Sisters of the Congregation of the Precious Blood, 1834–1844.* Dayton, OH: Sisters of the Precious Blood, 1945.

Smith, Ryan K. *Gothic Arches, Latin Crosses: Anti-Catholicism and American Church Designs in the Nineteenth Century.* Chapel Hill: University of North Carolina Press, 2006.

Swanton, S. S. *History of Mercer County, Ohio, and Representative Citizens.* Chicago: Biographical Publishing, 1907.

13.

The Puzzle of the Pope's Stone

The Washington Monument
2 15th Street NW
Washington, DC 20024

*Did you know that animus against
Catholics nearly prevented the
building of the Washington
Monument?*

Towering more than 550 feet above the National Mall in the heart of
the nation's capital is a striking monument in stone to the country's
first president. At the time of its completion, the obelisk was the tallest
structure in the world. The Washington Monument is a patriotic icon
for every visitor to Washington, DC.

It also holds a secret, buried within its tumultuous past—a secret
that reveals the anti-Catholic strain that runs through American history.

A Monument for General George

It may be hard for contemporary Americans to imagine, but there
was a time when the federal government was conscientious about
spending money. In the early nineteenth century, tax revenue was a
fraction of what it is today, and Congress doled out funds sparingly.

Even the project of honoring the nation's first president, the hero of the American Revolution, was looked on by many legislators as frivolous spending. So, a civic organization was formed, the Washington National Monument Society, to raise funds for the construction of a memorial to George Washington, which would be erected in the nation's capital city.

The District of Columbia was established by Congress in 1790, as required by the new Constitution. One of the two Catholic signers of the Constitution, Daniel Carroll of Maryland, was appointed to the commission that guided the development of the federal city that started rising from the lowlands around the Potomac River (and was soon named Washington in honor of the first president).[1] The grandiose plan initially envisioned by the French designer Pierre Charles L'Enfant never came to complete fruition, but the city's unique street arrangement, wide boulevards, and ample open spaces nonetheless endowed it with a monumental and ceremonial quality. From the beginning, L'Enfant called for permanent recognition of the country's great general and first president—most likely a statue. It would be a natural feature of a city destined to carry such symbolic importance. "Not only would the city serve as home to the national government," historian Sarah Luria observes, "it would provide a site where the abstract concept of nation could be experienced as a physical reality—something a citizen could point to, visit, and admire."

Which is not to say the location of the capital was an entirely pleasant spot. In the 1820s, there were still fewer than twenty thousand residents willing to brave the locale's sultry summers and gelid winters. (By comparison, New York and Philadelphia each boasted more than one hundred thousand residents by 1820, and nearby Baltimore was three times the size of Washington.) As late as the 1860s, citizens complained of the "truly fearful" state of Washington's streets, which became muddy morasses after the frequent rains. But the die had been cast, and the city on the banks of the Potomac would serve, for better or worse, as the nation's capital and home to its most significant national monuments.

The fundraising efforts of the Monument Society were successful in the 1830s, and architect Robert Mills was hired to design the tower—a fitting choice considering his recent appointment as architect of public buildings for the District of Columbia. Mills's original design carried a $1 million price tag, a figure exponentially larger than the funds on hand. Nonetheless, construction began. The cornerstone was laid on July 4, 1848, and the block structure began to rise from the Potomac plain. At that time, the National Mall was dominated by the white sandstone Capitol Building (whose dome was not yet complete) and the Seneca red-stone Smithsonian Institution (known as "the castle"). The giant obelisk would dramatically change the complexion of the capital city—if it could ever be completed.

The Pope's Stone

In 1849, the Monument Society, seeing that funds were running low, decided on a creative tactic: it would solicit donations of material from state and foreign governments. Contributions of granite, marble, and sandstone began arriving from across the United States and from around the globe. Fraternal organizations got involved, too. Stones were donated by the Grand Masonic Lodge of the District of Columbia, the Order of Odd Fellows Grand Lodge of New Jersey, the Sons of Temperance of North Carolina, and many others. In October 1853, a block of marble, 36 x 18 x 10 inches and engraved with the words "From Rome to America" in Latin, rolled up to the work site. It was a gift from Pope Pius IX. The stone had been taken from the ruins of the Roman Forum and shipped across the Atlantic.

The stone was supposed to be a goodwill gesture. The American ambassador in Italy, Lewis Cass Jr., had learned of the pope's intention to donate to the monument and had written to the Monument Society about it in 1852. The society's secretary, George Watterston, replied to Cass with an expression of "sincere gratification," assuring him that the stone would be placed "in a conspicuous position." When the matter became public, the initial reaction was one of welcome reflection. The stone, opined the *Massachusetts Barre Gazette*, "may be considered a voice from the ruins of once Imperial Rome that Peace alone can save the Republican Empire in America from the sad fate of the ancient, but now fallen Mistress of the World."

The tranquility did not last.

Nativism Rising

Catholic Americans had, from the time of the Revolution, been a small minority within the new nation. From approximately 25,000 in 1776 (1 percent of the total American population), Catholic numbers increased steeply toward the middle of the nineteenth century to 1.6 million (7 percent of Americans), the result of heavy German and Irish Catholic immigration. As the number and influence of Catholics increased in the 1840s, Protestant anxiety over the Catholic presence in America intensified. A series of violent encounters between Catholics and Protestants roiled several American cities in the 1840s. In 1844, Protestant mobs burned two Catholic churches in Philadelphia during the so-called Bible Riots.

Catholic churches were an increasingly common—and controversial—sight on the American landscape. There had been only 120 Catholic church buildings in the entire country in 1820, but their number increased twentyfold over the next forty years. In the fevered American anti-Catholic imagination, such edifices were not only symbols of Catholic presence—the "bloody hand of the pope" in the New World—but also imagined to be storehouses of arms and ammunition, stockpiled in preparation for a Catholic revolution that would turn the nation over to the rule of Roman clerics.

Anti-Catholic discontent crested in the 1850s, the first of several waves of anti-Catholic sentiment in US history. The phenomenon had its political manifestation in the creation of the Know-Nothing Party, which took its name from the answer its members were supposed to give when anyone inquired about the affairs of the secretive organization. Known officially as the American Party, the movement's primary concern was immigration, but in nineteenth-century America, anti-immigrant and anti-Catholic sentiment were often difficult to distinguish. The political program of the American Party included restrictions on immigration, the exclusion of immigrants from public office, and a long residency requirement for naturalized citizenship.

While the American Party gained steam, nativist agitators organized public rallies in Philadelphia, Washington, and Baltimore to demonstrate against the pope's stone. They circulated petitions to protest the inclusion of the block in the monument. One such document argued that "this gift of a despot, if placed within those walls, can never be looked upon by true Americans, but with feelings of mortification and disgust." It would become, in one historian's description of the stakes at play, "a symbol of foreign influence, papal power, and subversion of American life by Catholics."

Such sentiments ran contrary to those expressed by the honoree himself. In March 1790, the first president, responding to a congratulatory epistle from Bishop John Carroll, wrote a letter "To Roman Catholics in America," avowing that "all those who conduct themselves as worthy members of the community are equally entitled to the protection of civil government." Washington hoped that his fellow Americans would "not forget the patriotic part which you took in the accomplishment of their Revolution, and the establishment of their Government: or the important assistance which they received from a nation in which the Roman Catholic faith is professed."

But some did forget. On the night of March 5, 1854, a gang of ruffians snuck into the monument work site. They broke into the shed where donated blocks were stored, located the pope's stone, hauled it to the nearby Potomac River, and unceremoniously dumped it in.

When the news broke, Catholics and other Americans were appalled. The controversy provoked by the vandalism halted work on the monument for a decade. The Monument Society offered a reward for the finding of the perpetrators, but they were never arrested. In the election of 1854, nativist John Towers won the mayoralty of the District of Columbia, and the Monument Society itself was split in two when Know-Nothings tried to gain supremacy on the board of directors. In this divisive environment, Congress, which had been considering financial assistance for the project, closed its purse strings, and public support also faltered. By 1861, the country was distracted by more pressing matters.

Only after the Peace of Appomattox did construction resume. The Maryland marble used to complete the obelisk was a different color from the earlier materials, and the ten-year break in construction is visible on the structure to this day. Congress took control of the project in 1876.

By then, more than two hundred thousand people lived in the District of Columbia and the center of national government was growing as fast as the nation itself. Modern sewers had been installed, roads paved, and trees planted by the thousands. When the capstone was put in place in December 1884, the Washington Monument was the world's tallest building, surpassing even Cologne Cathedral in Germany.

Mysteries Solved?

What came before in this chapter are the basic facts of the story, generally accepted. Much remains in doubt. The assumption that those who removed the pope's stone were Know-Nothings motivated by anti-Catholicism has never been proved.

Mysteries persist. The vandals took measures to restrain the guard on duty, but there remain questions about why he didn't do more to stop the act (he was armed) and why it took him several hours to report the incident. Was he in on the job?

Most mysterious of all: What happened to the stone? It was a large block of marble, after all. The 1883 confession report published by the *Washington Post* claimed that it was indeed cast into the river but that some of the men had first chiseled off chunks to keep as tokens of their deed. The confessed thief—identified in the *Post* reports as "the saloonkeeper"—promised that the slab could be found if the river were searched at the location he pointed to. In 1892, the *Post* reported that the stone had in fact been found by a diver—but the elusive stone disappeared again a few days later!

In 1972, an eighty-six-year-old woman, Kathryn Wells, donated an eighteen-inch marble obelisk to the Smithsonian Institution. She asked that the museum do nothing to publicize the acquisition because it was connected to a "controversial event" in American history and she didn't want to impugn the reputation of those involved. That controversial event was the theft of the pope's stone in 1854. The little obelisk, Wells claimed, had been carved from a piece of Pius IX's Italian marble.

Wells had been hiding the stone in a closet in her home for sixty years. She said she had received it from a Confederate army officer, Joseph Ridgway. Ridgway's brother had apparently been one of the vandals. Was this one of the slivers hammered off as a souvenir before the slab was dropped into the Potomac? The National Park Service wasn't alerted to the existence of the Smithsonian stone until 1978, when a tourist mentioned it to a Washington Monument ranger.

Another purported piece of the stone came into the possession of Philip Hannan, auxiliary bishop of Washington, DC, from 1956 to 1965, and later archbishop of New Orleans. It was used as a paperweight, seemingly discarded during one of the bishop's moves, and has since disappeared. The coloration of the two alleged remnants of the stone did not match, but it remains uncertain what the color of the original marble was, given conflicting descriptions in the historical record. Yet another possible piece of the stone surfaced in 1973 in the possession of a Maryland collector.

Whatever the truth of these various claims and reports, the intentions of Pope Pius IX finally came to fruition in the late twentieth century, thanks to the dogged persistence of a Catholic priest from Spokane. Fr. James Grant, a decorated World War II veteran, happened upon the story of the pope's stone, was captivated, and dedicated many years to researching its details. In 1982, he commissioned the creation of a replica by the local Tresco Monument Company. With the cooperation of the relevant government officials, the block was installed in the Washington Monument at 340 feet. The stone, like most other donated blocks, is not accessible to the public, as the 898-stair ascent up the interior of the obelisk has been closed in favor of the elevator since 1976.

Yet there it sits, along the corridor, boldly displaying its inscription: *A Roma Americae.* From Rome to America.

Sources

Endres, David. "Know-Nothings, Nationhood, and the Nuncio: Reassessing the Visit of Archbishop Bedini." *U.S. Catholic Historian* 21 (Fall 2003).

Grant, James E. "The Washington Monument and the Pope's Stone II." Typescript, 1986.

Hodge, Paul. "Who's Got the Stone?" *Milwaukee Journal*, July 28, 1978.

———. "The Pope's Stone Mystery: Is the Evidence in Smithsonian?" *Washington Post*, June 1, 1978.

Jacob, Judith. *The Washington Monument: A Technical History and Catalog of the Commemorative Stones.* Washington, DC: National Park Service, 2005.

Luria, Sarah. *Capital Speculations: Writing and Building Washington, D.C.* Durham: University of New Hampshire Press, 2006.

Oxx, Katie. *The Nativist Movement in America: Religious Conflict in the 19th Century.* New York: Routledge, 2013.

"Rest in Peace: Father James Grant, 1923–2006." *Inland Register*, April 27, 2006.

Samuels, Ernest. *Henry Adams.* Cambridge, MA: Belknap Press of Harvard University Press, 1989.

Smith, Ryan K. *Gothic Arches, Latin Crosses: Anti-Catholicism and American Church Designs in the Nineteenth Century.* Chapel Hill: University of North Carolina Press, 2006.

Tindall, William. *Standard History of the City of Washington, From a Study of the Original Sources.* Knoxville, TN: H. W. Crew, 1914.

Veroske, Ariel. "The Mystery of the Pope's Stone." *Boundary Stones* (WETA's Local History Blog), July 16, 2013, blogs.weta.org/boundarystones/2013/07/16/mystery-popes-stone#-footnote-marker-7-1.

Washington, George. "Letter to Roman Catholics in America, c. 15 March 1790." Founders Online, founders.archives.gov/documents/Washington/05-05-02-0193.

14.

A Christmas Riot at the Corner of Eighth and Plum

Cathedral Basilica of St. Peter in Chains
325 W. 8th Street
Cincinnati, Ohio 45202

Did you know that the United States and the Vatican did not share full diplomatic relations until 1984?

The stately cathedral of St. Peter in Chains stands in a relatively peaceful section of downtown Cincinnati, at a distance from the hubbub of the stadiums, casinos, and nightclubs that line the Ohio River. Dedicated in 1845, the new cathedral served the exploding Catholic population of southwestern Ohio, where German immigrants formed the nucleus of a thriving local church. The structure was built in a Greek Revival style, its design intended to fit rather than flout the popular image of American public buildings at the time. There was no reason to goad anti-Catholic prejudice with an ostentatious, European-looking, Gothic hulk.

But on Christmas night, 1853, the quiet of the cathedral plaza was ruptured by angry shouts and gunshots. Anti-Catholic extremism had come to Cincinnati.

A Combustible Mixture

One element in the mix that exploded in 1853 was the nativism that swelled through much of the country in the 1850s (and burst forth in the affair of the pope's stone, chapter 13). The nativist movement took on different hues in different places. In Cincinnati, ironically, it was in large measure an intra-immigrant affair. Rather than a conflict between old American stock and newly arrived Germans, it was simply a change of battleground, from Europe to the New World. German Lutherans and German Catholics had been fighting each other over matters of religion since the sixteenth century. Why should they stop now?

But Protestant-Catholic tension was only part of the story. The donnybrook in Cincinnati was not simply a rehashing of the Wars of Religion. The leaders of the 1853 riots were "Forty-Eighters," that is, Germans consumed by the revolutionary spirit of 1848, which had swept Europe and had in some places (not Germany) overthrown monarchs in favor of democracy. The German revolutionaries were not, for the most part, devout Lutherans, but were instead agnostics or atheists—"freethinkers" in the terminology of the day.

Still, religious conflict played its role. The relationship between Protestants and Catholics in frontier regions like Cincinnati in the late eighteenth and early nineteenth centuries had generally been conciliatory. Confident Catholic leaders such as Fr. Stephen Badin, Bishop Benedict Joseph Fenwick, and Archbishop John Purcell engaged their Protestant counterparts in both friendship and debate. Differences were aired, to be sure, but the demands of building a common American community in the wilderness engendered more cooperation than conflict.

By the 1850s, the situation had changed. The frontier had receded beyond the Ohio River's confluence with the Mississippi, and with it the familiar patterns of religious conflict common on the Eastern Seaboard moved west. In 1832, the prominent Boston clergyman Lyman Beecher accepted the presidency of the newly formed Lane Theological Seminary and moved his family to Cincinnati. Shortly after arriving, he published an anti-Catholic tract, *A Plea for the West*. His series of sermons on the same topic, delivered in Boston in 1834, had been the impetus for the burning of an Ursuline convent by a Protestant mob. "The arrival of the Beechers," historian Margaret DePalma notes, "signaled a turning point in the debate between Protestants and Catholics in Cincinnati." The stridency of New England religious disputes was injected into the formerly cooperative frontier culture.

The "Butcher of Bologna"

The immediate cause of the strife in Cincinnati was a visit by a papal representative, Archbishop Gaetano Bedini, in 1853. The Italian prelate had been sent to the United States to assist with the settlement of the longstanding trustee controversy (see chapter 6). It was bad enough, from the perspective of nativist Protestants and German freethinkers, that the pope was meddling in American affairs. Worse was the choice of papal legate. Bedini had been the Holy See's secretary of state during the revolutions of 1848, which had not spared the Papal States.

While the revolutionaries rioted in Rome, Austrian forces reinstated papal authority in the north-central Italian region of Bologna. There, the revolution was forcibly suppressed and many rebels executed, among them a priest of the Clerics Regular of St. Paul (Barnabites), Ugo Bassi. Bedini was the legate who represented the pope in Bologna. The American press, gullibly accepting the story from biased immigrant radicals, began spreading stories that Bedini had something to do with the suppression and Fr. Bassi's murder. Bedini was labeled in some news reports as the "bloody butcher of Bologna."

The problem with this portrait is that it was entirely untrue. Bedini was assigned to Bologna, but he arrived there after the Austrian Empire's military had taken control of the region. He was powerless either to instigate or put a stop to political repression. But the distinction between his presence while bad things were happening and his agency as a cause of those bad things was lost on Americans susceptible to the virus of anti-Catholic bigotry.

For his part, Pope Pius IX viewed the American mission of Bedini as both a friendly gesture and an opportunity to gather intelligence. As the newly appointed apostolic nuncio to Brazil, Archbishop Bedini could rather conveniently (by the travel standards of the day) stop off in the US on the way to his new post. Bedini would be able to assess the trustee dispute in person and offer a fact-based solution. He would also personally deliver a "letter of good will" to President Franklin Pierce, expressing the Holy See's appreciation for the warm relations between America and the Papal States. An American diplomat to the Holy See, Lewis Cass Jr., gave assurance of "the cordial reception which Monsignor Bedini will receive" from the US government and a promise that President Pierce would receive Bedini's letter with "extreme pleasure." Cass offered no hint that Bedini's visit might provoke a backlash among some Americans.

For not the last time, however, there was a jarring disconnect between the intentions of the Church's leaders and the situation on the ground in the United States. Like his gift of "the pope's stone" for the Washington Monument (see chapter 13), Pius's gesture would be tragically misinterpreted.

No one involved seemed to foresee the possibility that Bedini's arrival would be a spark on dry tinder. Yet, homegrown Protestant nativism, imported European political tensions, and heated property disputes set the stage for a violent reaction. At the time, the only hint of trouble could be detected among the Catholic hierarchy itself, which was uneasy about Roman interference in its business. Although the pope's secretary of state, Cardinal Giacomo Antonelli, wrote a preparatory letter to the American bishops, he did not explain clearly that Bedini came to the United States with a dual charge as "envoy extraordinary" from the Holy See's secretary of state to the government of the United States and as "observer" from Propaganda Fide, the Roman congregation charged with overseeing mission territories.

In the latter role, it was clear that Bedini's visit was not to consist exclusively of expressions of goodwill and approval. His instructions were to "observe the state of religion there, the conduct of the clergy, and the abuses that have crept in." He was also to encourage missions to slaves and Native Americans. Finally, he was to address the trustee problem. The Propaganda Fide offered its own description as a backgrounder for Bedini's visitation: "The Trustees of that country have caused their bishops deep sorrow and brought about deplorable scandals." One source of the divisions within the American Catholic family, it continued, was that "native-born Americans hold themselves superior to those that have recently immigrated from Europe."

Bedini's visit was initially understated. Leaving Rome in early May, the prelate traveled first to Liverpool, where he boarded a ship for New York. The New York papers didn't even report his arrival on the last day of June 1853. After a few days with Archbishop John Hughes, the papal delegate departed for the nation's capital. He received a warm welcome from the Catholic clergy of Washington and enjoyed a pleasant visit with President Pierce. He delivered to the president a letter from Pope Pius IX, which reflected the pope's perception of the beleaguered status of the Catholic minority. "As we have been entrusted by Divine Commission with the care of the Lord's flock throughout the world," the missive read, "we cannot allow this opportunity to pass without earnestly entreating you to extend your protection to the Catholics living in your country, and to shield them at all times with your power and authority." The letter closed with effusive expressions of goodwill.

The papal delegate stopped at Visitation Convent, a monastery of nuns established in the 1790s. He took up residence at Georgetown, the college founded by Bishop Carroll in 1789, and attended its commencement ceremony on July 12. In Washington, Bedini got a glimpse of American bigotry. While he was celebrating Mass, he recounted later, "a Protestant lady had anxiously entered the church." She explained that she wished "to check if the Papal Nuncio had actually horns on his head."

At first, such incidents could be taken lightly, and the trip seemed to be a success. As Bedini's favorable impression of America became known, invitations began pouring in from around the country. Catholics—bishops in particular—were beginning to see the desirability of rubbing shoulders with the pope's advisor. Perhaps this was a golden opportunity to demonstrate to Rome the vitality and fidelity of American Catholicism. Bedini traveled to Baltimore, Philadelphia, Chicago, Milwaukee, and Detroit. After a tour of Canada, he made stops in Boston, Providence, and New Haven.

Although he was received courteously everywhere, there were also rumbles of discontent. In Philadelphia, he stayed at the parish of St. Mary's, puzzling some who wondered if the choice was a deliberate slight of the city's bishop (and future saint) John Neumann. In the same city, he was unable to arbitrate successfully the bitter trustee controversy at Holy Trinity Church. In Milwaukee, he was welcomed by many Protestants but also derided in liberal German publications. *The Detroit Free Press* published the false charge concerning his role in the murder of Ugo Bassi, and another scathing piece in the *Detroit Tribune* gained national attention and marked a decisive shift in the country's attitude toward the visit.

Matters grew more serious when, in September, Archbishop Hughes received word that a cabal of recent Italian immigrants were plotting to assassinate Bedini when he returned to New York. The informant who delivered this intelligence was himself murdered a week after Hughes went to the police with the threat. Alessandro Gavazzi, a former Barnabite priest and an exile from the failed Italian revolutions, began stalking Bedini during the tour, blaming the prelate for the death of his confrere Bassi and stirring up opposition.[1] As a result, the tour took on a surreal, uncomfortable quality. One historian describes the papal representative as being "greeted everywhere with a bizarre mixture of applause, deference, tumult, and hostility." In many cities, anti-Catholic demonstrators burned effigies of the archbishop.

Yet the tour continued as planned. From Quebec, Bedini went to New England. He encouraged Boston's Bishop John Fitzpatrick to dress more conspicuously by donning the pectoral cross. In Newport, Rhode Island, he met with a descendant of Charles Carroll of Carrollton. He visited the celebrated Catholic convert and intellectual Orestes Brownson at his home in Chelsea, Massachusetts.

Back in New York City on October 29, Bedini presided over the episcopal consecrations of new bishops for Burlington, Brooklyn, and Newark, in what was described as "the most brilliant ecclesiastical ceremony that New York had ever seen." The newly minted bishop of Newark was James Roosevelt Bayley, a convert like his aunt, St. Elizabeth Ann (Bayley) Seton.

Bedini continued to enjoy warm, even joyous, welcome in heavily Catholic settings. His December visit to western Pennsylvania—Frs. Gallitzin and Lemcke's bailiwick (see chapter 7)—was, as Bedini described it, "a most touching spectacle." A crowd of thousands paraded him into Loretto, led by a procession of five hundred men and women on horseback followed by fifty carriages. After a visit to St. Vincent Abbey, Bedini arrived in Pittsburgh.

The contrast with Loretto was stark. When Mass at the cathedral had ended, Bedini and Bishop Michael O'Connor were confronted by a hostile crowd. A protestor shoved the bishop, and another blew cigar smoke in the faces of both dignitaries. It was a portent of stormier days ahead.

Trouble in Cincinnati

Archbishop John Purcell of Cincinnati had been one of the first to issue an invitation to Bedini to come to his diocese. Finally, in December, the archbishop was able to fit the Queen City into his schedule. He arrived in Cincinnati on December 21.

On the same day, the newspaper of the German Forty-Eighters in Cincinnati, the *Hochwachter*, published a screed against Bedini. Referring to the Bassi case, it exclaimed, "Reader. Dost thou know who Bedini is? . . . A murderer, a butcher of men . . . the bloodhound of Bologna." It ended with a chilling exhortation, vague but threatening: "Germans, you are called for! Down with Bedini!"

Although the threat of violence hung over the city and the police were on alert, the first few days of the visit passed without incident. On Christmas Day, Bedini preached in the cathedral. At the same time, the German Forty-Eighters were meeting at Freeman's Hall to plan a demonstration. At ten o'clock that night, six hundred men and women began marching toward Bishop Purcell's home, eight blocks away, where Bedini was lodged.

One hundred Cincinnati police officers led by Captain Thomas Lukens had stationed themselves at the watchhouse located near the same intersection as the cathedral and the episcopal residence, Eighth and Plum. Meanwhile, a band of armed Catholic men kept vigil in front of the cathedral.[2] Toward them, to the steady beat of a vanguard of drums, the protesters menacingly approached. Among the banners were some that read "No Popery!" and "No Kings!"—classic Anglo-American slogans dating back to the colonial period. Others were more direct: "Down with Bedini!" Some of the marchers carried a scaffold with Bedini hanging in effigy.

As the mob neared the cathedral, the police advanced to meet them. A marcher fired a shot, and the two columns clashed in noisy combat. Several police officers and protesters were injured. One marcher was killed. Dozens were arrested.

After the Christmas night unrest, Bedini completed his visit to Cincinnati without further incident. The Sisters of Charity hosted him at St. Peter Asylum, where the orphan choir sang for him. On the Feast of the Holy Innocents—the twenty-fifth anniversary of his own first Mass in Italy—he ordained a priest in the orphanage chapel. He found comfort in his time at St. Peter's, and he later sent a thank-you note along with a monetary donation.

The archbishop was nonetheless shaken by the violence in Cincinnati and the forebodings of it elsewhere, and he hurried through the rest of his visit. He canceled previously planned trips to St. Louis and New Orleans and instead headed back east, making a stop in West Virginia. In Wheeling, Bishop Richard Whelan took a hard line. He instructed the mayor to send the message to protest planners that Catholics would provide their own protection. "The first one who dared to enter the cathedral," he warned, "would be immediately shot." When a mob did appear at the cathedral doors, they found an armed Catholic guard in place. Bedini passed through Wheeling unscathed.

He snuck out of the country in the darkness of February 4, 1854, rowing out to a waiting vessel in New York Harbor. "Never in the history of the United States," claims one study of the affair, "had the ambassador of a friendly country been forced to leave America in such an ignominious fashion." In a farewell letter to Archbishop Hughes, Bedini said that he had found most Americans to be friendly and speculated that it was exiles from Europe's revolutionary turmoil who had caused most of the trouble. But he also expressed disappointment that he had not witnessed a more vigorous defense of his reputation on the part of both the American bishops and the American government.

The Aftermath

What was to have been a friendly gesture by Rome toward the growing American Church turned into the pretext for the release of anti-Catholic animus, the severity and extent of which American Catholics had not guessed. The effects were far-reaching, says Fr. David Endres, professor of Church history at Cincinnati's archdiocesan seminary. "The America that skeptically greeted Bedini was not the same America that jeered his departure," he observes. "Bedini's mission had quite unknowingly ignited the competing tensions of the age: liberty and despotism, church and state, cultural pluralism and conformity." Their sharply differing views of Bedini were one factor exacerbating divisions between Catholics and other Americans as the nineteenth century progressed. The conflict helped stimulate a flourishing antipapal literature in the 1850s, as the mythology of the visit gave rise to extravagant claims—for example, that Bedini's aim had been to establish an American branch of the Inquisition! Conspiracy theorists linked the archbishop to the rise of the "Black Republicans" (antislavery politicians), abolitionism, and the disintegration of the Know-Nothing movement.

For Catholics, the importance of the episode at the time was reflected in the fact that a history of the Church in the United States published in 1857 devoted thirty pages to exonerating Bedini from the "butcher of Bologna" charges. One lasting effect was the tightening of ties between the American episcopate and Rome. Distrusting the hostile American environment as a sound training ground for priests, Bedini's report to the pope included a recommendation that a Roman seminary be created for the education of American priests. Five years later, the North American College was founded, and thousands of priests and bishops have passed through its doors in the years since.

In spite of the Bedini imbroglio, Catholic and non-Catholic Americans would learn to get along. They had to, for Catholic immigration was bringing additional thousands of "papists" into the country every year. These Catholics would be proudly American, but they were also devoted to their Holy Father in Rome.

Controversy over papal representation in the United States continued to flare up from time to time. In 1893, a permanent delegate from the Holy See was finally put in place with the appointment of Archbishop Francesco Satolli. It would be another hundred years, however, before full diplomatic relations between Vatican City and the United States were established. When Harry Truman attempted it in 1951, resistance was so stiff that he withdrew his nomination of General Mark Clark. Finally, in 1984, Ronald Reagan—with very little opposition—raised the US representative at the Vatican, William Wilson, to the rank of ambassador. On Rome's side, the then-apostolic delegate to the United States, Archbishop Pio Laghi, became nuncio. The two countries have exchanged ambassador-level delegations ever since.

Sources

Connelly, James F. *The Visit of Archbishop Gaetano Bedini to the United States of America (June, 1853–February, 1854)*. Rome: Libreria Editrice Dell'Università Gregorian, 1960.

D'Agostino, Peter. *Rome in America: Transnational Catholic Ideology from the Risorgimento to Fascism*. Chapel Hill: University of North Carolina, 2004.

DePalma, Margaret C. *Dialogue on the Frontier: Catholic and Protestant Relations, 1793–1883*. Kent, OH: Kent State University Press, 2004.

Endres, David J. "Know-Nothings, Nationhood, and the Nuncio: Reassessing the Visit of Archbishop Bedini." *U.S. Catholic Historian* 21, no. 4 (Fall 2003): 1–16.

Franco, Massimo. *Parallel Empires: The Vatican and the United States—Two Centuries of Alliance and Conflict*. Translated by Roland Flamini. New York: Doubleday, 2008.

Longley, Max. *For the Union and the Catholic Church: Four Converts in the Civil War*. Jefferson, NC: McFarland, 2015.

McCann, Mary Agnes. *The History of Mother Seton's Daughters: The Sisters of Charity of Cincinnati, Ohio, 1809–1917*. Vol. 2. New York: Longmans, Green, 1917.

Oxx, Katie. *The Nativist Movement in America: Religious Conflict in the 19th Century*. New York: Routledge, 2013.

Smith, Ryan K. *Gothic Arches, Latin Crosses: Anti-Catholicism and American Church Designs in the Nineteenth Century*. Chapel Hill: University of North Carolina Press, 2006.

15

The First Architect of the Northwest

PeaceHealth Southwest Medical Center
400 NE Mother Joseph Place
Vancouver, Washington 98664

*Did you know that Catholic sisters
founded the first hospitals in St. Louis,
Chicago, San Antonio, and many other
cities as the country spread west?*

PeaceHealth Southwest Medical Center serves the city of Vancouver, Washington, just across the Columbia River from Portland, Oregon. It is a modern health-care facility, replete with all the technology and amenities you would expect. Yet this sprawling complex was born as tiny St. Joseph Hospital in 1858. A plaque that hangs in the contemporary building honors the force behind that initial foundation: Mother Joseph of the Sacred Heart.

At the End of the Oregon Trail

Esther Pariseau was born in 1823 in Quebec. At her carriage-maker father's side, she learned about the tools and techniques of building with both wood and metal. From her mother she learned to garden, sew, and manage a household. She would need all those skills and more in the course of her eventful life. At the age of twenty she entered the newly formed Sisters of Charity of Providence in Montreal and took the name Joseph in honor of her father.

Mother Joseph's fellow Quebec native Augustin Blanchet was made bishop of Nesqually (now the Archdiocese of Seattle) in 1851. The diocesan see was located in Vancouver, in what was then the Oregon Territory. A fort had been erected there by the British Hudson's Bay Company to serve as a trading post with the Native Americans of the region. The race to colonize and control the Pacific Northwest—initially a three-empire contest among Russia, England, and Spain that had spurred the California mission enterprise (see chapter 4)—had boiled down to a border dispute between British Canada and the United States. Through the early nineteenth century, the two nations lodged competing claims against each other as their fur-trading companies vied for dominance in the resource-rich region.

By the 1840s, the American settlement of the Oregon Territory was well under way, even though the border dispute had not been finally resolved. Some settlers made the long, expensive journey around South America, braving the treacherous waters at Tierra del Fuego as well as the hazardous entry to port along the northern Pacific coastline. Others likewise went by water but crossed the jungle at the isthmus of Panama to re-embark on the Pacific side of the continent. Many others made the nominally shorter but no less arduous trek across the "Great Western Desert"—the Great Plains—along what became known as the Oregon Trail.

One of the champions of settlement was John McLoughlin, known as the "Father of Oregon." Despite his Scottish name, McLoughlin was, like Esther Pariseau, a native of Quebec. Born in 1784 of mixed Irish, Scottish, and French descent, he was baptized Catholic as Jean-Baptiste but was raised in the Anglican faith. In 1824, he was made "chief factor" or superintendent of the Hudson's Bay Company's Columbia District, which covered Britain's claims in the Oregon Territory. As such, he would receive and implement orders from the company's headquarters in Winnipeg and London.

McLoughlin settled at Fort Vancouver on the north bank of the Columbia River. His place of residence was built of the area's Douglas firs, and the massive installation covered nearly an acre—a fitting capitol for the burly, six-foot-four fur-company chief, who ruled the region as a benevolent despot. His arresting ashen hair and choleric personality provided reason enough for the name bestowed by the Chinook locals: "White-Headed Eagle."

Recognizing that Christianity brought with it a more placid and civilized community, McLoughlin welcomed the many and diverse missionaries who came into the territory. In 1838, he invited priests into the region to serve the growing Catholic population. When news of the arrival from Quebec of François Blanchet (Augustin's brother and the future archbishop of Oregon City)[1] and Modeste Demers (the future bishop of Vancouver Island) spread around the Columbia River fort, "from great distances Indians had flocked to Vancouver in awesome reverence to greet the Black-Robes, and the French Canadians had literally wept for joy at the scene." In 1842, in the midst of a personal crisis brought on by the murder of his son, McLoughlin returned to the faith of his baptism and received the sacraments from the Catholic missionaries.

As tensions increased between British and American interests in the 1840s, McLoughlin fostered good relations with the growing numbers of American settlers. During the 1844 presidential election, the status of Oregon became a polemical issue. Partisans of Democratic candidate James K. Polk wielded the slogan "54°40' or fight!" urging the US to insist on its northernmost latitude claims. Polk won the presidency, but there was no war with England over Oregon. With British settlers increasingly outnumbered by Americans in the Northwest and American tension with Mexico building in the Southwest, both sides were willing to compromise. The Oregon Treaty of 1846 set the border at the 49th parallel. McLoughlin then resigned from the Hudson's Bay Company, moved to Oregon City, and became an American citizen in 1849.

Meanwhile, the US Army set up a post in Vancouver and migrants from the East began pouring into the Willamette, Snake, and Columbia

Valleys. By 1860, the populations of Washington and Oregon exceeded sixty thousand. The soldiers, officers, and settlers were in desperate need of the institutions that served the more established populations of the East—schools, hospitals, churches. Bishop Blanchet had his hands full with the task of building and staffing churches, so he turned, as bishops always did, to women religious to fill the need for schools and churches. He naturally looked first to the French Canada he'd left behind. The Sisters of Providence answered the call.

Supplying Mercy, Charity, and Providence

In the work of tending the sick, Mother Joseph and her sisters stood in a proud tradition. It was Christianity that introduced into Western civilization the institution of the hospital. Religious orders were the main providers of such care from the early centuries of Christianity—mostly male religious at first, but later consecrated women predominated. English Sisters of Mercy had accompanied Florence Nightingale in her pioneering nursing service during the Crimean War. Nightingale later averred that the superior of the convent was "better qualified to be General Superintendent of the nursing corps" than was Nightingale.

In 1823, the University of Maryland opened the first modern hospital in the United States, the Baltimore Infirmary; on the staff were five Sisters of Charity from Emmitsburg. The same congregation supplied sisters when the Mullanphy Hospital in St. Louis opened its doors as the first hospital west of the Mississippi in 1828. These American Sisters of Charity were among the spiritual descendants of St. Vincent de Paul, who once told his Daughters of Charity in France, "When you leave your prayers for the bedside of a patient, you are leaving God for God. Looking after the sick is praying."

The Sisters of Providence, who borrowed their rule of life from the Sisters of Charity, displayed the same dedication in their apostolates. The congregation had its origins in Montreal with the work of Emilie Tavernier Gamelin. After the death of her husband and three children at a young age, Gamelin devoted herself to care for the sick, indigent, and orphaned. As her activities expanded, others joined her, and they formed a corporation, operating out of a building they called Providence House. In 1844, with the support of Bishop Ignace Bourget of Montreal, Gamelin and six other women took vows as Sisters of Providence. Esther Pariseau joined the congregation shortly thereafter. The sisters soon confronted the harsh realities of charitable nursing work in the nineteenth century. With other Catholic religious, the Sisters of Providence served the famine-fleeing Irish immigrants who arrived in Canada in 1847 on disease-ridden ships. Three sisters of the young congregation died of typhus, and many others were grievously weakened.

Bishop Augustin Blanchet knew the sisters well from his time in Montreal. He had witnessed their dedication to the poor, aged, and infirm. Their selfless love for God and neighbor would be a precious asset in the rugged conditions of the Northwest.

The first attempt to launch a Providence apostolate in Oregon had failed in 1853. Sr. Joseph was not among the group of sisters who, en route to Vancouver, only got as far as Oregon City. They found the place nearly deserted by former residents who had rushed off to find gold in California. Confused and unable to make contact with Bishop Blanchet, they abandoned the project and sailed off for a House of Providence in Chile.

Bishop Blanchet himself accompanied the sisters from Montreal for the second attempt in 1856, and this time Sr. Joseph was among the party. Awkwardly attired in out-of-style secular clothing for the journey (so as to avoid unwanted attention from anti-Catholic Americans), the bishop and six sisters made their way via the Hudson River to New York, where they were to embark for San Francisco. While dining in New York, a friendly waiter assured them that their religious garb would incite no violence. With relief they unpacked their black habits and wore them for the duration of the trip.

They avoided the hazardous passage through the Straits of Magellan by crossing the continent at Panama, where a newly built railway to accommodate increased traffic from East to West Coasts spared them the harrowing mule ride through the jungle. After a few days in San Francisco, they reentered the Pacific for the short trip to Vancouver. This last stage was not without peril. The entrance to the Columbia

River was notoriously dangerous in winter, and many vessels had come to ruin in what was called "The Graveyard." When a violent storm arose, the sisters thought the end had come. But they passed into harbor safely and arrived full of gratitude at the settlement at Fort Vancouver on the Feast of the Immaculate Conception, five weeks and six thousand miles since their departure from Montreal.

Building the Northwest

In a pattern that had been set earlier and was repeated countless times across the shifting American frontier throughout the nineteenth century, the sisters organized, constructed, and staffed the region's earliest social and charitable agencies. It was Catholic sisters who established the first hospitals in Chicago, Milwaukee, Boise, Salt Lake City, San Antonio, and many other places. By 1875, there were 160 Catholic hospitals across the country.

Almost from the moment of their arrival in Oregon Territory, the Providence sisters began taking in children whose parents were unable to care for them, as well as aged adults who could no longer care for themselves. They built a boarding school, Providence Academy. In June 1858, they opened St. Joseph Hospital, the first permanent health-care institution in the Northwest. Funding for the hospital came from Jews and Protestants as well as Catholics, an indication that everyone needed its services, and that the entire community would be served by it. Catholic health-care institutions, in particular, engaged non-Catholic America in the nineteenth century: "Their inherently public character," historian Christopher Kauffman observes, "fostered an accommodation to religious pluralism."

Even so, the sisters never downplayed the spiritual and even specifically Catholic character of their work. Reporting to Montreal, Mother Joseph wrote of the non-Catholic students in their new school. "Our little Protestants are not at all prejudiced," she exulted. "Their parents willingly allow them to go to church and learn the catechism." The sisters' devotion to the Miraculous Medal led them to display one at every Catholic bedside, and on at least one occasion hid one under the pillow of a non-Catholic patient. The first patient to expire at St.

Joseph Hospital converted to Catholicism. He "asked to be baptized on the Feast of St. Vincent de Paul," and his "edifying death," Mother Joseph reported, "appears to have made a favorable impression even among the Protestants of the town."

In 1859, Mother Joseph and her sisters organized as a corporation to enable the raising and administration of funds and the ownership of property in the cause of the many social services the Sisters of Providence had undertaken. That property multiplied in the 1860s as the sisters' activities expanded. Funding the construction of their institutions was always a challenge. The abandoned fort of the Hudson's Bay Company—over which John McLoughlin had reigned in recent memory—provided a bonanza of free lumber for some early structures.

More often, however, the sisters had to look farther afield for the material resources necessary for their apostolates. They would undertake "begging tours" of the surrounding region, excursions that Mother Joseph did not hesitate to join. It meant hundreds of miles on horseback, braving whatever terrain and elements nature offered. At one campsite, pitched in the midst of a torrential storm during which "we resigned ourselves to lying down in the mud as near to the fire as possible," a massive tree came down "two or three paces" from the tent in which they were sleeping. "You can understand," Mother Joseph wrote, "how fervent was our Te Deum." She also reported narrow escapes from wolves, a bear, a rattlesnake, a forest fire, and a tribal raiding party—who desisted when they noticed the group's crosses and the black robe of the Jesuit accompanying them. That was all in the course of a single trip through Washington Territory.

By 1865, there were thirty-one Sisters of Providence in the diocese, who were managing, besides St. Joseph Hospital, several schools and orphanages as well as St. John's Lunatic Asylum. The asylum afforded an improvement for its inmates, whose previous habitation had been jails. Mother Joseph designed and oversaw construction of a new, large hospital in 1874. In 1875, she established the first hospital in Portland, St. Vincent. At one of their hospitals, the sisters introduced a prepayment innovation that prefigured modern health insurance.

Over her lifetime, Mother Joseph would supervise the building of nearly thirty hospitals, schools, orphanages, and nursing homes in what are now the states of Washington, Oregon, Idaho, and Montana, as well as southwestern Canada. Sometimes known as "The Builder," she has also been called "the first architect of the Pacific Northwest."[2] Her work wasn't restricted to design and supervision; she knew how to use the tools of the trade and didn't hesitate to assist with carpentry or woodcarving.

Mother Joseph of the Sacred Heart died on January 19, 1902. Over the span of forty-six years, she had witnessed monumental growth at the scene of her labors. There were more than 250 Sisters of Providence, in addition to other Catholic religious orders working in the region. The combined populations of the states of Oregon and Washington had swelled from 13,000 to nearly one million.

Mother Joseph's last recorded words were "Do not say, 'Ah! This does not concern me, let others see to them.' My sisters, whatever concerns the poor is always our affair." The Sisters of Providence are still active in the Pacific Northwest, organized as the Mother Joseph Province. She has been honored by the state of Washington as one of its two representatives in the National Statuary Hall Collection in the US Capitol. Still, one suspects that few of the thousands of people who each day utilize the services of PeaceHealth know that the technological marvels of modern medicine they encounter stand on the foundation of a few women, shrouded in black habits, praying Rosaries and pounding nails at the end of the Oregon Trail.

Sources

Dary, David. *The Oregon Trail: An American Saga.* New York: Alfred A. Knopf, 2004.

Dunn, Philip. "On a Mission from God: Nuns' Healing Spirit Tamed the Frontier." In American Hospital Association, *Health Care.* Chicago: AHA Press, 1999.

Ferngren, Gary B. "Healing the City: How Christians Helped the Sick and Poor in the Roman Empire's Cities." *Christian History,* no. 124, (Fall 2017): 17-20.

"History of the Congregation of the Sisters of Providence." providenceintl.org/en/search-requests/history-of-the-congregation/.

Hyde, Anne Farrar. *Empires, Nations, and Families: A New History of the North American West, 1800–1860*. New York: Ecco Press, 2012.

Kauffman, Christopher J. *Ministry and Meaning: A Religious History of Catholic Health Care in the United States*. New York: Crossroad, 1995.

McCrosson of the Blessed Sacrament, Sr. Mary, with Sr. Mary Leopoldine and Sr. Maria Theresa. *The Bell and the River*. Palo Alto, CA: Pacific Books, 1957.

Montgomery, Richard G. *The White-Headed Eagle, John McLoughlin: Builder of an Empire*. New York: Macmillan, 1934.

"Mother Joseph of the Sacred Heart: A Miraculous Vancouver Life." N.d. Rosemere Neighborhood Association, www.rosemerena. org/home/wp-content/uploads/2009/04/mother-joseph-of-the-sacred-heart.pdf.

"Pioneer, Leader, Woman of Faith." Providence Archives, www2.providence.org/phs/archives/history-online/MJSH/Pages/Pioneer. aspx.

Schoenberg, Wilfred P., SJ. *A History of the Catholic Church in the Pacific Northwest, 1743–1983*. Washington, DC: Pastoral Press, 1987.

Ward, Jean M., and Elaine A. Maveety, eds. "Mother Joseph of the Sacred Heart, S.P. (Esther Pariseau)." In *Pacific Northwest Women, 1815–1925: Lives, Memories, and Writings*. Corvallis: Oregon State University Press, 1995.

16.

A Hermit and a Holy Hill

The Basilica and National Shrine
of Mary Help of Christians
1525 Carmel Road
Hubertus, Wisconsin 53033

*Did you know that each year,
five hundred thousand pilgrims visit
this shrine near Milwaukee?*

As the longest route in the National Trails System, the North Country Trail winds more than 4,500 miles from New York to North Dakota. Hikers passing along the trail in southeastern Wisconsin, where it is part of the statewide Ice Age Trail, can glimpse a majestic, two-towered brick edifice perched on a nearby hilltop. It's the Basilica of the National Shrine of Mary Help of Christians, and its location has come to be known as Holy Hill.

The Early Days of Butte des Bois

Catholicism came early to this region of the country. In the days when it was easier and faster to travel by water than by land, the Indian country that was accessible from the Great Lakes via the rivers that emptied into them was prime real estate for the missionary enterprises of Jesuits, Franciscans, and others. Jean Nicolet, an envoy from the founder of New France, and a friend of Samuel de Champlain, first made contact with Wisconsin's Indigenous peoples at Green Bay in the 1630s. The Jesuit Jacques Marquette famously explored the Mississippi River with his companion Louis Jolliet. Some accounts, possibly apocryphal, have Marquette setting foot on Holy Hill in 1673 and bestowing the title that would be used by French settlers: Butte des Bois, or Hill of the Woods.

Through the efforts of missionaries such as the Jesuit Claude Allouez, many natives of Wisconsin were exposed to Christianity by the end of the seventeenth century, though the Fox and other native tribes remained resistant to evangelization. In 1763, control of the region passed from France to Britain as a result of the treaty ending the French and Indian War. The British period was brief, for revolution broke out in the American colonies in 1775. The native tribes of southern Wisconsin joined others in pledging their support to the patriot cause represented by General George Rogers Clark at Cahokia (Illinois) in 1778—part of the same negotiation process in which Pierre Gibault (see chapter 5) had played a role. At the close of the Revolution, the Treaty of Paris set the northern border of the new nation at the top of the Great Lakes, and Wisconsin became part of the United States.

American settlers remained far away, however, as they moved into Ohio, Kentucky, and Tennessee during the early years of the new republic. Many British remained, continuing to conduct their lucrative trade in furs—beaver especially—until they were evicted after the War of 1812. At that point, the area was still dominated by Native Americans, with a few *habitants*—descendants of French colonists—scattered among them. But change was on the way. The US Army began building forts throughout tribal territory, including Wisconsin, as the nation sought to establish its authority. During the 1820s and 1830s, a series of conflicts and subsequent treaties gradually pushed the Indigenous peoples farther west or onto reservations. The last Native American cession, the Menominees', occurred in 1848, and within a few years the tribe was relegated to a reservation in northeastern Wisconsin (today, Menominee County).

Meanwhile, other land issues also had to be settled. Based on their original grants, many of the colonies along the Eastern Seaboard had maintained claims to land in the West. New York, Massachusetts, and Virginia all professed control of parts of Wisconsin. The Land Ordinance of 1785 transferred all such western claims to the national government, which then undertook the systematic process of surveying and selling its vast new holdings in what became known as the Northwest Territory. The project, starting in southeastern Ohio, finally reached Wisconsin in 1833. The ancestral land of the Fox, the Ojibwa, and the Winnebago was now open to sale, and immigrants were on their way.

Holy Hill and Its Hermit

When Wisconsin officially became a territory of the US in 1836, there were about 11,000 non-Indigenous people in the area. By 1840, there were 30,000. With the tribal lands opened up, agriculture gradually replaced trapping as the primary economic activity. Immigration, improved transportation, and government promotion of western settlement cooperated to spur massive growth. About two-thirds of the state's population in the mid-nineteenth century were migrants from elsewhere in the United States. The other third were foreign immigrants: Irish, British, German, and Norwegian settlers who added diversity to the region's ethnic and religious makeup. In 1850, two years after statehood was achieved, the population was 305,000.

For a time, the missionary activity of the French period tapered off. From 1728 to 1823, there was no Catholic priest serving the Wisconsin region. As settlers arrived, however, so did new missionaries. Outstanding figures such as the Italian Dominican Samuel Mazzuchelli and the Slovenian "Snowshoe Priest," Frederic Baraga, were among those who labored in the Wisconsin mission field.

As in many other places in the United States, the small native Christian communities of Wisconsin were eclipsed by swelling numbers of immigrant Catholics and their offspring over the course of the nineteenth century. The Catholic Diocese of Milwaukee was created in 1843. Just northwest of the city, the Hubertus area in Washington County—named for St. Hubert—was first settled by Irish, whose presence is attested to in place names such as Erin Township and Donegal Road. The Irish also first dedicated the locale's most prominent geological feature—the Butte des Bois, known by the English as Lapham's Peak—to the Virgin Mary and began calling it St. Mary's Hill. After reports of miraculous healings there in the 1850s, it was also called Miracle Hill.

By the 1850s, Germans rivaled Irish as the area's principal ethnicity. Funneling through Milwaukee, they settled in parishes such as St. Boniface and St. Augustine. The pastor of these parishes, Francis Paulhuber, was one of a number of Austrian priests who came into the diocese to serve the German-speaking Catholics. In 1855, he purchased from the government the parcel of land that contained the hill. Paulhuber predicted that the rocky eminence would one day become "one of the most noted places in all this land . . . a place of worship and pilgrimage when tens of thousands shall come to do homage to the Virgin Mary and her Son."

Fr. Paulhuber did not live to see his vision become reality—he soon returned to Austria—but his successors labored to bring the idea into being. In 1858, Fr. J. B. Hasselbauer arranged for a cross of white oak to be erected at the summit. It was fashioned by Roman Goetz, a prominent parishioner and longtime caretaker of the property, who welcomed pilgrims from his log cottage aside the hill's ascent. During the pastorate of Fr. George Strickner, parishioners of St. Augustine and St. Boniface constructed the first place of worship atop the hill, a small chapel made of timber and stone. It was dedicated on May 24, 1863, the Feast of Mary, Help of Christians.

It was around this time that nearby residents discovered the mysterious character who would become known as "The Hermit of Holy Hill." His name was François Soubrio and his native tongue was French, but when farmers suddenly became aware that someone was living nearby as a hermit, no one knew who he was, where he came from, or how long he'd been there. One rumor claimed that he'd murdered a loved one and then fled to the wilderness of the Great Lakes to find peace with God.

The hermit's answers to inquiring neighbors were at first brief and evasive, as he spoke neither German nor English fluently. He lived in a crude dugout near the top of the hill, wore a cape and hat, and carried a staff and a book. He spent his time praying and meandering about the woods. After the neighbors built a hermitage for him, he became friendlier and began to share his story.

He had left France as a young man to try to earn a fortune that would enable him to win approval from the father of the woman he intended to marry. From Quebec to New York to Baltimore to Charleston, François traveled ever farther south in a seemingly fruitless quest for gainful employment. Luck finally came in Charleston, where he managed to procure a sizable income.

Worried about the failure of his beloved to return his letters, he returned to her home in Mannheim, Germany. There he found that a terrible drama had unfolded in his absence. The girl's father had died, and she had married François's best friend. This friend had been responsible for conveying his letters to her and had deceived her into believing that François had met an untimely demise in America. This husband had died in a dissolute state, leaving a destitute young widow and child.

François did not remain in Germany. With his spirit crushed, he spent ten years as a sailor on commercial vessels, then tried his luck in California during the gold rush. After stops in Charleston and Quebec, he became fascinated with the Great Lakes region and set out for Wisconsin. There he stayed at Miracle Hill until he departed the area in 1881. Where he went or how his days on earth ended, history has not recorded.

François's legacy lived on in more changes to the name of Miracle Hill. In the 1860s, some referred to it as Hermit's Hill, after the captivating Soubrio was discovered living there. A poem about Soubrio published in the 1880s—"Hermit of Holy Hill"—popularized yet another name for the landmark, and this one stuck. Like millions of pilgrims ever since, the region's residents perceived something transcendent about the three-hundred-foot-high pile of rocks and gravel left behind by the retreat of the glaciers many centuries before. It has been known as Holy Hill ever since.

The Shrine on Holy Hill

The hill's popularity as a place of pilgrimage and healing gradually increased. In 1878, Fr. Ferdinand Raess, pastor of nearby St. Hubert Parish, led a seven-mile procession culminating in the placement in the shrine of a life-size statue of Mary, Help of Christians (henceforth known as Our Lady of Holy Hill). By that time, the need for a bigger church was clear, and Raess petitioned Archbishop John Martin Henni of Milwaukee for permission to build. Fieldstone excavated for the leveling of the hill's summit was used to construct the foundation, and the two hundred thousand bricks needed to raise the walls were made from a clay bed in the vicinity. The original chapel was razed to make room for the new church, whose cornerstone was laid in 1879. The new building was christened as the Church of St. Mary Help of Christians by Milwaukee's Archbishop Michael Heiss on September 8, 1881.

In 1903, Pope Leo XIII formally designated the church as a Catholic shrine. By 1906, Archbishop Sebastian Messmer deemed it necessary to have priests in residence to serve the spiritual needs of the visitors. As the shrine was not canonically a parish of the archdiocese, entrusting the task to a religious order was the most sensible solution. Messmer invited Discalced Carmelites from Bavaria to become custodians of the shrine, and a Carmelite monastery was added on the property of Holy Hill.

The Carmelites, an ancient religious order, had their origins on another holy hill: Mount Carmel in Israel, where the prophet Elijah worshipped the Lord. The Carmelite coat of arms thus features a hill with a cross atop—an appropriate symbol for the custodians of Holy Hill.

The burgeoning Catholic population of the region and the shrine's continuing popularity made construction of a third, even larger church necessary in the 1920s. This building was constructed in a neo-Romanesque style, with stone arches traversing the nave and also marking off the aisles to either side. Several windows from the earlier church were preserved and installed in the new edifice. At the heart of the shrine is a forty-ton marble altar surmounted by an ornate bronze tabernacle and covered by a white stone canopy supported by red marble columns. The two steeples at the front of the shrine soar above the deciduous forest below, with a third, shorter spire rising from the apse. On July 19, 1931, the church was solemnly dedicated.

Its appeal has endured. In the words of one longtime visitor, "Holy Hill gives a tiny glimpse of heaven when you walk in the door." Many pilgrims have also continued to find healing at the shrine, giving rise to its reputation as "the Lourdes of Wisconsin."

In 1938, Cardinal Samuel Stritch came from Chicago to preside at a Pontifical High Mass celebrating the diamond jubilee of the establishment of the shrine. In 2006, the year marking one hundred years of Carmelite stewardship, the church was named a basilica by Pope Benedict XVI.

Some half a million visitors come each year to seek spiritual regeneration at Holy Hill. Like Moses at Sinai, Elijah at Carmel, the apostles at Tabor, and countless others through the ages, they have found that God's presence is often manifested on a mountain—even a small one in Wisconsin.

Sources

Avella, Steven M. *In the Richness of the Earth: A History of the Archdiocese of Milwaukee, 1843–1958*. Milwaukee, WI: Marquette University Press, 2002.

"History." HolyHill.com, www.holyhill.com/basilica/history/59-history.

LeCount, J. M. *Holy Hill: Its History—Authentic, Legendary, and Prehistoric*. Hartford, WI: J. M. LeCount and Son, 1891.

Nesbit, Robert C. *Wisconsin: A History*. Madison: University of Wisconsin Press, 1973.

O'Neill, Eddie. "O Holy Hill, the Basilica Is Brightly Shining." *National Catholic Register*, December 13, 2006.

Rainey, William Francis. *Wisconsin: A Story of Progress.* New York: Prentice-Hall, 1940.

Rosario, Cornel. *Inside Holy Hill: Basilica of the National Shrine of Mary, Help of Christians.* Hubertus, WI: Holy Hill Basilica, 2009.

Rummel, Leo, OPraem. *History of the Catholic Church in Wisconsin.* Madison, WI: Knights of Columbus, 1976.

17.

A General Absolution before Battle

Monument to Fr. William Corby, CSC
Gettysburg National Memorial Park
Hancock Avenue
Gettysburg, Pennsylvania 17325

Did you know that a priest memorialized at Gettysburg also served two terms as president of the University of Notre Dame?

Amid the innumerable plaques, statues, and markers that dot the hills and woods surrounding the town of Gettysburg in what is now a national memorial commemorating the Civil War's best-known battle, there is a life-size bronze of a Catholic priest, standing, his hand raised in blessing.[1] It was in large measure the scene depicted there that made Fr. William Corby "the most famous of all Catholic chaplains" to serve during our nation's bloodiest conflict.

A People Divided

Corby was born in Detroit in 1833, a second-generation Irish immigrant. In 1853 he went to the decade-old University of Notre Dame and while there decided to join its founding order, the Congregation

145

of Holy Cross. Following ordination, he taught at Notre Dame and also served local parishes around South Bend.

When the War between the States erupted, Corby volunteered to serve as a chaplain, one of seven Holy Cross priests to enlist. Like the rest of the country, American Catholicism was split by the Civil War. The Catholic Church never formally broke in two as did many Protestant denominations, but it still suffered deeply from internal divisions. By and large, Catholic laypeople, parishes, and clergy in the South took the side of the Confederacy, while northern Catholics favored and fought for the Union. Catholics Philip Sheridan and William Rosecrans led Union armies into battle, while Maryland-born Catholic Raphael Semmes was a Confederate navy captain. William Tecumseh Sherman, the scourge of Georgia, was raised in the Catholic household of Senator Thomas Ewing of Ohio and married Ewing's daughter, and their son became a Jesuit priest (though William himself did not become Catholic until on his deathbed). The Catholic general P. G. T. Beauregard commanded the Confederate forces at Charleston and thus gave the order to fire on Fort Sumter on April 12, 1861—the first shots fired in the Civil War.

The predominantly Catholic Irish were the largest immigrant group at the time, and they served in large numbers on both sides. There were thus Irish Catholic units in both armies. The best known of these in the North was the Irish Brigade. It was composed of one regiment from Massachusetts, one from Pennsylvania, and three from New York, including the famous "Fighting 69th" Infantry Regiment of New York. After the Battle of Bull Run, it was commanded by Brigadier General Thomas Francis Meagher, an exile from the Irish nationalist struggles against Britain. The brigade fought in some of the fiercest battles of the Civil War, including Antietam and Fredericksburg. One of the Irish Brigade's chaplains was Fr. William Corby.

Civil War Chaplains

Catholic priests were active as chaplains on both sides of the conflict, and Catholic sisters were likewise indispensable as nurses for both the Blue and the Gray. Some 20 percent of all Catholic sisters served as nurses during the war, around seven hundred in total from twenty different religious communities. About fifty priests served in the Union army and thirty in the Confederate.[2] David Power Conyngham, an Irish journalist who first covered and then served in Corby's unit, praised the priests and sisters who "on the battlefield or in the hospital" offered their "attention and services . . . to all alike, regardless of their religion, their complexion, or their nationality."

To Catholics in the field, the chaplain was a fount of solace in the midst of squalor and inhumanity. Conyngham admired the chaplains who "had volunteered to partake with him all the hardships, dangers and privations of a soldier's life in time of war." After the war, Conyngham collected testimonials from surviving officers. The impressive list of correspondents who contributed endorsements included General Ambrose Burnside, who observed that "the Catholic clergy engaged in army work were eminently distinguished for the self-sacrificing and zealous manner in which they performed their duties"; General Joseph Hooker, who "always found the Catholic chaplain faithful, attentive, and zealous" and "by his pious example and religious teachings . . . greatly softened and Christianized the tone and actions of the men"; and General Robert E. Lee, who gave credit to both the priests—"kind and attentive to the temporal and spiritual wants of the men"—and the sisters—who "devoted themselves to the sick and wounded."

As a group, Catholic chaplains were almost universally held to be self-sacrificial servants of their flocks. The Union general Benjamin Butler praised the Episcopalian and Roman Catholic priests for "their correct deportment, persevering industry, unaffected piety, restless activity, and sound moral instruction." The Catholics in particular, Butler observed, "were remarkably zealous."

One of the chief duties of the Catholic chaplain was to provide sacraments. Holding a Mass for wartime armies could be an extraordinary affair. After the war, Conyngham described one such memorable event in almost mystical terms. It was a Christmas midnight Mass in 1861, offered outside Washington, DC, where the Irish Brigade was encamped. The men erected a makeshift chapel out of the trunks and branches of pine and cedar trees. As the voices of the chaplain celebrants

> rose in psalmody and hymn, and as the prostrate worship-
> pers humbly bowed their heads in response and muttered
> their silent prayers, there was something wildly grand in
> the ceremony. The glare of the candles suspended from the
> trees, the flickering, feeble light barely making the gloom of
> the night visible, the sigh of the wind and the gentle patter-
> ing of the falling snow and sleet, the surpliced priests, the
> soft tinkling of the bell, and the low responses of the atten-
> dants and pious worshippers, all combined to add a solemn
> sanctity to the celebration that we have never experienced
> inside the walls of the most stately edifice.

That Mass was the calm before the storm for the Irish Brigade. They were soon embroiled in a series of gruesome battles, and the work of the chaplains grew grimmer. In camp, Conyngham recalled "often seeing at early morning a crowd of men outside the priest's tent waiting to go to confession, and the afternoon another crowd, some sending money home to friends, others waiting to have him, 'Just write a letter home.'" In the crucible of war, the Sacrament of Confession took on urgency for even marginal believers. After all-day marches, with battle imminent, the priest would face a line of penitents who wanted to clear their consciences before taking desperately needed rest.

Then there was the war itself. At Fredericksburg, two-thirds of the Irish Brigade was cut down on the merciless battlefield. The chaplains crept among the human ruins, giving both spiritual and physical comfort. The ministry was not without danger. Though Corby was unscathed, his clothing took two rebel bullets. Another chaplain was gravely wounded by a wayward shot.

Gettysburg

By the summer of 1863, the Irish Brigade's fighting strength, initially several thousand, had decreased to 530. In July, after marching long and hard, the miserable soldiers, now led by Colonel Patrick Kelly, arrived in south-central Pennsylvania near the town of Gettysburg. Union forces were gathering to try to stop the advance of Lee's Army of Northern Virginia. For his part, Lee hoped by this bold invasion of the North to secure recognition of the Confederacy by England and France and further dishearten a war-weary Union.

On the morning of July 2, the brigade assembled in a position near Cemetery Ridge, supporting the long defensive line commanded by Daniel Sickles. With combat imminent, Fr. Corby judged that the situation justified the use of general absolution. That meant that, instead of requiring individual Confession as was normal, Fr. Corby would ask the men to repent of their sins to God and then he would grant them forgiveness as a group. The soldiers were gathered in a tranquil meadow, but sounds of battle already filled the air around them as the bearded priest mounted a rock so as to be more easily seen by the crowd.

As one of the officers recalled the scene later, Corby explained the situation, informing the soldiers that they could be absolved of their sins by "making a sincere Act of Contrition and firmly resolving to embrace the first opportunity of confessing." The men had been standing, but "as he closed his address, every man, Catholic and non-Catholic, knelt on his right knee, his head bared, hat in left hand, right hand upon his rifle, and bowed his head." The priest finished with a Sign of the Cross from his raised right hand and the words of forgiveness in Latin: "*Dominus noster Jesus Christus vos absolvat . . . in nomine Patris, et Filii, et Spiritus Sancti. Amen.*"

"I do not think," the officer reflected, "there was a man in the brigade who did not offer up a heart-felt prayer."

Corby insisted later that his benevolent act was "intended for all— in quantum possum [so far as my power allows]—not only for our brigade, but for all, North or South, who were susceptible of it and who were about to appear before their Judge."

Within an hour, the Irish Brigade was engaged, and the soldiers of the beleaguered unit, at peace with God but at war with their fellow man, began dying. They held their line until, vastly outnumbered, they gave way before the hollering rebels. By the end, the already decimated unit had lost another three hundred men. It was the end of the Irish Brigade, for a time. After Gettysburg, the unit was disbanded until its numbers could be reinforced.

The Aftermath

The significance of Corby's absolution, like the Battle of Gettysburg itself, endured beyond the first days of July 1863. Some effects were manifested quickly. A week after the battle, a non-Catholic Union officer approached Corby and said, "I would like to know more about your religion." The fellow had been present on July 2, and, he observed, "While I have often witnessed ministers make prayers, I never witnessed one so powerful as the one you made that day."

The poignancy of the event for those involved also did not diminish with time. After the war, Corby returned to South Bend and became vice president and then president of the University of Notre Dame. He served two terms, so he was both the third (1866–1872) and the sixth (1877–1881) president of the institution.

But he went back to the site of those dramatic events one more time. Corby was reunited with the veterans of the Irish Brigade during the twenty-fifth-anniversary observance of the Battle of Gettysburg in 1888, when fifty thousand survivors from across the nation gathered at the scene, which had become a national memorial. A monument to the Irish Brigade was dedicated during the gathering, on July 2. The bronze Celtic cross, standing nearly twenty feet tall, was fashioned by an Irish Confederate veteran of Gettysburg. Fr. Corby blessed it.

"The emotions that filled my breast," he wrote later, "when I met the surviving officers and men once more on the field that drank in the blood of so many of our dead companions may be more easily imagined than described. I shall never forget that meeting."

Corby died in 1897. In 1910, he was given his own monument at Gettysburg, a bronze statue featuring his act of absolution, sculpted by fellow Irish Catholic Samuel Murray. Thanks to several popular memoirs and the memorial statue, the incident has become a part of Civil War lore. It appears, for example, in the 1993 film *Gettysburg*. In a brief scene, the Union officers preparing for action on the morning of July 2 come upon a large group of soldiers receiving a blessing from a priest whose back is turned to the camera.

Thus, one of the iconic images of a bloody and brutal conflict, which brought an end to "America's original sin," the appalling institution of slavery, is that of a man of God, his hand raised in an act of blessing and forgiveness.

Sources

Conyngham, David Power. *Soldiers of the Cross: The Heroism of Catholic Chaplains and Sisters in the American Civil War*. Edited by David J. Endres and William B. Kurtz. Notre Dame, IN: University of Notre Dame Press, 2019.

Corby, W., CSC. *Memoirs of Chaplain Life*. Chicago: La Monte, O'Donnell, 1893.

Longley, Max. *For the Union and the Catholic Church: Four Converts in the Civil War*. Jefferson, NC: McFarland, 2015.

McClarey, Donald R. "Father Thomas Ewing Sherman." *American Catholic*, September 15, 2010.

18.

A Catholic Conspiracy to Kill a President?

Grave of Dr. Samuel Mudd
St. Mary's Catholic Church
13715 Notre Dame Place
Bryantown, Maryland 20617

Did you know that many Americans thought that Abraham Lincoln's assassination was a Catholic conspiracy?

Bryantown, Maryland, is an unincorporated community located on State Route 5, a major thoroughfare that leads north to Washington, DC, and south toward the peninsulas of southern Maryland, where the Calverts and other Catholic settlers founded St. Mary's City (see chapter 2). Bryantown is dominated by its Catholic church, St. Mary's. The current parish dates to 1793, but there was Catholic liturgy in Bryantown as early as the 1650s.

On the grounds of St. Mary's is a large cemetery, a testament to the Catholic history of the region. Among the tombs is an unremarkable gray stone engraved with the names Dr. Samuel Alexander Mudd and Sarah Frances Mudd. The date of the earlier deceased—Samuel, 1883—belies the contemporary look of the stone. In fact, the original tombstone was replaced in 1940, and it can be viewed at the Samuel Mudd House in nearby Waldorf. Dr. Mudd is the most famous area resident because, in 1865, he participated in what has credibly been called "the most sensational crime in American history." He helped to kill the president of the United States, Abraham Lincoln.

Or maybe he didn't.

The guilt of Samuel Mudd is one of the great, unsettled debates of American history, and the Lincoln assassination connects a bewildering array of political, social, and religious factors in a complex web of intrigue. Catholics were in the thick of it.

Samuel Mudd and Jack Booth

Samuel Mudd was born December 20, 1833, in Charles County, Maryland, the fourth of ten children. He was educated at Georgetown College, the Jesuit school in the District of Columbia, and obtained a degree in medicine from the University of Maryland, Baltimore. In the 1850s, Mudd began practicing medicine in Charles County, married his childhood sweetheart, Sarah Frances Dyer, started a family that would eventually consist of nine children, and began managing a small tobacco farm, where he owned five slaves.

A few years later, the nation was torn apart by the Civil War. Maryland was a border state where loyalties were divided, but Mudd was a proslavery stalwart and thus a southern sympathizer. In 1862, he wrote a letter to the well-known Catholic convert and intellectual Orestes Brownson, explaining his reasons for canceling his subscription to Brownson's *Quarterly Journal*. Brownson had written vigorously against slavery and in defense of the war aims of the North, affirming the Catholic Church's disapproval of human enslavement. Mudd objected strenuously to Brownson's assertions and declared that the South was fighting to defend states' rights.

Ominously, in light of later events, Mudd targeted Lincoln as the source of the conflict that roiled the nation: "I confidently assert, that if there was any other man at the head of the government of true conservative and constitutional principles, the Revolution would immediately cease so far as the South is concerned." He further predicted that the South was capable of standing up to the northern bullies. "She is possessed of every ingredient to make her self-sustaining and powerful—all she wants is a little more time," he insisted, "and if the war should be protracted, all the better for her future, because her resources will be brought out."

Like many southerners, Mudd's optimism concerning the capacity of the Confederacy to keep pace with the war machine of the North proved unfounded. His belief in the threat posed to slavery, however, was accurate. In 1864 the state of Maryland abolished slavery, costing him his labor force and undermining the financial viability of his farm. He decided to sell the property and rely on his medical practice.

There was at the time a young actor who was wandering the area, ostensibly intending to purchase real estate. His name was John Wilkes Booth, and he was in fact planning an escape route from Washington, where he and his collaborators intended to kidnap Abraham Lincoln and force the Union to release southern prisoners.

In December 1864, Booth and Mudd met after Mass at St. Mary's Church. Was their connection innocent, with Mudd merely courting a prospective property buyer—or was it more sinister, with Booth recruiting the doctor to assist in the conspiracy? This is the critical question in the mystery of Dr. Samuel Mudd.

It wasn't their only meeting. The government's star witness in its prosecution of the conspirators after the assassination, Louis Weichmann, testified that Mudd rendezvoused with Booth at a Washington hotel in January 1865, and there was spotty evidence that they got together on other occasions.

Booth had been active in creating a small circle of dedicated conspirators, including John Surratt, the son of a widowed boardinghouse proprietor. Mary Surratt, whose story was told in the 2010 major motion picture *The Conspirator*, was the first woman to be executed by the federal government. She and her son were Catholics from southern Maryland. (Mary's tavern was the main attraction in the town of Surrattsville—which was promptly renamed following the proprietor's conviction and execution.)

The Surratts were not one of Maryland's old Catholic families. Much of their ancestry is unclear, but John Surratt's biographer guesses that the first American Surratts may have been Huguenots fleeing persecution in Catholic France—one of many ironies in this story. As a child, Mary Surratt, born Mary Elizabeth Jenkins, attended the Academy for Young Ladies in Alexandria, Virginia, a school operated by Mother Seton's Sisters of Charity. Mary decided to convert from Episcopalian to Catholic during her time there. She married John Surratt Sr. in 1840, and their third child, John Jr., was born in April of 1844. Like the other children, he was baptized at St. Peter's Catholic Church in the District of Columbia.

"From all indications," historian Kenneth Zanca writes, "Mary Surratt took her Catholicism very seriously." Through Mary's influence, her mother, her mother-in-law, and her brother and his family all entered the Church. Priests were among Mary Surratt's close friends and confidants. She aided Fr. Joseph Finotti, SJ, as he raised funds for the building of a new church in Oxon Hill, Maryland. Fr. Bernadine Wiget helped with her sons when she grew concerned about the influence of their alcoholic father.

In 1859, John Jr. enrolled at St. Charles College, an institution founded by Charles Carroll of Carrollton as a preparatory school for future priests. The young Surratt was there in 1860 when Abraham Lincoln was elected president and sectional politics raged in Maryland. A classmate later recalled that the young Surratt "was a pronounced friend of the Southern cause from the start, yet I do not recall that he ever made himself offensive to anyone by the persistency of his views."

In August 1862, John Sr. died, leaving Mary a widow. She asked her son to come back home, and he left his classmates at St. Charles, never to return. Mother and son devoted themselves to their farm and tavern. Failing to make ends meet, they decided to move into the District and manage a boardinghouse on H Street, not far from Ford's Theatre. Priests and sisters were among its patrons. It was a popular gathering place.

The final meeting between Booth and Mudd occurred on April 15, 1865. On the previous day, Good Friday, Booth had entered Ford's

Theatre and shot Abraham Lincoln as he watched the play *Our American Cousin*. With the surrender of the Confederate Army on April 11, the motive of prisoner exchange had evaporated. In its place welled the frustration and fury of defeat. Booth had vowed to destroy the man who symbolized the end of the Confederacy and the southern way of life.

When Booth leapt from the viewing box—or perhaps in a riding accident during his escape—he broke his leg.[1] He managed to make his way to Mudd's house in Maryland (the place, now a museum, where the original tombstone is preserved). After Mudd treated Booth, the assassin and his coconspirator David Herold resumed their flight from the relentless manhunt. Booth would be cornered and shot by federal troops a few days later.

Samuel Mudd and Mary and John Surratt were among those implicated and captured in the dragnet of the federal investigation of the assassination. A total of eight conspirators were tried and found guilty. Four, including Mary, were hanged. Four, including Mudd, were imprisoned.

A Catholic Conspiracy?

The Catholic connections of some of the accused were not lost on a distraught, conspiracy-minded public. David Herold, who accompanied Booth on his escape, had attended Georgetown College. The Jesuit link was a suggestive one. Members of the Society of Jesus, champions of the Catholic Counter-Reformation, had been antagonists of Protestantism since the sixteenth century. Shortly after the assassination, a letter addressed to War Secretary Edwin Stanton from a former Protestant Civil War chaplain tried to connect the dots and helpfully suggested where the fugitive might be found:

> John M. Surratt is a Roman Catholic, once patronized . . . by the priests of Georgetown. . . . As the Papal government only has shown favor to the Southern Rebellion, and the loyalty of a large proportion of the Catholic clergy is, to say the least, questionable, is not the presumption fair, that

Surratt is harbored in some of their secret sanctuaries, more
likely in Georgetown?[2]

Surratt was in fact in Canada at the time. He had fled immediately
and was the only major conspirator to escape punishment.

Stanton's tipster, though perhaps motivated by irrational anti-Catholicism and not quite accurate as to either the position of the Catholic Church on the Confederacy or the geographical location of Surratt,
did shrewdly guess somewhat close to the mark. Surratt in fact had
the assistance of priests during his exile from the United States. Stanton, for his part, directing the search for Booth and his accomplice,
had already issued orders to scour the "counties of Prince George,
Charles and St. Mary's" in Maryland, a region "noted for hostility
to the Government and their protection to Rebel blockade runners,
Rebel spies and every species of public enemies." Southern Maryland
happened to be both the historic heart of American Catholicism and
also a hotbed of Confederate sympathy. There was plenty of grist for
the mill of those who were determined to view the Lincoln conspiracy
as a Catholic plot.

The anti-Catholicism of the 1850s—manifested in the Bedini riot
and the affair of the pope's stone (see chapters 13 and 14)—had been
tempered by the Civil War. Indeed, part of the motivation for the nativism of the Know-Nothings—the "American" Party—was to solidify
a national American identity and preserve the Union. It didn't turn
out that way, as the pioneering historian of nativism, John Higham,
notes: "The division between North and South, which nativists endeav-
ored to submerge, soon submerged nativism." Nativism, including
its anti-Catholic component, would not long remain under water,
however. Even as northern Catholic opposition to the war and eman-
cipation kept northern Protestant suspicion toward Catholics kindled
during the conflict, Catholic involvement in the Lincoln assassination
furnished fresh fuel for antipapist fires afterward.

Mary and John Surratt's Catholic connections were not merely historical. In Canada, John lived in the house of a priest in a remote village in the province of Quebec. In September 1865, he fled to England,
where he lodged at a Catholic oratory in Liverpool. The following

spring, he moved again, this time to Italy, where he joined the Papal Zouaves, a short-lived military unit composed of volunteers from around the world who banded together to defend the territorial claims of the papacy as the Papal States were besieged by Italian nationalists during the 1860s.

The anti-Catholic narrative had problems, though. While Maryland was the cradle of Catholicism in the British colonies, it was also a den of anti-Catholic sentiment. Secretary of State William Seward, the other victim of the April 14 plot, was a detested figure in southern Maryland, in part because of his friendliness to Catholics and other immigrants. There is also the fact that, once papal authorities learned the identity of Surratt, they placed him under arrest with the intention of extraditing him for trial in the United States.

But the desperate Surratt escaped from his Roman captors, scrambled into the Italian countryside, and eventually ended up in Egypt. There he was at last apprehended by American officers. In what some continue to view as a miscarriage of justice, the jury—on the strength of testimony that insisted Surratt was not in Washington on the day of Lincoln's assassination—failed to convict Surratt and he went free. He got married, had children, and taught at a Catholic school in Emmitsburg, Maryland. He lived until 1916 and was buried at a Catholic cemetery in Baltimore.

The Conspiracy Theory Lives On

During Mary Surratt's trial, five Catholic priests appeared as character witnesses for the accused. Fr. Jacob Walter, her parish priest, joined Mary's daughter in a frantic final attempt to stay the execution. "You cannot make me believe," he wrote later, "that a Catholic woman would go to Communion on Holy Thursday and be guilty of murder on Good Friday." Their efforts failed.[3] On the morning of the hanging, Mary appeared in the company of Frs. Walter and Wiget. They spiritually and physically supported the middle-aged woman, who fainted as she approached the scaffold. They were present as the trap door opened and her mortal life ended. Her body, with those of the other conspirators, remained in government custody for several years but was finally interred in 1869 at Mount Olivet, a cemetery of the Archdiocese of Washington.

Protestant disgust at Catholic involvement in the plot prompted Congress to take action as well. It passed a ban on funding for an ambassador to the Vatican that stood for over a hundred years. The beleaguered Pope Pius IX was in the process of losing the Papal States—the Church's sovereign possessions for over a thousand years (the efforts of the Papal Zouaves came to naught)—and thus the need for a diplomatic mission to the pope seemed diminished in any case.

The notion of a Catholic assassination conspiracy, far from petering out, actually gained momentum in the postwar era. One of the most flamboyant anti-Catholics of the nineteenth century, ex-priest Charles Chiniquy, was its chief proponent. His 1885 screed, *Fifty Years in the Church of Rome,* has been called the "main witness" for the prosecution against the Church and the first "systematic development" of the assassination as a "Catholic grand conspiracy."

There had been rumblings of an unseemly affinity between Catholicism and Confederacy during the war. The southern government made overtures to Pope Pius IX, and he replied in a friendly though diplomatically noncommittal way. The supposition of natural alliance between what they saw as two enemies of freedom was confirmed in the minds of papal detractors by Pius's sympathetic gesture of sending a letter to Jefferson Davis, the imprisoned former president of the Confederacy, after the war.

Chiniquy heated this simmering controversy to a boil by fabricating Lincoln quotations, which in turn became stock items in the anti-Catholic literature of subsequent decades. "I do not pretend to be a prophet," the president allegedly said, "but though not a prophet, I see a dark cloud on our horizon. And that dark cloud is coming from Rome." During the war, Chiniquy claimed, Lincoln declared, "It is not against the Americans of the South, alone, I am fighting, it is more against the Pope of Rome." In Chiniquy's telling, Lincoln thought the First Amendment would need to be curtailed for Catholics because they are "sworn and public enemies of our constitution, our laws, our liberties, and our lives."

The editors of one Lincoln collection describe Chiniquy as "the biggest liar in Lincoln literature," but no matter: *Fifty Years* was a huge success. It reached forty editions by 1891, and among its publishers was the major evangelical press Fleming H. Revell. Chiniquy spread his message by spoken as well as printed word. He was a popular draw on the lecture circuit until his death in Quebec in 1899.

A Chiniquy pamphlet summarizing the case for a Catholic conspiracy made the rounds during the election of 1890. The secular *Los Angeles Herald* denounced it as "too silly for any sane man or woman's attention," but conceded that it was "widely circulated." The nativist American Protective Association rehashed Chiniquy's claims in its magazine in the same decade. The tale long outlived the teller. In the 1910s, an abridged version of Chiniquy's account, titled "The Assassination of Abraham Lincoln by Romanists," was published in the anti-Catholic periodical *The Menace*, circulation 1.5 million. The fundamentalist Jack Chick Publications republished the story once again as "The Big Betrayal" as late as 1981, and both *Fifty Years* and the Jack Chick article remain easily available online, preserving the Catholic conspiracy theory for generations to come.

His Name Was Mudd

Samuel Mudd was sent to an American prison in the Dry Tortugas, west of the Florida Keys. At first he tried repeatedly to escape, but he eventually submitted to his fate. He distinguished himself by his service as a physician during a yellow fever outbreak, and this among other factors was cited in President Andrew Johnson's pardon decree of February 8, 1869.

Mudd returned to his family in Maryland and lived out the rest of his days in peace. When he died in 1883, he was buried in the parish cemetery. One granddaughter, Cecilia, joined the Congregation of Holy Cross, taking the name Sr. Samuela. She died at the congregation's convent at Notre Dame, Indiana, in 2003. A grandson, Richard, devoted himself to clearing his grandfather's name, going so far as to petition Presidents Jimmy Carter and Ronald Reagan. Both responded similarly, expressing their personal opinion that Mudd was innocent of any serious wrongdoing but also insisting that they had no power to formally overturn a federal conviction. "As President," Reagan wrote, "there is nothing I can do. Presidential power to pardon is all that is in a President's prerogatives and that, of course, was done by President Andrew Johnson."

Did Mudd willingly participate in the conspiracy to assassinate Abraham Lincoln? The definitive answer will likely never be known. It's a secret Mudd took to his grave—the one that lies in the cemetery of St. Mary's Catholic Church in Bryantown, Maryland.

Sources

Hatch, Frederick. *John Surratt: Rebel, Lincoln Conspirator, Fugitive.* Jefferson, NC: McFarland, 2016.

Higham, John. *Strangers in the Land: Patterns of American Nativism, 1860–1925.* 2nd ed. 1955; rpr. New Brunswick, NJ: Rutgers University Press, 1988.

"History of St. Mary's Cemetery." www.stmarysbryantown.com/history-of-st-marys-cemetery.

"January 13, 1962: Letter from Mudd." *American Catholic,* posted by Donald R. McClarey, Jan. 13, 2012, the-american-catholic.com/2012/01/13/january-13-1862-letter-from-mudd/#more-35110.

Kauffman, Michael W. *American Brutus: John Wilkes Booth and the Lincoln Conspiracies.* New York: Random House, 2004.

Kurtz, William B. *Excommunicated from the Union: How the Civil War Created a Separate Catholic America.* New York: Fordham University Press, 2016.

Longley, Max. *For the Union and the Catholic Church: Four Converts in the Civil War.* Jefferson, NC: McFarland, 2015.

Obituary for Sr. Samuela Mudd, CSC. *South Bend Tribune,* March 7, 2003, www.rootsweb.ancestry.com/~instjose/obits/m/muddsistermsamuela.htm.

Roscoe, Theodore. *The Web of Conspiracy: The Complete Story of the Men Who Murdered Abraham Lincoln.* Englewood Cliffs, NJ: Prentice-Hall, 1960.

Sobiech, Michael. "Chiniquy's Lincoln: Aiming Booth's Bullet at the Roman Catholic Church." *American Catholic Studies* 127, no. 4 (2016): 23–47.

Steers, Edward, Jr. *Lincoln Legends: Myths, Hoaxes, and Confabulations Associated with Our Greatest President.* Lexington: University Press of Kentucky, 2007.

Zanca, Kenneth J. *The Catholics and Mrs. Mary Surratt: How They Responded to the Trial and Execution of the Lincoln Conspirator.* Lanham, MD: University Press of America, 2008.

19.

A Sister of Charity in the Wild West

Sr. Blandina Gardens
133 N. Commercial Street
Trinidad, Colorado 81082

*Did you know a Catholic sister won
the respect of Billy the Kid?*

Her life had all the adventure of a stock character out of a Hollywood western: stagecoach rides, lynch mobs, runaway horses, and murderous outlaws. But she was neither a pioneering homesteader nor a woman of doubtful virtue. Blandina Segale was a Catholic Sister of Charity, and her story is entwined with the history of one of America's great western highways, the Santa Fe Trail.

Considering that she lived on the margins of civilization during the nineteenth century, we know a lot about Sr. Blandina. In diaries and letters to her family, she left us a rich memoir full of fascinating details and amazing tales.[1] Scholars have questioned the veracity of these accounts, and in fact there are discrepancies with the known historical record that must be acknowledged. Still, it's reasonable to assume that, allowing for some exaggeration in the telling and some errors resulting from careless recording and faulty memory, Sr. Blandina's remarkable story is largely reliable.

From Italy to the American West

Rosa Segale was born in Cicagna, Italy, in 1850. When she was four years old, her family immigrated to the United States, settling in the bustling Ohio River hub of Cincinnati, which had already been the site of a diocese for nearly thirty years and was home to a community of Elizabeth Ann Seton's Sisters of Charity. In 1852, when the Emmitsburg congregation affiliated with the Daughters of Charity in France, some sisters from the Cincinnati group, with the assistance of Bishop John Purcell, chose to become a diocesan congregation. This split would mean, among other things, that the future Sr. Blandina would be garbed in the relatively modest, bonnet-like habit of the Cincinnati Sisters of Charity rather than the spectacular cornette that was adopted by the Emmitsburg sisters.[2]

In 1865, a bishop in need once again called upon the nuns. Bishop Jean-Baptiste Lamy of Santa Fe appealed to the Sisters of Charity to open a hospital in New Mexico. Four sisters were sent, and they soon expanded their operations to include an orphanage, an industrial school for girls, and outreach to the impoverished. In Santa Fe, as elsewhere, Catholic women religious provided the personnel and resources necessary to establish the region's first educational, healthcare, and social welfare institutions.

Meanwhile, in 1866, Rosa and her sister Maria Maddelina had both joined the Sisters of Charity. Maria became Sr. Justina, and Rosa, taking the name of an early Christian martyr, became Sr. Blandina. Following a teaching stint in Steubenville, Ohio, Blandina was assigned to work on the frontier, serving the handful of Hispanic and Anglo Catholics—as well as their non-Catholic neighbors—who lived in and around Trinidad, Colorado. After opening a novitiate in Santa Fe in 1870, the Sisters of Charity had expanded their mission to the nearby mining town of Trinidad. By 1900, there would be ten thousand Catholic sisters working throughout the American West.

The Santa Fe Trail

The Spanish name of the town, honoring the Holy Trinity, reflected the heritage of the southwestern United States. The area had been part of New Spain until the Mexican Revolution, and part of Mexico until the Mexican-American War. Now, Trinidad was a stop on the Santa Fe Trail, one of the arduous tracks that brought settlers from the more populated East into the plains, deserts, and mountains of the West.

The chief city of the region, which gave the trail its name, was also a legacy of the Spanish era. From the time of the conquistadores, men had dreamed of finding riches in the bleak but beautiful expanses of the Southwest. Sante Fe was founded in 1607—the year an English party settled Jamestown—as La Villa Real de la Santa Fe de San Francisco de Asís: The Royal City of the Holy Faith of St. Francis of Assisi. The name was impressive, but Santa Fe's growth was destined to be outpaced by that of communities in more hospitable and strategic locales in New Spain, such as California, Mexico, and Texas.

The explorations of Zebulon Pike in the first decade of the nineteenth century reignited interest in the wealth that might lay untapped in the arid lands of southern Colorado, New Mexico, and Arizona. The earliest traders defied not only the elements and hostile tribesmen but also the wrath of the Spanish authorities, who forbade private commerce between its own territories and the US. When the enterprising Auguste Chouteau (see chapter 5) attempted to flout this ban in 1817, he was captured and imprisoned by the Spanish.

Mexican independence in 1821 released government restraints on trade, and Chouteau participated in negotiations with the Plains tribes to open the trail to American commerce. By the end of the decade, the route from the Missouri River to Santa Fe was a thoroughfare for the exchange of goods between Mexico and the United States. That commerce was facilitated by Senator Thomas Hart Benton of Missouri, who enjoyed a cozy relationship with the irrepressible Chouteaus of St. Louis. In 1825, Benton pushed legislation through Congress to sponsor surveying and marking of the trail from Missouri to the Mexican border. Although the passage remained extremely hazardous, the attractions of the Southwest outweighed its dangers in the eyes of many restless Americans. By the 1840s, a steady stream of settlers heading west were using the Santa Fe Trail, hoping to navigate successfully the perils of Comanche raids, mercurial weather, and scarce water supplies.

A School in the West

It was late in the life of the Santa Fe Trail, December 1872, when Sr. Blandina alighted from a stagecoach and for the first time beheld the dusty, remote town in which she was to labor. She joined four other sisters who were already residing at a simple convent in Trinidad. She described the existing church as "an adobe structure—with a pretense of a gable roof and double pretense of having been shingled; mud floor, mud walls, wooden candlesticks." And there was a row of pews, "if you can call eight planks nailed together, pews."

One of the main tasks of the sisters was to provide schooling for the settlement's children. In the desperate situation of the American frontier, sectarian differences did not figure as strongly as they might have back east, where Protestant families had a variety of educational options. In Trinidad, parents could send their kids to the sisters or they could train them at home; there were no other possibilities. In an arrangement that was not unique to Trinidad, therefore, the Sisters of Charity were the staff and faculty of a public school, maintained with public funds.

In rural Colorado in the 1870s, schools were dependent on the largesse of the local community. When Blandina became convinced of the need for a new structure to replace the cramped and aging hovel that had so far served as a school, she decided to take matters into her own hands. Mounting the roof of the old school with a crowbar, she began prying off the clay shingles. A wealthy local woman happened by and cried out, "For the love of God, Sister, what are you doing?" When Blandina explained that she was demolishing the building so as to construct a more suitable structure, the woman promised to provide the men and supplies necessary. Blandina was assisting with the plastering when she encountered the local pastor, accompanied by a visiting bishop, Joseph Machebeuf of Denver. Blandina put down her hod-bucket and greeted the dignitary, who remarked, "I see how you manage to build without money."

Teaching remained the primary mission of the sisters. The classroom brought its own adventures.

One of her older students burst into the school one day in a panic, to retrieve his younger sister. His father had been thrown in jail for shooting a man, and a mob was waiting outside. The instant the wounded man "breathes his last," the boy explained, "the mob will go to the jail and drag Dad out and hang him." Sr. Blandina proposed a conciliatory visit between the shooter and the victim. The son warned that there was no way to get the two together with the mob standing between, but Blandina insisted. A nervous sheriff reluctantly agreed to make the attempt, and so an odd procession began from the jail to the victim's room across town. Advancing together were, on one side, the grizzled, six-foot-four-inch lawman; on the other side, the habited nun, barely five feet tall; and in between them the dejected prisoner. "The crowd made way," Blandina reported. The shooter asked forgiveness from the victim, and it was granted. The perpetrator returned to his cell and, spared mob justice, awaited sentence from the circuit court judge.[3]

On another occasion, the regular coach driver failed to show up at the school for a field trip into the mountains. Not wanting to disappoint the schoolgirls, Blandina took the reins herself. She had deposited all of the girls but one at the campsite when the horses hitched to her wagon began to run wild. She managed to keep them on the road for a while, holding fast though the reins cut into her hands. Then, perceiving that to hazard the road ahead at such breakneck speed would mean certain death, she pulled with all her might to force the team to the left onto level ground.

Sr. Blandina was knocked unconscious by the jolt of bringing the horses to a stop. When she came to, she found the wagon broken apart and the horses grazing nearby. She located the child who had accompanied her on the wild ride near a piece of the damaged vehicle, "blood oozing from her nose and no sign of life." Sr. Blandina begged the Blessed Mother to intercede for the girl. When Blandina returned after fetching the horses, the injured pupil was sitting up and able to speak. The two had begun to struggle toward town when they were met by a helpful passerby.

Billy the Kid

Although education was the sisters' primary apostolate, the exigencies of western life required that they be prepared to perform whatever work of mercy was demanded. They distinguished themselves by their care of the sick. It was this service that led to one of Sr. Blandina's most spectacular encounters.

Reality and myth are interwoven in the stories of the outlaws of the American West, but that gangs of desperadoes prowled the plains and mountains seeking easy prey is true enough. There were a number of gang leaders who went by the name "Billy the Kid," William Bonney being only the most famous of them.

In 1876, a henchman of Billy the Kid—whether it was Bonney or some other Billy is uncertain—was injured by a gunshot taken during a quarrel with a fellow outlaw. He was left to die, and none of the area's four physicians would lift a finger on his behalf. Sr. Blandina, in contrast, visited him frequently over the ensuing weeks, offering both physical and spiritual comfort.

While the fellow was incapacitated, Billy the Kid and his men returned to Trinidad to visit their comrade and to exact vengeance on the town's doctors. Having been apprised of Sr. Blandina's efforts, Billy offered that she might request a favor of him. She asked him to spare the lives of the four physicians. He agreed, and left town peacefully.[4]

New Mexico and Beyond

Near the end of 1876, Blandina was informed that she and another sister had been assigned to a new mission territory: Santa Fe, the terminus of the famed westward trail. She spent five years in Santa Fe before moving on to Albuquerque. Ever solicitous of those in need, without regard to faith, ethnicity, or economic means, Blandina defended Mexicans and Native Americans who were sometimes treated as second-class citizens by the Anglo-Americans who now ruled the land. In one case, she confronted the mother of two men who were trying to take advantage of New Mexicans' lack of expertise in the English language and American law. "Your sons are trying to steal land and call it lawful," Blandina scolded her. "You may tell them there is a Vigilance Committee which will be highly pleased to meet them."

In 1880, the Atchison, Topeka, and Santa Fe Railroad linked the region to the nation's continental rail network. (The archbishop of Santa Fe, Jean-Baptiste Lamy, was a key figure in convincing the railroad not to bypass the city.) The advent of the rail line, however, marked the end of an era—in the words of a local newspaper head-line, "The Old Santa Fe Trail Passes into Oblivion." When Blandina returned to Trinidad in 1889, she remarked that it "has lost its frontier aspect."

The development of Colorado proceeded rapidly, and the Old West, a place in which Sr. Blandina had thrived, gradually passed away. Now afforded the luxury of choosing from among other quali-fied teachers, the school board demanded that the faculty of "Public School Number One"—the Sisters of Charity who had established it—change their "mode of dress." No longer were religious habits a welcome uniform for public-school teachers. Sr. Blandina replied to the board's chairman with characteristic cheek: "The Constitution of the United States gives me the same privilege to wear this mode of dress as it gives you to wear your trousers. Good-bye."

Blandina said good-bye to the West in 1894, spending the rest of her long life in her hometown of Cincinnati.[5] There, she and Sr. Justina founded the first Catholic settlement house in the United States, as a place to serve poor Italian immigrants. The wide-ranging services the sisters offered included catechesis; visitations to homes, hospitals, and prisons; emergency relief; an employment bureau; and a home for girls.

One of the abuses they tackled was human trafficking, known at the time as "white slavery." Blandina, in her usual fashion, confront-ed the problem directly by publicly accosting the madam of a local brothel and threatening to take her to court. The media attention she generated helped shine a light on a previously neglected problem.

Sr. Justina died in 1929. Blandina retired to the congregation's infirmary in 1933. On January 23, 1941, she celebrated her ninety-first birthday, and died one month later.

Given her extraordinary life and outsized personality, it isn't surprising that Sr. Blandina has enjoyed sporadic bursts of attention. Her letters were first published as a magazine serial from 1926 to 1931 and then a year later in book form, a release that received notice in the *New York Times Book Review*. She has been featured in comic books and on a 1966 television series that called her "The Fastest Nun in the West." In 2014, the Archdiocese of Santa Fe formally opened her cause for canonization.

Sources

Butler, Anne M. *Across God's Frontiers: Catholic Sisters in the American West, 1850–1920.* Chapel Hill: University of North Carolina Press, 2012.

Dary, David. *The Santa Fe Trail: Its History, Legends, and Lore.* New York: A. A. Knopf, 2000.

Hyslop, Stephen G. *Bound for Santa Fe: The Road to New Mexico and the American Conquest, 1806–1848.* Norman: University of Oklahoma Press, 2002.

Mahoney, Benedicta. *We Are Many: A History of the Sisters of Charity of Cincinnati, 1898–1971.* Cincinnati: Sisters of Charity, 1982.

Metz, Judith. *Women of Faith and Service: The Sisters of Charity of Cincinnati.* Cincinnati: Sisters of Charity, 1997.

Nordhaus, Hannah. "The Fastest Nun in the West." *Smithsonian* 47 (November 2016): 35–37, 90–94.

Segale, Blandina. *At the End of the Santa Fe Trail.* 1932; Albuquerque: University of New Mexico Press, 1999.

20.

The Murder of an Archbishop in Alaska

Archbishop Charles John Seghers's Burial Site
St. Andrew's Cathedral
740 View Street
Victoria, British Columbia V8W 1J8

Did you know that a Catholic bishop was murdered by a traveling companion in the hinterland of Alaska?

On an evening late in November of 1886, four men settled into their bearskins to try to keep warm in the uninhabited hut they had appropriated for the night. They were worn out from a long day trekking across the snow-covered tracts of western Alaska. They went to sleep knowing they would reach their destination, the trading-post town of Nulato, the next day. In the early hours of the morning, one of the men got up and said he was going out to get some firewood. Instead, he returned with a gun. He aimed it at one of the other men and delivered a single shot through his heart. Thus came to a violent end the extraordinary life of Archbishop Charles John Seghers.

Missionary to the Northwest

Seghers was born in Belgium in 1839. Orphaned at a young age, he was raised by his uncles. Drawn to the prospect of a life spent spreading the Gospel in distant, pagan places, he enrolled in the American Seminary of Louvain, an institution founded for the purpose of recruiting and training men from Europe's Francophone nations for missionary service in the United States. He was ordained in May of 1863, and by September he was on a ship crossing the Atlantic, bound for the seventeen-year-old Diocese of Vancouver Island.

The see city of Victoria was a study in diversity. There were Catholics of many different nationalities and ethnicities, white Protestant Americans of various denominations, some Jews, some Chinese, and a large population of native islanders. Those of European descent were mostly transients on their way to work the gold fields of the Fraser River, the longest river in British Columbia. This combustible assortment managed an uneasy coexistence, characterized by cooperation in a colorful array of vices. Against this daunting set of challenges stood Bishop Modeste Demers and a handful of priests. Demers had arrived in Oregon Territory in 1838 as a companion of François Blanchet. When the Church erected three new dioceses to cover the Oregon Territory in 1846, Blanchet became the first bishop of Oregon City, his younger brother Augustin was made bishop of Walla Walla, and Demers was appointed to Vancouver Island.

When he first arrived, the learned and diligent young Fr. Seghers was a welcome reinforcement. Seghers took up his duties as rector of the cathedral and de facto administrator of the diocese during Bishop Demers's frequent travels. But Seghers's missionary zeal impelled him to set out on evangelistic quests whenever he had the opportunity. He visited Native Americans around Vancouver Island, some of whom had never seen a priest. On these journeys he proved himself capable of bearing the harshest physical conditions and material deprivation, a quality indispensable for ministers on the northern shores of the Pacific.

Following Demers's death in 1871, Seghers was made bishop of Vancouver Island. Far from providing him with an excuse to relax, the appointment freed him to pursue his missionary aspirations in the place he had long desired to work: Alaska. The Diocese of Vancouver Island included that vast territory, whose native peoples dwelled in some of the most remote locations on earth.

Apostle to Alaska

Russia was the first western nation to establish contact with Alaska. From the eighteenth century, explorers, fur traders, and Russian Orthodox missionaries were active in the Aleutian Islands and along the west coast of the mainland. In response to Russian advances, the Spanish made brief sorties into Alaska. A few place names—Valdez, Cordova, Malaspina[1]—are all that remain of the Spanish effort. A lasting Catholic presence would not be established until the time of Seghers and his contemporaries.

The Russian Orthodox missionaries established Mikhailovosk (Fort St. Michael) in 1799, and refounded it as New Archangel after its destruction by native warriors. It is today the city of Sitka on the Alaskan panhandle. The Orthodox made substantial inroads in Alaska, in particular among the Aleut islanders. Russian activity was limited to coastal areas, however. Even more challenging would be penetrating the vast Alaskan interior. That possibility was opened up to American missionaries when the United States purchased Alaska in 1867.

Seghers reconnoitered Alaska during a brief journey in the first year of his episcopate. By 1877, he had sufficiently put affairs in order in Victoria that he could manage a longer trip into the far north. From the old Russian settlement of St. Michael, he and his travel companions—another priest, Joseph Mandart, and four native assistants—ventured up the Yukon River into the interior. As they went, the bishop made use of his facility with languages, learning both Russian and native dialects. This eliminated the serious problem of unreliable translators, who could do damage with careless renderings of theological concepts—such as enumerating the Trinity as "Father, Son, and Mother."

The party survived the manifold dangers of winter travel in Alaska: temperatures reaching forty-two degrees below zero (F), plunges through ice into deathly cold waters, and hostile local shamans who sensed a challenge to their authority. Anywhere an opportunity presented itself, Seghers gathered the local people and explained the basic truths of Christianity. By the time Seghers returned to Victoria in September of 1878 after more than a year away, he had made contact with some thirty thousand Alaskan natives.

There was news waiting for him when he returned. Pope Pius IX had died, and his successor, Pope Leo XIII, had a new assignment for Seghers: coadjutor of Oregon City, heir-apparent to the pioneering bishop of the Pacific Northwest, François Blanchet.

An Oregon Interlude

Seghers departed his beloved flock at Vancouver Island with sadness but set out at once on an apostolic visit of his new diocese, which, if not quite the unfathomable size of Alaska, was yet enormous. The diocese, based in Portland, encompassed the states of Oregon, Montana, and Idaho. Seghers made his way across the mountains and plains, laboring as he went. "When I am preaching, I rest from riding," he wrote; "when I am riding, I rest from preaching."

An efficient administrator as well as a competent theologian, Seghers quickly put both the financial and spiritual affairs of the archdiocese on sound footing. His emphasis on Catholic education was noteworthy. Three years before the bishops of the United States issued their clarion call to Catholic schooling at the Third Plenary Council of Baltimore (1884), Seghers and his suffragans promulgated an equally strident exhortation to pastors and parents to provide a fully Catholic education to their Catholic children.

In preparation for the Third Plenary Council, the archbishops of the United States went to Rome in 1883 to meet with Pope Leo XIII and Cardinal Giovanni Simeoni, prefect of the Congregation De Propaganda Fide. There Seghers, now himself an archbishop, learned that his successor in Vancouver Island, Bishop Jean-Baptiste Brondel, had been transferred to become the bishop of the new Diocese of Montana. A suitable replacement for Victoria had not been found. Seghers wrote to Simeoni, pleading that he be restored to the Diocese of Vancouver Island. His request was granted.

The people of Alaska had always remained close to Seghers's heart. In short order, he assigned priests to the relatively accessible posts of Wrangel and Sitka, but the more remote areas would require more extensive preparations. After making sure that Vancouver Island itself had been adequately provided for, Seghers made plans for an apostolic voyage to the Alaskan interior in 1886.

The Final Voyage

With two Jesuits, a Catholic layman, and a contingent of native porters, Seghers set off for the headwaters of the Yukon River tributaries in northern British Columbia. The layman in the party, Frank Fuller, had been attached to the Jesuit De Smet mission in Idaho. The Jesuits didn't trust him—they thought him mentally unstable—and urged Seghers not to allow him to be part of the group. But Fuller begged to be included, and there was nothing in his demeanor to foretell the breakdown to come. Seghers overruled his Jesuit companions and permitted Fuller to join the expedition.

It was a strenuous journey, taking them into the Arctic Circle. Threats abounded from wildlife, river rapids, and bone-chilling cold. The man whom American newspapers had described as "a gentleman of high culture and refinement" took his part in the humblest tasks. During one period, when he was left alone at camp during a lengthy portage, the archbishop spent a day cleaning and mending cloth items—including undergarments: "I had to remain under my blankets to subject some of my clothing to the necessary repairs, perfectly safe from any intruder's visit."

The group made their way by foot and canoe to Harper's Place, the junction of the Yukon and Stewart Rivers. Wishing to both serve that region and hasten on to Nulato, far down the Yukon, the missionaries made the difficult decision to split up. Frs. Louis Robault and Pascal Tosi would remain, while Archbishop Seghers, Fuller, and two native guides would proceed to Nulato.

There was no sign of trouble with Fuller until the group reached the village of Nuklukayet, west of the junction. There they encountered a trader named Walker, who apparently harbored some animosity toward Catholic missionaries. It is believed that he poisoned the already troubled mind of Fuller, activating a paranoid fear that Archbishop Seghers was plotting the demise of his companion.

During their time at the village, Seghers began to notice Fuller's increasing agitation and erratic behavior and recorded his observations in his diary. On October 16 he wrote forebodingly, "Had a strange conversation with brother [Fuller] who, for the third time, is giving proof of insanity."

They pushed on toward Nulato, camping on a high crag on the north bank of the Yukon. There they hunkered down in a poor hut roofed with turf. "Without light, without ventilation," it was "unspeakably squalid and comfortless."

The last words in Seghers's diary are dated November 25. Three days later, Fuller shot and killed the archbishop, with whom he had traveled for four months. The rifle used was allegedly the victim's own.[2]

The natives of Alaska, his fellow priests, and the people of Vancouver Island and Oregon were all stunned at the news of the prelate's death. Yet grief gradually gave way to celebration of his faith and his achievements. A non-Catholic Victoria newspaper eulogized: "Do you wish to see his monument? Look around! . . . above all, you see it—the light in darkness—in the great work which he has himself done among the Indians." The arduous life and tragic death of this zealous evangelist were the labor that gave birth to the Church in Alaska.

Sources

Baets, Maurice de. *The Apostle of Alaska: Life of the Most Reverend Charles John Seghers* (Vie de Monseigneur Seghers, [1894]). Translated by Mary Mildred, SSA. Paterson, NJ: St. Anthony Guild Press, 1943.

Jamieson, Patrick. *Victoria, Demers to De Roo: 150 Years of Catholic History on Vancouver Island.* Victoria, BC: Ekstasis, 1987.

Naske, Claus-M., and Herman E. Slotnick. *Alaska: A History of the 49th State.* Norman: University of Oklahoma Press, 1987.

Steckler, Gerard, SJ. *Charles John Seghers, Priest and Bishop of the Pacific Northwest, 1839–1886.* Fairfield, WA: Ye Galleon, 1986.

21.

A Catholic Mission and an Indian Tragedy at Wounded Knee

The Heritage Center on the
Pine Ridge Indian Reservation
100 Mission Drive
Pine Ridge, South Dakota 57770

*Did you know that through the activity
of an American saint, an East Coast
business fortune funded an array of
Catholic missions in the West?*

On December 29, 1890, a confrontation between a regiment of US Cavalry and a group of Lakota (Sioux) Indians on their reservation in South Dakota erupted into violence. When the melee ended, more than two hundred Native American men, women, and children lay dead, along with nearly thirty soldiers. The conflict is known to history as the Wounded Knee Massacre or the Battle of Wounded Knee.

The following day, a much less deadly contest between the Lakotas and American troops occurred—the last armed engagement in the long, heartbreaking history of American–Native American conflict. It is known as the Drexel Mission Fight. The site takes its name from a saint who, though she lived two thousand miles away, dedicated her life to the betterment of the long-suffering native peoples whose plight was exemplified in the tragedy at Wounded Knee.

Catholic Indian Missions

Evangelization of Indigenous people had long fired the imagination and resolve of Catholic missionaries such as Isaac Jogues, Jacques Marquette, and Junípero Serra (see chapters 3 and 4). Even so, in most tribes, the preaching of the Gospel was challenging at best. Language barriers, cultural differences, and the local inhabitants' natural suspicions—aggravated by the abuses of European explorers, settlers, and sometimes missionaries themselves—all conspired to make evangelization a difficult and often dangerous affair.

Yet there was progress in many places, as testified by the Catholic mission churches that dotted the reservations of the western United States—where, by the late nineteenth century, Native Americans were largely confined. The Catholic priests and sisters who worked on the reservations were constantly hampered by a shortage of personnel and material resources. The Catholic immigrants who made up the bulk of the American Church were struggling to get by as it was. Having dedicated their meager resources to building schools and churches in the cities of the Eastern Seaboard, the Great Lakes, and the West Coast, they were mostly uninterested in contributing to the missions that were scratching out their existence on the Great Plains.

The US government, meanwhile, was mostly unhelpful. Dominated by Protestants, its Bureau of Indian Affairs favored the creation of non-Catholic missions and sometimes even placed communities of already baptized Indigenous Catholics under the authority of Protestant clergy. Anti-Catholic sentiment in the bureau reached an apex in the late nineteenth century during the tenure of Commissioner Thomas Jefferson Morgan. Morgan set in motion a plan to divest "sectarian" schools located on reservations of all federal support—support that had been vital for Catholic schools serving an impoverished clientele. By 1901, Catholic schools were on their own, facing the need to raise funds from a distant, mostly working-class Catholic laity.

Cardinal James Gibbons of Baltimore lamented the result. "Deprived of Government help," he declared, "the numerous schools, nurseries of Catholicity and civilization, which were flourishing among the tribes, are on the verge of destruction."

Beginning in the 1880s, however, this financial strain would be eased by one enormous source of relief. In Philadelphia, the heiress of the Drexel estate committed her considerable fortune to the betterment of Native Americans and African Americans.

St. Katharine Drexel

Katharine Drexel's grandfather was an Austrian immigrant who married into a venerable Philadelphia Catholic family and started a brokerage firm that would enable his son, Katharine's father, to acquire a fortune and catapult him into the ranks of high society. Katharine's mother, a Quaker, died shortly after Katharine's birth in 1858, but Francis Drexel made a happy second marriage, and Katharine's home life was materially comfortable, emotionally warm, and devoutly religious. Her parents were role models for their children. The busy banker made time every day to pray, and Emma Bouvier Drexel distributed goods and money to the city's needy.

Katharine's response to her good fortune was marked by gratitude and fraternal charity. "I love my country with all my heart," she wrote at age sixteen, "the people, the habits, the cities, everything!" Her diaries reveal a child who was exuberant, precocious, and somewhat mischievous, but also serious about her spiritual life. As much as she loved the country under whose flag her family had so richly benefited, she was also acutely sensitive to the injustices that marred it. Her concern for those left behind—in particular, Native Americans and African Americans—would inspire her life's apostolate.

Katharine knew that she would dedicate her fortune to this cause, but she wasn't at first certain about how God wanted her to do so. She made her debut in Philadelphia society in 1879. Six years later, both her stepmother and her father were dead, leaving the three Drexel sisters as stewards of an inheritance of $14 million (the equivalent of more than $300 million today).

But Katharine was not destined for a life in society. After discerning a call to consecrated religious life, she followed the advice of her spiritual director and decided to found a new congregation—one dedicated to redressing the injustices that troubled her beloved nation. On February 12, 1891, she made her profession, becoming the first Sister of the Blessed Sacrament for Indians and Colored People. Her family's estate in northeast Philadelphia became the first motherhouse for Katharine and her thirteen novices and postulants.

For forty-six years Katharine served as superior of the Sisters of the Blessed Sacrament, her leadership a case study in grace building on nature. She brought to the order all of the discipline, social dexterity, and business savvy that had been instilled by her upbringing. Though she controlled vast sums of money, she lived in poverty and wouldn't permit others to coddle her. On her many travels across the country to oversee new foundations and the endeavors that had benefited from her funds, she rode coach class and packed meals to save money. When she died at the age of ninety-seven in 1955, Cardinal Richard Cushing of Boston described her as "the greatest benefactor of the Home Missions of the Catholic Church in the United States."

The Lakota Missions

One of the many beneficiaries of Katharine Drexel's largesse was Holy Rosary Mission on the Pine Ridge Reservation, a Lakota refuge in South Dakota.[1] Beginning in the seventeenth century, a series of Catholic missionaries—including Jesuits Jacques Marquette, Claude Allouez, and Joseph Marest, and Franciscan Louis Hennepin—had worked among the Sioux peoples of the upper Midwest, but the suppression of the Society of Jesus in the late 1700s brought a temporary halt to that project.[2] The celebrated Jesuit missionary Pierre De Smet reestablished a Catholic connection with the Sioux in 1839 and first made contact with the Oglalas in 1849. De Smet's relationship with the Oglalas deepened during the Laramie Treaty negotiations in 1851, when the Jesuit became a trusted intermediary between the local tribes and the US government. De Smet befriended the Lakota chief Sitting Bull, Custer's future nemesis.[3]

Thus, when the government under President Ulysses Grant began the practice of assigning tribes and reservations to the exclusive administration of particular denominations, the Lakotas complained when they were matched with Episcopalian missionaries. During a visit to the nation's capital in 1877, Lakota chiefs requested Sina Sapa ("Black Robes") to serve their people and educate their children. When, in 1879, a Benedictine from St. Meinrad Abbey in Indiana tried to honor the Pine Ridge Lakotas' desire for Catholic priests, the government agent ordered him to leave the reservation. The undaunted monk set up shop two miles to the south in Nebraska, where the Lakotas came to visit him and receive the sacraments.

Eventually, the government acceded to the Lakotas' wishes, and the reservations of South Dakota were opened to Catholics. In 1886, Fr. John Jutz, SJ, founded St. Francis Mission on the Rosebud Agency of the Department of Indian Affairs (predominantly Oglala) and the following year established Holy Rosary Mission at Pine Ridge (predominantly Brule). A few years before she founded the Blessed Sacrament congregation, Katharine Drexel visited Holy Rosary, met the Lakota chief Red Cloud, and agreed to fund the construction of a school. The compound became known as the Drexel Mission.

The Lakota and other Plains Indian tribes were at the end of a decades-long, losing battle against the encroachment of American settlement on their ancestral lands. They enjoyed fleeting successes—the defeat of General Custer at the Little Bighorn was the most famous—but, in the words of historian Martin Gitlin, "such triumphs merely served to hasten their demise due to white backlash that strengthened and prioritized government resolve to either kill off the Indians or place them securely on reservations that grew smaller and smaller as the nineteenth century marched on."

In the 1880s, at one reservation—Standing Rock Agency, on the border of the Dakotas—a group of Lakotas, with their esteemed leader Sitting Bull, began the practice of performing the Ghost Dance, a ceremony connected to a religious movement popular among the Plains tribes at the time. Some nervous observers—including the new and inexperienced government agent of the Pine Ridge

Reservation—interpreted the dance as being a prelude to war. The stage was set for the disaster to come.

Wounded Knee

On December 15, 1890, a contingent of Standing Rock reservation police—themselves members of the Lakota tribe—attempted to arrest Sitting Bull on suspicion of fomenting rebellion. Sitting Bull resisted, a quarrel ensued, and shots were fired. The beloved Sioux chief was killed, struck down by his own people.

In response, several hundred Lakotas fled to the Cheyenne River Reservation, joined another band led by Spotted Elk (later known as Big Foot), and then continued south toward Pine Ridge, the site of the Drexel mission. Facing arrest, however, they surrendered to American forces and were escorted to an encampment at Wounded Knee Creek. On December 29, an attempt by the soldiers to disarm one of the detainees caused the Lakota's weapon to discharge, setting off a chaotic chain of events as tribe members fled and soldiers fired. Even one of the soldiers, who claimed that the Lakotas fought back furiously, admitted that the conflict degenerated into a massacre. "When the shelling started," he recounted,

> all red women and children in the camp had immediately taken flight. Unrestrainedly, they threw themselves into carts or rushed desperately away—some up the valley to the right, others again in wild panic towards the ravine down whose sides they blindly rode, drove, or precipitated themselves, only to be massacred against the rugged rocks at the bottom or to be shot down without mercy by the skirmish line on the opposite side.

Among those caught up in the chaos was a Catholic missionary, Fr. Francis Craft, who was wounded so severely by shot and blade that reports initially circulated that he'd been killed. Fr. Craft's career among the Lakotas was characterized, in the words of his biographer, by "the zeal of St. Paul, the idealism of Don Quixote, and the flair of Cyrano de Bergerac."

Craft, the descendant of a Mohawk chief, was born in New York City and raised as an Episcopalian. As a teenager, he was injured at the Battle of Gettysburg, and in his twenties, he found himself fighting for the French in the Franco-Prussian War. (He was in Europe to study medicine.) Ever spoiling for a fight, he raised a contingent of American mercenaries for the Cuban War for Independence in 1871, where he was grazed by bullets and slashed by bayonets. Later that decade—for reasons unexplained but possibly through the influence of the Irish he fought with in Cuba—he converted to Catholicism. Determined to evangelize the people with whom he considered himself kin, he initially sought to follow in the footsteps of the great Jesuit missionaries of America but later left the Society of Jesus and was ordained to the diocesan priesthood in Omaha in 1883.

He was sent immediately to the Rosebud Agency. The mission demanded both physical and mental toughness, and Craft looked the part. Over six feet tall, "as keen, sinewy, and powerful as a stag," he was already "an experienced horseman and expert marksman" when he arrived among the Lakotas. By 1890 he was an expert in their language and culture, an adopted member of the tribe, and a trusted counselor. In a letter published in an eastern journal, he deplored the Lakotas' poor treatment and noted that his companions were "not fools, but men of keen intellect." As such, they perceived and rebelled against injustice. The savvy missionary could not have been surprised when violence erupted a few days later.

Injured survivors of the Wounded Knee fight were treated at the nearby Episcopal church. To alleviate crowding there, Fr. Jutz of the Holy Rosary Mission offered the services of his Catholic school to care for wounded children.

In the days following the massacre, the Lakotas on the Pine Ridge Reservation ambushed soldiers sent in to keep order. They burned the government school and even fired on white doctors and nurses searching the area for survivors. Many of the Lakota warriors wanted to attack the Drexel Mission but were dissuaded by their elders. "Red Cloud used all his influence," writes a Drexel biographer, "to convince them that the black robes always acted kindly toward the Indians."

The respectful treatment accorded to Native Americans by past and present priests such as De Smet and Craft was remembered and honored, and Catholic missionaries and their buildings were singled out for protection.

Nicholas Black Elk

During the fighting at Wounded Knee, a Lakota medicine man named Black Elk was struck by a bullet in the abdomen, leaving "a long deep scar." As a child, he had taken scalps from the enemy during Custer's debacle at Little Bighorn. Later, he performed in Buffalo Bill's Wild West Show, touring throughout the United States and Europe—where he met Queen Victoria—before returning to Pine Ridge. Two years after his survival of the Wounded Knee Massacre, he married Katie War Bonnet, who converted to Catholicism shortly thereafter. They had three children, all baptized Catholic, before Katie's death in 1903.

The following year, Black Elk joined the Church, taking the name Nicholas, and he served for more than twenty years as a catechist—an important post amid a shortage of ordained missionaries. As catechist, he instructed others in the faith, led Corpus Christi processions, and preached and presided at prayer services when a priest was unavailable. According to the testimony of his daughter, he always had a rosary in his hand.

He was still at Pine Ridge in 1931 when he was interviewed by a Nebraskan poet. The resulting publication, *Black Elk Speaks*, is one of the best-known firsthand accounts of Native American life in our country's history. The book sparked a revival of interest in Native American religion—somewhat ironically considering that its subject was a devout Catholic. "I say the Apostle's Creed and I believe every word of it," Black Elk wrote in 1934. "I tell my people to stay in the right way which Christ and His church have taught us." Sixty-seven years after his death in 1950, Nicholas Black Elk's cause for canonization was formally introduced by the Diocese of Rapid City.[4]

The relationship between Native Americans and the Catholic Church in America has been complicated. But the labors of Fr. Francis Craft, the generosity of Katharine Drexel, and the faith of Black Elk display the potential that existed for not merely peaceful coexistence but even a genuine integration of native people and culture with the universal Church in a way that respected the essence of both. The Catholic Sioux Congress, an annual gathering inaugurated in 1890, provided a means for the Lakotas to achieve this integration. In 1931, Pine Ridge hosted the congress. The central gathering space at which Mass was celebrated was a large area encircled by pine branches—an arrangement that resembled the lodges in which the Lakotas tradition- ally held their sacred ceremonies, such as the Sun Dance. The Catholic mission at Pine Ridge is a marker of both the tragedy and the promise of Native American life in the United States.

Sources

Armstrong, Mark. "Was Chief Sitting Bull a Catholic?" *CatholicLane. com*. April 17, 2011.

Black Elk Speaks: Being the Life Story of a Holy Man of the Oglala Sioux, as Told through John G. Neihardt. Lincoln: University of Nebraska Press, 2000.

Duffy, Consuela Marie. *Katharine Drexel: A Biography*. Cornwells Heights, PA: Mother Katharine Drexel Guild/Sisters of the Blessed Sacrament, 1966.

Enochs, Ross. *The Jesuit Mission to the Lakota Sioux: Pastoral Theology and Ministry, 1886–1945*. Kansas City, MO: Sheed and Ward, 1996.

Foley, Thomas W. *Father Francis M. Craft: Missionary to the Sioux*. Lincoln: University of Nebraska Press, 2002.

Gitlin, Martin. *Wounded Knee Massacre*. Santa Barbara, CA: Green- wood, 2011.

Greene, Jerome A. *American Carnage: Wounded Knee, 1890*. Norman: University of Oklahoma Press, 2014.

Holler, Clyde, ed. *The Black Elk Reader*. Syracuse, NY: Syracuse Uni- versity Press, 2000.

Markowitz, Harvey. *Converting the Rosebud: Catholic Mission and the Lakotas, 1886–1916*. Norman: University of Oklahoma Press, 2018.

Russell, Samuel L. "Father Francis M. J. Craft—Missionary Wounded in Battle." *Army at Wounded Knee*. February 14, 2014. armyat-woundedknee.com/2014/02/14/father-francis-m-craft-missionary-wounded-in-battle/.

Steltenkamp, Michael F. *Black Elk: Holy Man of the Oglala*. Norman: University of Oklahoma Press, 1993.

_____. *Nicholas Black Elk: Medicine Man, Missionary, Mystic*. Norman: University of Oklahoma Press, 2009.

22.

"There Are No Bad Boys"

Boys Town
14100 Crawford Street
Boys Town, Nebraska 68019

Did you know that the founder of Boys Town ended up in Omaha because he was sent there to recover from a nearly fatal bout of pneumonia?

The sprawling campus sits on a bluff overlooking downtown Omaha. A stone tower announces the site: Boys Town. The institution's motto announces its purpose: Saving Children, Healing Families. It's been serving this purpose since its foundation by an optimistic Ireland-born priest in 1917.

Fr. Edward Flanagan was working among the poor families of Omaha when he realized that the troubled men he was serving were often past the point of rehabilitation. He needed instead to focus his attention on the boys who were growing into dysfunctional adults. He further recognized that this corruption was due in large part to their surroundings. "There are no bad boys," Flanagan insisted to all who cast a skeptical eye on his programs, "only bad environment, bad training, bad example, bad thinking."

Fr. Flanagan Comes to Omaha

Edward Flanagan was born in Ireland in 1886. The boy, his parents, and his eleven brothers and sisters recognized his calling to the priesthood early in life. His older brother, Patrick, ordained in Ireland, went to the United States to serve the growing Catholic population in Nebraska. Eddie decided to follow in his footsteps and complete his seminary studies in America. In 1904, he arrived in New York to do just that. After a stay at Mount St. Mary's Seminary in Emmitsburg, Flanagan returned to New York to complete his preparation for the priesthood at the archdiocesan seminary at Dunwoodie. But all did not go as planned. A bout with pneumonia nearly took his life, and he was forced to move west to drier air. His brother—they now called him Fr. P. A.—welcomed him to the bustling new city of Omaha.

Omaha lay on the eastern edge of what had been known in the nineteenth century as the Great American Desert. It was so called because the rainfall was not what Europeans and eastern Americans were accustomed to, but it was adequate to support the growth of copious prairie grasses. These in turn fed immense herds of grazing animals, most notably the American bison, which roamed the plains by the millions. The buffalo was the prize over which the Great Plains' Indian tribes fought—among them, the band that gave its name to the principal city of Nebraska.

The region became part of the United States through the Louisiana Purchase, and Lewis and Clark passed through the future site of Omaha as they paddled up the Missouri River in 1804. The fur trade soon came to Nebraska, and white settlement gradually increased. By the 1850s, the area's residents were eager to organize as a political entity, and once the thorny questions of slavery (Kansas-Nebraska Act) and Native American rights (Treaty with the Omaha) had been worked out (temporarily and unsatisfactorily, on both counts), Nebraska became a territory in 1854. The young settlement of Omaha would be its capital.

Two years later, the first religious structure in the city, St. Mary's Catholic Church, was built. It was still the only Catholic church in 1859, when Fr. James O'Gorman, the head of the new vicariate apostolic of Nebraska, arrived. By that time, there were about four thousand people in Omaha and its environs.

The steamboat had already improved transportation along the Missouri River markedly, but in 1863 Omaha got its big break when the Union Pacific Railroad announced plans to make the city the launching point for its westward push across the continent. The prairies surrounding Omaha, which had supported legions of buffalo, proved equally adept at feeding beef cattle, and once the innovative steel plow managed to break through the sod, the fertile soil produced vast quantities of corn and other crops. Omaha rapidly became a center of transportation, meatpacking, and agricultural exchange. Nebraska's population soared from twenty-nine thousand in 1860 to half a million by 1890. Meanwhile, in 1867, it became the thirty-seventh state. By the turn of the twentieth century, the Omaha that Flanagan encountered had all of the characteristics of a booming American city: progress and opulence alongside the depression and poverty of those who had been left behind.

Flanagan's Home for Boys

After a period of recovery in his new hometown, Edward Flanagan was sent by Bishop Richard Scannell to Rome to study. But again, plans fell through. The putrid air of the Eternal City reaggravated the seminarian's lung problems and he was forced to return to Omaha. Another period of recovery—working meanwhile as a bookkeeper at an Omaha meatpacker—put his health problems behind him for good. Flanagan undertook a final seminary course of study, this time in the clear air of the Austrian Alps at the University of Innsbruck. He was ordained there on July 26, 1912.

Working as a parish priest back in Omaha, Flanagan made efforts to assist homeless, aimless men. The project to help troubled youth started humbly. He rented a two-story brick boardinghouse on Dodge Street for ninety dollars a month—he barely scraped together the first month's rent and trusted that the rest would come—and welcomed his first five boys. Three were homeless orphans and two were lawbreakers consigned to the priest by juvenile court. The staff consisted of two sisters and a novice of the School Sisters of Notre Dame.

From the start, Flanagan's Home for Boys followed certain principles. For example, there would be no discrimination based on race, ethnicity, or religion. Fr. Flanagan saw God's grace as indispensable to the success of his project, and so he insisted that the boys practice their faith. But that faith might be Catholicism or Methodism or Judaism.

By the time two weeks passed, there were twenty-five boys in residence, and in less than a year, a hundred. By 1921, Flanagan was desperate for more space, a piece of property where his vision could take full flight, permitting ample room for dormitories, sports facilities, and the agricultural work that both provided food for the institution and taught the boys skills and responsibility.

He knew what he wanted: Overlook Farm, a 94-acre tract that was at the time located on the outskirts of the city. He persuaded the current owner, a warmhearted businessman, to accept a small down payment and a promise to pay the rest as donations to Boys Town permitted. With an appropriately interfaith committee (one Catholic, one Protestant, and two Jews) leading the way, Boys Town's first major fundraising campaign commenced, an effort to raise more than $200,000 to erect the buildings that would fill the new property.

Among the schemes Flanagan hatched to promote the project was "The Show Wagon," a bright red circus wagon pulled by a team of horses, which hauled a touring company of boys about the Nebraska countryside. The boys would present a two-hour routine consisting of singing, dancing, and comedy. Building goodwill by such promotions was essential, as not every Omahan was enthusiastic about a racially and religiously diverse campus full of "troublemakers" in their backyard.

But Flanagan didn't see them as troublemakers. He knew that bestowing responsibility induced responsible behavior, so he granted the boys broad authority over their own affairs. They held elections and chose their own mayors, council members, and commissioners. Flanagan's faith paid off in the reform of countless troubled youths.

The Village of Boys Town

A second building campaign in 1929 completed the physical plant of Boys Town. It was the year of the great stock market crash—exquisitely bad timing—but somehow the money came anyway. The governor of Nebraska, the mayor of Omaha, the bishop of the Diocese of Omaha, and other notables participated in the gala celebrating the dedication of the new buildings. The complex, now consisting of a school, gymnasium, dormitories, and administrative buildings, housed several hundred youngsters. It became the Village of Boys Town in 1934, when a United States post office was installed there.

An archway and tree-lined drive led from the main road to the buildings of Boys Town. Boys who heard about the promise of a new life at Flanagan's town traveled from across the country to the outskirts of Omaha. During the Great Depression, five to ten boys per day passed beneath the arch and trudged up Birch Drive, hoping that Boys Town would offer an improvement over whatever troubles they had left behind.

By 1938, the experiment was notable enough to have drawn the attention of Hollywood. Two big stars of the day, Spencer Tracy and Mickey Rooney, were cast in the leading roles for the film production of *Boys Town*, and its world premiere was held in Omaha. Tracy won an Oscar for his efforts. He donated the trophy to Boys Town, and it can be seen today in the museum that is part of the village complex.[1]

In 1943 Boys Town adopted its famous logo: a boy carrying a smaller boy, accompanied by the caption, "He ain't heavy, Father— he's my brother."[2] During World War II, so many soldiers who were former Boys Town citizens listed Flanagan as their next of kin that he was named "America's Number One War Dad." In the aftermath of the war, the priest toured Japan, presenting a sound vision for family life and recommending improvements to Japanese child-welfare practices.

On May 14, 1948, on another such tour in Germany, he suffered a heart attack. He died the following morning. His tomb was suitably placed in the chapel at Boys Town.

Over the years, the Boys Town organization has changed and adapted, extending its work to girls and expanding throughout the world. But the home campus in Omaha remains the spiritual center of the apostolate, and a Catholic priest has always held the position of executive director. In the American imagination, the midwestern prairie has always carried with it the threat of peril and the challenge of hard labor but also the promise of new beginnings. Fr. Flanagan's enterprise for boys was thus properly placed in a metropolis of the Midwest, and his legacy is the thousands of young people who have found the hope and courage to become better human beings through their experience in a hilltop village in Omaha.

Sources

Clooney, Nick. *The Movies That Changed Us: Reflections on the Screen*. New York: Atria Books, 2002.

Dustin, Dorothy Devereux. *Omaha & Douglas County: A Panoramic History*. Woodland Hills, CA: Windsor Publications, 1980.

"History." BoysTown.org.

Oursler, Fulton, and Will Oursler. *Father Flanagan of Boys Town*. Garden City, NY: Doubleday, 1949.

23.

The Churches of Quincy, Illinois, and the First Black Priest

Fr. Augustus Tolton Gravesite
St. Peter Cemetery
3300 Broadway Street
Quincy, Illinois 62301

Did you know that no American seminary would accept the man who would become the nation's first Black priest?

There are four historic churches in Quincy, Illinois, that have connections to Quincy's most celebrated Catholic citizen: St. Boniface Church, founded in 1837; the Church of St. Peter, whose origins date to 1838 as St. Lawrence O'Toole; St. Francis Solanus, established in 1860 by German Franciscans; and St. Joseph's Church, founded seven years later. But when this future illustrious resident arrived in Quincy in 1862, he was far from the center of attention. He was a fugitive slave who would work his way through seemingly insurmountable obstacles on the path to the priesthood. He is Augustus Tolton, America's first Black priest.[1]

195

A Child of Slavery

Before he ever set foot in St. Peter's Church in Quincy, Tolton was carried into St. Peter's Church in Brush Creek, Missouri. The baptismal record there gives the details: "A colored child born April 1, 1854. Son of Peter Tolton and Martha Chisley. Property of Stephen Eliot. Mrs. Stephen Eliot, sponsor; May 29, 1854. Father John O' Sullivan."

Martha Chisley grew up in Kentucky, on the large plantation of Catholic slave owners Mr. and Mrs. Stephen Burch. In 1849, the Burches' daughter, Susan, married Stephen Eliot, who had recently acquired a farm in Ralls County, Missouri. As a wedding gift, Susan gave her new husband a group of slaves from her parents' plantation, among them the sixteen-year-old Martha Chisley. Like countless other enslaved persons before her, Martha was torn from her family at the whim of her owners. She traveled west with the newlyweds to their new home.

Peter Paul Tolton, an enslaved worker on the Hager estate adjacent to the Eliot farm, was a bright, assertive young man who kept abreast of the news and understood that the institution of slavery was under threat. He was planning to escape to the free North when he had an encounter that changed his mind. He met Martha Chisley in a field, caring for a fellow laborer, and fell in love.

Martha and Peter Paul were married by Fr. John O'Sullivan at St. Peter's, a log church nearby. The slaveholders agreed to an arrangement whereby the couple would live at the Eliot farm while Peter Paul continued to work at the Hager place. The Toltons would have three children: Charley in 1853, Augustus in 1854, and Anne in 1859.

On the Way to Freedom

Two years after Anne's birth, the Battle of Fort Sumter ignited the war that would bring an end to the enslavement under which the Toltons and millions of other Black Americans suffered. Peter Paul grew restless again. He laid plans to escape and join the Union army, promising to return to the family when the war was over. With Martha's blessing and a mixture of sadness, fear, and excitement, Peter Paul fled the farm and found his way to the St. Louis headquarters of the US Army. He would never see Martha or the children again.

More than a year passed with no word of Peter Paul's fate. Eight-year-old Charley and six-year-old Augustus were already full-time laborers, enduring the harsh treatment meted out to field slaves. Martha resolved to escape with her children.

There had long been an "underground railroad" in operation, conducted by northern abolitionists and sympathetic southerners. They helped slaves cross borders to freedom and aided them in finding homes and employment. What to do about the steady stream of fugitive slaves passing from south to north had been one of the contentious issues that led to the Civil War.

It's impossible to pinpoint the number of enslaved persons who escaped to northern states or other countries, or the number who were assisted by northern sympathizers through the underground railroad. The distinguished historian Eric Foner guesses that between one and five thousand slaves escaped per year from 1830 to 1860. What is certain is that "all fugitive slaves faced daunting odds and demonstrated remarkable courage."

Located just up the Mississippi River in the free state of Illinois, Quincy was a center of abolitionist activity. Dr. Richard Eells, a prominent abolitionist and agent in the underground railroad, lived there until his death in 1846. Another doctor and Presbyterian minister, David Nelson, was also active in the abolitionist movement in the Quincy area. The Nelsons established a farm for the support of fugitives just southeast of Quincy. After Nelson's death in 1844, his widow, Frances, continued to operate a safe house for escaping slaves through the antebellum period. Thus, a community of free Blacks developed in Quincy, just thirty miles north of the Missouri farm where Martha Tolton and her children were held as property.

The 1850 Fugitive Slave Act made running away dangerous, but the situation changed in the 1860s. Lincoln's election, followed by the outbreak of war, led to an explosion in escapees. Escaping slaves were an asset to the North and a detriment to the South, so there was no reason for northern authorities to prevent their flight. By 1862 the need for an underground railroad had disappeared, as slaves were escaping by droves across lines into Union territory. "Far more slaves—men, women, and children, of all ages—escaped to Union lines than had reached the free states and Canada during the preceding thirty years," Foner writes.

It was during this free-for-all period that Martha decided to run. One night, under cover of darkness, she made her move. She carried twenty-month-old Anne while the boys walked hand in hand behind. They hurried across the fields of eastern Missouri over the course of several days, hiding in plain sight among field hands working farms during the day, and then moving on after nightfall. Soon they reached the landmark that was both their goal and their most imposing obstacle: the wide Mississippi River.

In Hannibal, the group was nearly captured, but some Union soldiers disputed the jurisdiction of the would-be slave catchers and secured their release. Martha located a dilapidated rowboat and stowed the children on board. As she desperately rowed across the wide river, shouts came from the Missouri side and Confederate partisans began firing at the boat. With the children cowering on the floor, Martha strove gamely to pull the boat across. Finally, they made it. Mother and children clambered onto free soil and gave thanks. "Now you are free," she announced. "Never, never forget the goodness of the Lord."

A New Life in Quincy

Martha and the children settled down in the Black district of Quincy, sharing lodging with a widow and her child. She and the two boys got jobs at the big tobacco factory. They also started attending church. A number of Black Catholics worshipped at the German parish, St. Boniface, where they congregated in one section of designated pews. Since 1858, the pastor had been Fr. Herman Schaeffermeyer. The bright and attentive Augustus gradually became fluent in the German language.

The family continued to face hardships. The tobacco production work was grueling. Augustus's brother, Charley, died of pneumonia during the winter of 1863. And prejudice against Black people was not restricted to slave states. As the Toltons were about to discover, it had even infected their beloved faith community.

Martha wanted Augustus to have a religious education, so she enrolled him in St. Boniface's parish school. It was the first time a Black student had attempted to join the all-white school. Fr. Schaeffermeyer was encouraging, and the School Sisters of Notre Dame who ran the school welcomed him with open arms. The rest of the community was another matter.

Catholics of African descent have been part of the American experience from the beginning. Servant of God Mary Lange formed the first religious order for African Americans, the Oblate Sisters of Providence, in Baltimore in 1828. But the place of Black Catholics in the Church was often ambivalent. On one hand, Black Americans shared with Catholics a status as a minority, often misunderstood and discriminated against. On the other, white Catholics frequently shared in the prejudices of their white, non-Catholic neighbors. The historian Stephen Ochs found that the Catholic Church in the United States "lost many of its own black members in the nineteenth century, because it did not allow blacks to participate fully and freely in the life of the church."[2]

The Toltons experienced this racial tension dramatically. The experiment at St. Boniface School lasted less than a month. Augustus was physically and psychologically tormented by fellow students. Parents pledged to withdraw their children and halt their financial support for the school. Fr. Schaeffermeyer and the sisters received anonymous threats. Martha decided to pull Augustus out of the school and to avoid St. Boniface parish altogether.

The Toltons next began attending the Irish parish in Quincy, St. Peter's. It had been established in 1838 to serve a small English-speaking Catholic community, but it had grown quickly as Irish immigrants arrived to work on the construction of the Northern Cross Railroad. The parish was managed with an iron fist—and a loving heart—by its pastor, Fr. Peter McGirr. McGirr's congregation displayed the same prejudices that St. Boniface's parishioners had, but at St. Peter's they were not tolerated. Catholics of any ethnicity or race were welcome, and Fr. McGirr brooked no opposition to this tenet. "Christ died for all," he would declare, and the argument was over.

When Fr. McGirr discovered that Augustus was attending a poorly equipped public school, he insisted that the boy transfer to St. Peter's. McGirr enlisted the support of the teachers, again the School Sisters of Notre Dame, who demanded that the other children treat Augustus with respect. McGirr refused to receive rectory visitors if their purpose was to protest the integration of the school, and he preached pointed homilies that exhorted his parishioners to charity toward all.

Could There Be a Black Priest?

Augustus served as an altar boy, and his spiritual devotion was clear to all. When he was sixteen years old, he received his First Communion. Fr. McGirr discerned the possibility of a special calling. One day he asked Augustus, "How would you like to be a priest?"

The boy was at first nonplussed. He had never seen a Black priest. He didn't know it was possible. The pastor assured him that it was. From that point, the desire and determination to become a priest were rooted ineradicably in Augustus's soul.

After Augustus graduated from St. Peter's in 1872, Frs. McGirr and Schaeffermeyer conspired to find a path to ordination and concluded that the nearby community of Franciscans would be the perfect venue for his further education. The two priests were as devastated as Augustus when they received a negative reply from St. Francis Monastery.

A short time later, Fr. Schaeffermeyer left St. Boniface to join the Franciscans himself. In a letter to his replacement, he noted that a separate fund had been established in the parish accounts for the education of Augustus and concluded: "I trust that you will do what you can for the Negro, as he is indeed very worthy. I promised to help him, and now I request you to carry out my promise." It was a request that the new pastor at St. Boniface would honor faithfully.

Fr. McGirr did not give up hope either. One by one he approached every Catholic seminary in the United States with an inquiry about Augustus, and one by one they replied to his letters with variations on a theme: "We are not ready." No seminary in the country was ready to accept a former slave as a student and thereby jeopardize its funding, enrollment, or maybe even its physical safety.

Acceptance to Seminary

Stymied in their search for a cooperative seminary, the two Quincy priests shifted strategy. The new pastor of St. Boniface, Fr. Francis Ostrop, offered to McGirr the services of Ostrop's new assistant, Fr. Theodore Wegmann. Wegmann was an outstanding scholar willing to train Augustus in the subject areas needed for priestly formation.

During this period, the Quincy priests learned of a new possibility. St. Joseph's Society for Foreign Missions—popularly known as the Mill Hill Fathers in England and later the Josephites in the United States—had been founded in England in 1866. Their apostolate was missionary service in English-speaking regions, and they accepted a call from the American Church to take on the missionary field of former slaves. With the blessing of Archbishop Martin Spalding, the Josephites arrived in Baltimore in 1871 and took over management of St. Francis Xavier Church.

Fr. McGirr inquired, but the Josephites did not yet have a seminary in the United States. Augustus would be welcome at their house in London, but that seemed far from home and of uncertain financial feasibility. In consultation with the priests, Augustus decided to continue studies with Fr. Wegmann.

After several years of private tutoring, Augustus gained entrance to a new college in Quincy, St. Francis Solanus. There he gained yet another clerical supporter, Fr. Michael Richardt, OFM, the pastor of St. Antonius Church just outside Quincy. With Richardt's encouragement, Augustus organized a Sunday school for young Black Catholics. Augustus's dedicated work among African Americans at the newly formed St. Joseph's School reinforced his desire to become a priest, as he recognized that he could do much more to promote the faith among his people if he were ordained. As he passed his twenty-fourth birthday, he pressed his mentors on the matter.

They had not been idle, but every path terminated in a dead end. The Franciscans of Teutopolis could not accept him; their provincial forbade it. No diocesan seminary was yet admitting Blacks. Even the Josephites were wavering: appreciating that African American priests were desperately needed in the United States, they did not want to train Augustus in their English seminary, which prepared men for the mission field in Africa.

Into this gloomy milieu Fr. McGirr brought a glimmer of hope. The bishop of Alton had written to Rome, recommending Tolton's admission to the College of the Propaganda Fide, the Church's mission seminary. Yet Rome's answer was the same as that of the Josephites: he was needed in the United States. He should be educated in an American seminary.

Fr. Richardt decided that the situation called for his last, desperate play. He would write to the superior general of the Franciscan order, who knew personally the prefect of the Propaganda Fide. The last string was pulled—and this time, it did the trick.

Studies in Rome

To get to integrated Rome, Augustus went through Jim Crow America. He left Quincy in February 1880, joining other Black passengers on the segregated railcar to Chicago. From there he traveled to New Jersey, where he stayed with some nuns for a few days while he waited for his ship.

The costs of his voyage were in part defrayed by support from Fr. Ostrop, the former pastor of St. Boniface, who had never forgotten his pledge to Fr. Schaeffermeyer to assist Augustus. He would continue to send monetary gifts throughout Augustus's stay in Rome.

Shortly after he boarded *Der Westlicher* in the port of Hoboken, Tolton was surprised to hear a familiar voice call his name. It was a German Franciscan whom he had met in Quincy. Passengers on the twelve-day voyage aboard the steamer were treated to the spectacle of three white Franciscans in brown robes and a Black American gentleman conversing merrily and singing hymns in German.

On the night of March 10, 1880, Augustus finally arrived in Rome. His home for the next six years would be the Collegium Urbanum De Propaganda Fide. He was greeted there by the prefect, Cardinal Giovanni Simeoni, and given the seminarian's uniform: black soutane with red sash and biretta with red trim. In the college, he encountered Africans and Italians; Indians and Irish; Filipinos and South Americans. All were treated equally, and all treated one another with respect. "For the first time, in his life," Tolton's biographer observes, "Augustus sensed the sublime delight of the brotherhood of man under the fatherhood of God."

Established by Pope Urban VIII in 1637, the College of the Propaganda Fide was the seminary for the Vatican office that oversees the Church's missionary activities.[3] As such, the college trained priests for service in far-flung mission territories. In the pre–Vatican II period, Holy Orders consisted of seven distinct steps. Augustus passed through the minor orders of porter, lector, exorcist, and acolyte during 1884 and 1885. By early 1886, he had completed the first two major orders, subdeacon and deacon. He was now ready for the final step.

The day before his ordination to the priesthood, Augustus received a shock. Everything he had been told and inferred during his seminary years had seemed to point toward a mission to Africa. He was excited about the prospect of spreading the Gospel in the land of his ancestors. But when assignments were announced, Cardinal Simeoni had a surprise. It had been decided that Augustus was needed in the United States. Illinois would be his mission territory. With disappointment, he obediently accepted.

The Priest

On April 24, Holy Saturday of 1886, Augustus Tolton attained the goal toward which he had striven since childhood. The ceremony, presided over by Cardinal Giovanni Parocchi, took place in the oldest church in Rome, the Basilica of St. John Lateran, which serves as the cathedral of the Diocese of Rome. The following day, Easter Sunday, pilgrims to St. Peter's Basilica witnessed the first Mass celebrated by the first African American priest. He was assisted at the altar by Cardinal Simeoni.

By early July, Tolton was back in America. His first stop was St. Mary's Hospital in Hoboken, where the sisters were delighted to host an event that they placed in their community's records for July 7, 1886: "The first Mass in the United States [celebrated] by the first African-American priest and ex-slave."

The new priest was a sensation everywhere he went. He celebrated his first solemn High Mass at St. Benedict the Moor, a Black parish in New York City. The local press reported that people of color from across the city and beyond came to fill the church and witness the former slave intone the Latin chants in a sonorous voice.

A crowd of cheering locals welcomed him when he arrived in Quincy a few days later. On July 18, he celebrated his first High Mass in the city at St. Boniface Church. A parish priest reported that "the crowd was larger than we ever had before for any occasion." Following Mass, Fr. Tolton addressed the gathering as his mother, Martha, looked on proudly from the front pew. More than twenty-five years earlier, she and her children had crept out of the slave quarters, fled across the wide Mississippi with hunters on their heels, and collapsed, exhausted and starving, in the refuge of Quincy.

"Above all," the beaming priest said, "I want to thank my mother."

On July 25, Tolton was formally installed as pastor of the fourth Quincy church to which his life was connected, St. Joseph, which had been designated to serve the Black Catholics of the city. Fr. Tolton labored untiringly, but he made little headway in building a vibrant Black parish. Protestant evangelists had already secured the allegiance of a large number of the city's African Americans. One year into his pastorate, Tolton reported to the Propaganda Fide that "the number of Negro Catholics has not increased." He also mentioned that some were urging him to move to Chicago, where a large and growing population of Black Catholics would welcome his presence. The prefect replied that Tolton was "giving complete satisfaction," and "we advise you to stay there."

Although St. Joseph's had a faithful core of Black parishioners, Tolton's parish gradually attracted a much larger number of white attendees. The Rome-trained priest gained a reputation as a fine singer and an excellent preacher, whose "rich and full voice," as one local newspaper put it, "falls pleasantly on the ear." The white congregants were an important source of financial support for the indigent parish. St. Joseph's became a model of integration in a segregated world: white and Black children served together at the altar, and white and Black musicians sang together in the choir.

This success also provoked conflict, however. Fr. Michael Weiss, the pastor of St. Boniface, resented St. Joseph's appeal to white Catholics. In part, the reason may have been financial—chagrin at the generous donations to St. Joseph's that might have instead been going toward paying down St. Boniface's formidable debt. Also, in part, the reason may have been racism. Tolton heard reports that Fr. Weiss was not above referring to him as "the n— priest."

Weiss's resentment evolved into a blatant campaign against Tolton. Tolton summarized the situation in a report to the Propaganda Fide: "He is persecuting me." In a letter to a Josephite priest in Baltimore, Tolton intentionally left out the unedifying details. "The facts I have kept hidden," he wrote, "and will never let them out through fear of it greatly injuring the success of the mission among the colored race."

"The Church for Our People"

Whenever his schedule permitted, Tolton acceded to requests from around the country to speak to Catholic audiences eager to learn about the first Black priest and the importance of ministry to Catholics of color. Some of the content of his speeches was preserved and reconstructed in a mission journal in 1945. It provides insight into how Tolton could remain so loyal to a Church in which he was so often degraded.

First, there was the example of the priests of Quincy's churches during Augustus's formative years. "I was a poor slave boy, but the priests of the Church did not disdain me. It was through the influence of one of them that I became what I am tonight." Those priests had also prepared Tolton for the trials that he would confront, and advised him how to respond: "It was the priests of the Church who taught me to pray and to forgive my persecutors."

Second, there was the experience of the universal Church in Rome. At the College of the Propaganda Fide, "I found out that I was not the only Black man there. There were students from Africa, China, Japan, and other parts of the world. . . . The Church which knows and makes no distinctions in race and color had called them all."

Finally, there was the appeal of the Church itself, the divine dimension that was its essence, regardless of human failings. From the School Sisters of Notre Dame Tolton had "beheld for the first time the glimmering light of truth and the majesty of the Church." The Church, he concluded, "is broad and liberal. She is the Church for our people."

Fr. Tolton needed to muster all of his love for the Church in the dark days of 1889, when his treatment in Quincy was at its nadir. Fr. Weiss persuaded the bishop to support his dictate that the African American priest cease ministering to anyone other than Black Catholics. Yet the Black community in Quincy was desperately poor, and the Catholics among them were beleaguered by constant pressure from Protestant denominations. It was impossible for Tolton to engender a successful parish in these circumstances.

Transfer to Chicago

Aware that the growing Black community in Chicago was eager for a pastor of its own, Tolton wrote to Archbishop Patrick Feehan, who assured him of a warm welcome in the Windy City. With the approval of both bishops and the prefect of the Propaganda Fide, Tolton's transfer to the Archdiocese of Chicago was soon consummated. On December 19, 1889, Tolton departed for a new mission field. He would never again set foot in any of the churches of Quincy, Illinois.

For the next eight years, Tolton tended to the spiritual needs of the Church in Chicago. He encountered some of the same obstacles that he had faced in Quincy, but he persevered. He orchestrated the construction of the first church for Black Catholics in the city, St. Monica's. The building was never completed due to lack of funds and the rapidly shifting demographics of Chicago in the postwar period, but its impressive beginning was nonetheless a point of pride for the impoverished parish. Tolton's value as a minister of the Church is manifest in an anecdote he related to Katharine Drexel. "Just last Sunday night," he recounted, "I was called to the deathbed of a colored woman who had been away from her duties for nine years because she was hurled out of a white church and even cursed by the Irish member. Very bad indeed! She sent for me and thanked God that she had a priest to send for."

In July 1897, Fr. Tolton left his parish for a few days to make a spiritual retreat with the other priests of Chicago at St. Viator's College in Bourbonnais, Illinois. He had returned to Chicago by train and begun to walk toward the rectory in the sweltering heat when he collapsed on the sidewalk. He was rushed to Mercy Hospital, where he died that evening, July 9. The cause of death was determined to be heatstroke and uremia. He was forty-three years old.

The half-completed Church of St. Monica, overflowing with priests and parishioners, was the site of the solemn requiem Mass, but Chicago would not be Tolton's final resting place. He had asked to be buried in the priests' lot in the cemetery at St. Peter's in Quincy, the church where he had received his First Communion and Confirmation, and the home of his beloved mentor and intrepid supporter, Fr. Peter McGirr, who had died in 1893.

The life of Augustus Tolton revolved around the churches of Quincy, and they remain as monuments to the pathbreaking priest. A large, concrete cross marks Tolton's gravesite. Its inscription reads in part, "Rev. Augustine Tolton, The First Colored Priest in the United States."[4] In 2011, the Archdiocese of Chicago, joined by the Dioceses of Springfield, Illinois, and Jefferson City, Missouri, initiated Tolton's cause for canonization, and in June 2019, Pope Francis promulgated the decree of heroic virtue, bestowing the title Venerable.

Sources

Burke-Sivers, Harold. *Augustus Tolton: The Slave Who Became the First African-American Priest*. Irondale, AL: EWTN Publishing, 2018.

Collins, William H., and Cicero F. Perry. *Past and Present of the City of Quincy and Adams County, Illinois*. Chicago: S. J. Clarke, 1905.

Davis, Cyprian, OSB. "Black Catholics in Nineteenth Century America." *U.S. Catholic Historian* 5, no. 1 (1986): 1–17.

Foner, Eric. *Gateway to Freedom: The Hidden History of the Underground Railroad*. New York: W. W. Norton, 2015.

Hemesath, Caroline. *From Slave to Priest: A Biography of the Reverend Augustine Tolton (1854–1897), the First Black American Priest of the United States*. San Francisco: Ignatius Press, 2006.

Ochs, Stephen J. *Desegregating the Altar: The Josephites and the Struggle for Black Priests, 1871–1960*. Baton Rouge: Louisiana State University Press, 1993.

"Our History." Mill Hill Missionaries, millhillmissionaries.com.

Perry, Joseph N. "Father Augustus Tolton, 1854–1897." Archdiocese of Chicago, n.d., tolton.archchicago.org/documents/1604561/1604725/Tolton+Biography+-+PDF/d8d2f8ac-b0c6-4180-b474-0ea68b4849ba.

Raboteau, Albert J. "Black Catholics and Afro-American Religious History: Autobiographic Reflections." *U.S. Catholic Historian* 5, no. 1 (1986): 119–27.

Snodgrass, Mary Ellen. *The Underground Railroad: An Encyclopedia of People, Places, and Operations*. Vols. 1–2. London: Routledge, 2015.

24.

The Saint of the Immigrants

The National Shrine of St. Frances Cabrini, Chicago
2520 N. Lakeview Avenue
Chicago, Illinois 60614

Did you know that Cardinal George Mundelein of Chicago was the main celebrant at both Frances Cabrini's funeral Mass and her Mass of beatification?

Tucked away behind the high rises along Chicago's Lakeview Drive is an oasis of peace, a small park and a chapel honoring the first United States citizen to be canonized by the Catholic Church. As immigrants from eastern and southern Europe poured into American cities in the late nineteenth and early twentieth centuries, the American Church—and its need for schools, orphanages, and hospitals—grew rapidly. Mother Frances Cabrini's zeal to meet this need took her across the continent as she founded institutions in New York, Chicago, Denver, Seattle, and many other places. Her national shrine stands on the ground occupied by the hospital where she spent her final years on this earth—living, working, and dying in service to her fellow immigrants.

An Immigrant Church

America is a nation of immigrants, it's often been said. American Catholicism, it might as well be said, is a church of immigrants. The character and culture of Catholicism in the United States changed dramatically over the course of the nineteenth century as waves of German and Irish Catholics washed into the little Anglo-American Church that had been established by the colonial Catholics of Maryland and Pennsylvania. The face of the Church was transformed again beginning in the late nineteenth century as immigrants from other parts of Europe—especially Italy and the domains of the Austro-Hungarian Empire—poured into America's cities. Frances Cabrini was one of them.

Maria Francesca Cabrini was born in July 1850 in northern Italy, the tenth of eleven children in a devoutly Catholic farm family. She was educated by Sacred Heart sisters and intended to join their community, but they declined her application, possibly because of her fragile health. Her parents, who were in their fifties when Frances was born, died during her late teen years. Now on her own, she obtained a position as a teacher in a small town nearby.

A couple of years later, her spiritual director induced her to assist an emerging religious community that managed an orphanage called the House of Providence. The situation was a formidable challenge, as Frances was charged with overcoming the mismanagement and disruptive personalities of the existing leaders. The place nonetheless served as the cradle of Frances's own religious venture, as she and a small group of other Sisters of Providence separated themselves from the original community in 1880 to form a new religious institute, the Missionary Sisters of the Sacred Heart (MSC). Recruits came quickly, and the new community founded a second house in 1882.

As the title of the order indicates, Mother Cabrini envisioned a battalion of sisters dedicated to working in missionary lands. When she took her vows, Frances added "Xavier" to her name in honor of the great sixteenth-century Jesuit missionary to Asia. Her determination in the face of obstacles was reflected in the words of St. Paul to the Philippians, which developed from her own personal motto into the standard of the whole order: "I can do all things in him who strengthens me." Mother Frances believed that she was destined to evangelize the enigmatic empire to which St. Frances Xavier had never gained entrance: China.

A critical step toward her vision was obtaining the approval of the Church for her activities. With that intention, she went to Rome to meet with the pope. One of her first stops was the Jesuit Church of the Gesù, which contained a shrine dedicated to St. Francis Xavier. She also met Bishop Giovanni Scalabrini, who was becoming increasingly concerned about the spiritual plight of Italian immigrants to the United States.

Scalabrini urged Frances to fix her sights on America rather than China. In March 1888 she had a private audience with Pope Leo XIII, who saw the United States, with its masses of immigrants and few priests or religious to serve them, as a fertile missionary field. "Not to the East, my daughter, but to the West," the pontiff said. The decision was made. The lives of Frances Cabrini, hundreds of MSC sisters, and millions of Italian immigrants would be shaped by Leo's guidance.

Arrival in New York

On March 31, 1889, Frances and her sisters arrived at New York Harbor. The towering figure of Liberty, erected three years earlier, was still copper in color. Like so many other immigrants, they were heartened by the sight as they coasted into the estuary. "After twelve days of sickness and tribulation," one of Cabrini's companions recalled, "we saw the beautiful Statue of Liberty. . . . Oh, how happy Mother was."

About fifty thousand Italians were immigrating to the United States annually, and the number was rising. By the first decade of the twentieth century it would be two hundred thousand, creating what sociologists Nathan Glazer and Daniel Patrick Moynihan called "modern history's greatest and most sustained movement from a single country." During peak periods, fifteen thousand Italians might arrive at Ellis Island in a single day. All told, five and a half million Italians came into the United States between 1820 and 1920.

Before 1880, most of the newcomers were from northern Italy—often literate, skilled tradesmen who were relatively high on the socioeconomic ladder. In the heyday of Italian immigration over the succeeding forty years, however, there was a dramatic demographic shift as the overwhelming majority of immigrants came from Sicily and the southern half of the Italian peninsula. These were predominantly agricultural peasants with little education or exposure to the world outside their villages. From the ports of Palermo, Naples, and Genoa, they boarded crowded boats to cross the Atlantic and settle in crowded Italian neighborhoods in cities such as San Francisco, Chicago, Cleveland, Philadelphia, and especially New York, where there were about one hundred thousand Italian immigrants at the time of Cabrini's arrival.

In his 1945 biography of Cabrini, Theodore Maynard claimed of the Italians that "probably no race, not even excepting the Negroes, has been so poorly thought of in the United States." The former slave Booker T. Washington toured Sicily in 1911 and similarly concluded that "the Negro is not the farthest down." He found that "the condition of the colored farmer in the most backward parts of the Southern States in America" was "incomparably better than the condition and opportunities" of the Sicilian peasant. In the United States, Italians filled openings in dangerous and odious industries such as mining, construction, and textiles. In New York's horrific Triangle Shirtwaist fire of 1911, more than half of the 145 textile workers who died were Italian immigrants. Overall, more than a third of textile workers died before the age of twenty-five.

Italians were oppressed by more than just low economic status. Boardinghouse signs in some cities welcomed potential renters with the message, "We do not rent to Negroes or Italians." Italians were driven out of towns in Pennsylvania and lynched in southern states such as Louisiana and Mississippi. The most notorious incident occurred in New Orleans in 1891, when a mob killed eleven Italian immigrants who had been accused but then exonerated in the murder of a police chief.[1]

So, the MSC sisters had plenty of opportunity for their charitable apostolate among a marginalized and downtrodden people. Besides the obvious subsistence needs, there was demand for education, health care, and assistance navigating the strange legal and economic systems of their new nation. Foremost, from the sisters' point of view, was the spiritual need. Like ministry to African Americans, it was a problem that had drawn the attention of the American bishops gathered at the Third Plenary Council of Baltimore in 1884, who called for immigrants to be served by priests capable of speaking their native language. The vast majority of Italian immigrants were Catholic, but in America they confronted a priesthood dominated by Germans and Irish. Italians who practiced their faith were often herded into church basements, kept separate from the wealthier, assimilated Catholics worshipping above. They also encountered non-Catholic Christians for the first time. "There are here plenty of Protestants who are heretics, but they have a religion, too," a nineteen-year-old Italian observed. "Many of the finest churches are Protestant," he added, "but they have no saints and no altars, which seems strange." If most Italians found Protestant practices odd, that did not guarantee that they would remain connected to the Catholic Church. Separated from the old country's communal support, many drifted from the practice of the faith. The MSC sisters aimed to reverse this trend.

They got off to a rocky start. The sisters arrived in New York to find no convent ready to receive them—evidently the result of miscommunication caused by the plodding mail system of the day. They spent the first night at a miserable boardinghouse. In early May, the first two orphans—one of whom would later join the Missionaries of the Sacred Heart—arrived at the sisters' new Asylum of the Holy Angels on 59th Street. The number of children under their care soon grew to four hundred. In the meantime, they branched into education, taking charge of St. Joachim's School. A short while later they expanded yet again, when the sisters were asked to manage a hospital being organized to care for the neglected Italian immigrants of the city.

That project initially failed, but Cabrini spearheaded the formation of another hospital a year later; it was her first "Columbus Hospital" and would endure for more than a hundred years. Frances chose the name "Columbus" with deliberation: Italians would recognize it as their own (Christopher Columbus being the "first Italian immigrant"), and it would appeal to secular and religious Italians alike. The sisters had just enough money for ten cheap beds, which they furnished with homemade mattresses. Maynard expresses the modesty of their enterprise: "Their pharmacy consisted of a dozen bottles of medicine. . . . As the Sisters had no money left to buy beds for themselves, they slept on the floor."

The earliest of Mother Cabrini's American foundations had been made; there would be many more.

The Founding of Chicago's Columbus Hospital

As the first decade of the new century progressed, Mother Cabrini saw the need to push west across the burgeoning United States. Many Italians were working in the mines of Colorado, so she and her sisters established a home in Denver. Even more significantly, in 1903, they purchased the North Shore Hotel in Chicago, a monumental six-story building near Lincoln Park that had been ruined by bad management yet remained an attractive location on the lake. The sellers attempted to cheat the presumably naïve women religious by cutting off parcels of the property at the end of the block for later development, but the detail-oriented, business-savvy Cabrini caught the undisclosed change before the sale documents were signed, and the would-be chiselers backed down.

Thus began Chicago's Columbus Hospital. It was dearly needed in a city growing by leaps and bounds. Many years earlier, the site of the Midwest's greatest metropolis had been brought to the attention of the world by a Catholic priest. On their return from the famous expedition exploring the Mississippi River in 1673, the Jesuit missionary Jacques Marquette and his companion, Louis Jolliet, were guided by Native Americans to the portage route that connected the Mississippi to Lake Michigan via the Chicago River. In the early nineteenth century, the US Army built Fort Dearborn nearby, and the town of Chicago was incorporated in 1833. With its ideal location as a transportation and trade hub, the "Emporium of the West" saw mind-boggling growth during the nineteenth century. By 1890 it had more than a million residents, and by 1900 only New York had a larger population.

Chicago's vast stockyards, meatpacking plants, lumberyards, railroad yards, and steel mills created an endless demand for labor, which attracted an endless stream of immigrants from the American East and the rest of the world. In the 1880s, Italians began arriving in large numbers. During the first two decades of the twentieth century, first- or second-generation immigrants constituted a whopping 80 percent of the city's population.

The Chicago that Cabrini and her sisters confronted was one rife with problems. It was known to be America's capital of radicalism, where social revolution and labor unrest were endemic. Two of the country's most combative labor conflicts—the Haymarket Riot of 1886 and the Pullman Strike of 1894—had occurred there within recent memory. Growth had outstripped sanitation infrastructure, with disastrous results for public health. There were repeated outbreaks of typhoid during the 1880s and 1890s; in 1885 a wave of typhoid, cholera, and dysentery led to the deaths of more than a tenth of the city's inhabitants. In the twentieth century, Al Capone and other criminal celebrities generated the city's lasting reputation for danger and violence.

The manifest urban problems also made Chicago a center of reform. Jane Addams and Ellen Gates Starr founded the settlement house movement there, which was designed to offer assistance to the impoverished and uneducated urban masses, immigrants prominent among them. The Sacred Heart sisters joined the ranks of those doing battle with these problems by offering, as they had in New York, health care, education, and other services—even though Cabrini's sisters and Addams's social workers were stridently opposed to each other on some political and religious matters, most notably the question of public versus parochial schools.

After a frantic two-week sprint to complete renovation work on the former hotel, Chicago's Columbus Hospital opened for business on February 26, 1905. Four thousand people attended a dedication presided over by Archbishop James Quigley. Mother Cabrini proudly described the facility to a correspondent, mentioning that it included operating rooms, x-rays, and a training college for nurses, all "governed according to the hygienic laws of modern surgery." She added, "The medical faculty of the city classifies our hospital as one of the first order." On the dedication day, she agreed to sit for a formal portrait—a rare concession for her. The photograph is the best-known image of the first American citizen-saint.

In that same year, the Missionaries of the Sacred Heart celebrated the twenty-fifth anniversary of their founding. There were nearly a thousand sisters in fifty houses across eight countries. Mother Cabrini would travel widely, but from that time her home base was her room in Chicago's Columbus Hospital.

By 1914, the hospital was treating more than two thousand patients a year. The Columbus Extension Hospital in the heavily Italian Vernon Park neighborhood, which the sisters opened in 1911, served another 1,500 patients annually. By that time, the original hospital had added children's wards and a state-of-the-art obstetrical department.

As dedicated to outreach as the MSCs were, their work always remained Christ-centered. "The mission of the Institute," Cabrini reminded her sisters shortly after the turn of the century, "is worldwide evangelization—to inflame all people with the love of Jesus Christ." Prayer remained the heart of their lives. Mother Frances embedded six hours of prayer and contemplation into the sisters' daily schedule. Arduous charitable labor was to be spiritually rooted: "The more the work, the greater the need for prayer."

"To Die of Love"

In 1909, Mother Cabrini became a United States citizen. In March 1911, she steamed across the ocean for the twenty-second and final time, returning to the United States from Italy. Her health was failing, but she continued to travel to attend to business from New York to Seattle to Los Angeles. When she arrived in Chicago on April 18, 1917, she was diagnosed with malaria. She was well enough in June to receive several distinguished visitors to Columbus Hospital, including the apostolic delegates to the United States and Australia, an Italian diplomat, and Archbishop George Mundelein of Chicago. But she experienced a slow decline, and on Saturday, December 22, she was too ill to rise for Mass. She died in the chair in her room at the hospital later that day.

Mother Cabrini was soon known as "the saint of the immigrants." With the blessing of Pope Pius XI, the cause for her canonization was inaugurated shortly after her death. The Catholic Church's usual process for canonization involves two miracles. One of those miracles occurred at one of Cabrini's hospitals in New York. In March 1921, a nurse accidentally used the wrong bottle of silver nitrate solution to treat the eyes of newborn Peter Smith. At fifty times the normal strength, the acid quickly destroyed his eyes, and a doctor reported dejectedly that the boy would be blind for life. The sisters on staff began praying through the intercession of their deceased superior, Mother Cabrini.

The next morning, the damage to the eyes was visibly less. A doctor examined the infant and found that he could see! When Cabrini was beatified in 1938, a seventeen-year-old Peter Smith was present at St. Peter's Basilica in Rome. He said, "I for one know for certain that the age of miracles has not passed." Peter Smith went on to become a priest, as did his younger brother, John Frances Xavier Smith. Ten Chinese postulants of the Missionaries of the Sacred Heart were also present at the Rome ceremony. Mother Cabrini had gone to China after all.

More miracles led to Cabrini's canonization in 1946. In 1950, Pope Pius XII, in admiration of the woman who "dedicated herself to the arduous work of materially and spiritually assisting the immigrants," declared Frances Xavier Cabrini "the Heavenly Patroness with God of all the Immigrants."

Cabrini's national shrine was originally built in 1955 as a chapel inside the hospital. Restored and renovated, today it features a main altar made of black onyx and marble, which holds a glass reliquary containing one of Cabrini's arm bones. Paintings depicting the saint's life adorn the walls around the altar. The Columbus Hospital room where Frances lived and died was preserved largely intact and is exhibited in the shrine. In the adjacent garden is a statue of the Sacred Heart of Jesus that once stood at the hospital's entry.

Although Mother Cabrini's hospitals in New York and Chicago are no more, the spirit of the patroness of immigrants endures. The United States continues to attract multitudes of immigrants, and the Catholic Church continues to invoke her example. On the World Day of Migrants in 2017 (the centenary year of Cabrini's death), Pope Francis praised "this courageous sister" who "dedicated her life to bringing the love of Christ to those who were far from their homelands and families," and prayed that "her witness helps us to take care of our foreign brothers and sisters, in whom Jesus is present, often suffering, rejected and humiliated."

Sources

Francis. Angelus Message. St. Peter's Square, January 15, 2017. Vatican.va.

Maynard, Theodore. *Too Small a World: The Life of Francesca Cabrini.* Milwaukee: Bruce Publishing, 1945.

National Shrine of St. Frances Xavier Cabrini. CabriniNationalShrine. org.

Pacyna, Dominic A. *Chicago: A Biography.* Chicago: University of Chicago Press, 2009.

Petrina, Catherine M. *The Italian Americans.* San Diego: Lucent Books, 2002.

Rademacher, Nicholas. "Commemorating the Centennial of Mother Cabrini's Death." *American Catholic Studies* 128, no. 3 (2017): 111–24.

Shane, C. J., ed. *The Italians.* San Diego: Greenhaven Press, 2005.

Sullivan, Mary Louise. *Mother Cabrini: Italian Immigrant of the Century.* New York: Center for Migration Studies, 1992.

Treece, Patricia. "Mother Cabrini's First Miracle." *Catholic Exchange,* November 14, 2016. catholicexchange.com/mother-cabrini-first-miracle.

25.

The Birth of a Political Dynasty

John F. Kennedy Birthplace
83 Beals Street
Brookline, Massachusetts 02446

Did you know that both of President John F. Kennedy's grandfathers were Massachusetts state senators?

Shortly before he married Rose Fitzgerald in October 1914, Joseph Kennedy purchased a nine-room colonial revival at 83 Beals Street in the Boston suburb of Brookline. The marriage united two wealthy, politically powerful Irish Catholic families, but the best was yet to come. The children of Joe and Rose would include a United States senator, a United States attorney general, and a United States president. John Fitzgerald Kennedy—born May 29, 1917, in the second-floor bedroom of the Beals Street home—was the first Catholic president.

Politics in the DNA

"Since their arrival in this land," one account avows, "the Kennedys have been exemplars of the Irish Catholic immigrant experience in America." Joe's father, Patrick Joseph (P. J.) Kennedy, was born in Boston to Irish immigrants who had fled the potato famine of the 1840s, and worked his way from dockworker to prominent businessman. His wealth and social connections provided a springboard to politics, and he was elected to a succession of terms in the Massachusetts house and senate. He would continue to exert influence on Democratic politics until his death in 1929.

Rose's father, John F. Fitzgerald, was also born in Boston to Irish immigrants of the 1840s. After an education at the elite Boston Latin School, he became active in the Democratic Party. He was elected mayor of Boston in 1905 and would later serve in the US House as a representative from Massachusetts (and, briefly, in the state senate as well). His reputation as a glad-handing and histrionic politician furnished his enduring nickname, "Honey Fitz." Rose attributed to her mother, Mary, the "most precious gift" of "deep faith in the Church and its teachings and practices."

In the summer of 1907, the Fitzgerald and Kennedy families both vacationed at Old Orchard Beach in Maine. P. J.'s son Joe, seventeen, and Honey Fitz's daughter Rose, sixteen, fell in love. The romance was not immediately blessed by the families.[1] For several years, the teenaged couple, abetted by Honey Fitz's chauffeur, arranged to meet secretly at dances, parties, libraries, and lectures. But the elders eventually relented, and Joe and Rose were married in an inconspicuous service conducted by Cardinal William O'Connell in his private chapel on October 7, 1914.

The Dynasty Is Born

Rose remembered the Beals Street residence as "a nice old wooden-frame house with clapboard siding . . . on a small lot with a few bushes and trees." She was fond of the "sense of openness in the neighborhood, with a vacant lot on one side of us and another across the street, and fine big shade trees lining the sidewalk." At the time, she wrote, the home "seemed just right, beautiful and comfortable, a dream realized."

The gray house on tree-lined Beals Street was in fact a sign of the new family's upward mobility and assimilation. The base of both the Kennedys' and Fitzgeralds' political and financial power was in the ethnic enclaves of Boston, but there were few Irish Catholic families in Joe and Rose's Brookline neighborhood. The home was nonetheless adorned with symbols of their Irish and Catholic heritage, and the children would be taught to embrace their background with pride. The friction between attachment to their ethnic and religious heritage and ambition to succeed in a WASP-dominated[2] culture would be a constant source of dramatic tension in the lives of the Kennedy clan.

Joe Jr. was born at a summer cottage in 1915, so John Fitzgerald was the first born in the Beals Street home. He was sickly as an infant and chronically ill as he grew up. As a baby, he slept in the nursery, in a bassinet that would successively cradle all nine of the Kennedy offspring. The first daughter, Rosemary, was born the following year, 1918. Slower to reach physical and intellectual developmental markers than her siblings, she experienced learning difficulties when she reached school age and was privately tutored through most of her childhood. Kathleen, Eunice, and Patricia followed in 1920, 1921, and 1924. Before the birth of Eunice, the Kennedys moved to a larger home a few blocks away. The last child born in Brookline was Robert, in 1925. The births of Jean (1928) and Edward (1932) would complete the family.

From the beginning there were strong forces both pulling apart and holding together the rapidly growing family. Overwhelmed by the responsibilities of motherhood and upset by rumors of her husband's extramarital dalliances, Rose briefly abandoned the family at Beals Street in January 1920 and moved back into her parents' home. But family pride and religious commitment would always be centripetal forces counteracting the stresses of infidelity and family discord. Honey Fitz urged his daughter to return to her husband and children. Before she did so, Rose went on a Catholic retreat, seeking the spiritual sustenance to shoulder her burdens.

Rose remained faithful to her familial obligations ever after, a pillar of unity amid the storms that often buffeted the family. She also remained faithful to her religious obligations, the main conduit maintaining the Kennedy family's connection to the faith of their forebears.

Catholicism and the Kennedys

One and a half million Irish, some 90 percent of them Catholic, immigrated to the United States during the famine years (1845–1855). Desperately poor and thus lacking the resources to take up farming, the Irish congregated in urban neighborhoods in cities such as Philadelphia, New York, and Boston, where they faced discrimination much like that endured later by Italians (see chapter 24). In this environment, the Church represented a source of both spiritual and material sustenance; thus "the great majority of Irish Catholic immigrants not only remained loyal to the Church but eventually became more faithful practitioners than they had been back home." The Church remained a lodestar in the Irish universe.

Although the Kennedys exhibited varying degrees of devotion to the faith, their lives were enmeshed with the Catholic Church. Inconsistency in Catholic practice began at the top. The family attended Mass together regularly on Sundays, but Joe's observance of the ritual and moral codes of the Church extended little further. Even so, he would have recourse to his faith in times of exigency, as when two-year-old John—called "Jack" by his family—battled scarlet fever and Joe dropped into church in the middle of the day to implore God to spare his son.

Rose, meanwhile, was a frequent visitor to church, bringing the children along for weekday prayer. She prayed the Rosary often and reminded her children to observe holy days. She aimed to make "God and religion a daily part of their lives." That effort was at least partially successful. Robert and Eunice were notably devout throughout their lives. Jean assisted Maryknoll priest Fr. James Keller, who founded the Christopher movement, a Catholic outreach designed to sanctify American public life.

The matter of Jack's faith has been a topic of extensive discussion. That Catholicism was an essential component of his identity is undeniable. Friends and aides attest that he prayed daily and attended Sunday Mass regularly. At the same time, his transgressions against the Church's sexual norms are well known. In public life, he seemed to calibrate his level of religiosity to the intended audience, and his policy stands on Catholic-related issues (e.g., parochial school funding, contraception) appeared to have more to do with political calculation than any principled commitment to Church teaching.

Regardless of the vagaries of each Kennedy's personal attachment to the faith, the family was certainly connected to the Church institutionally. P. J. and Honey Fitz cultivated a warm relationship with Boston's archbishop and a fellow son of Irish immigrants, Cardinal William O'Connell. Joe and Jack would do the same with O'Connell's successor, Cardinal Richard Cushing. Joe had close connections with Pope Pius XII through friends in Rome, and he served as a liaison between the Roosevelt administration and the Vatican. He orchestrated Roosevelt's appointment of a personal envoy to the Holy See in the 1930s, helping to cement the image of a Democratic Party friendly to Catholic interests.

By that time, the Kennedys were no longer in Massachusetts. In 1937, frustrated at the continued shunning by the Brahmin elite despite Joe's political and economic stature, Joe and Rose forsook the suburbs of Boston for those of New York. The "social and economic discrimination was shocking," Joe recalled, and he didn't want his children "to go through what I had to go through when I was growing up there." The family moved into a twenty-room mansion in the affluent neighborhood of Riverdale in the Bronx.

Triumph and Tragedy

Soon after the Kennedys relocated, the governor of New York, an Irish Catholic named Al Smith, lost his bid for the US presidency to Herbert Hoover. The exact impact of religion on the race remains contested, but there's no question that Smith's Catholicism was a political target during the campaign, and that many Catholics took his defeat as a slap in the face. Paulist Fr. James Gillis, in his "we shall not wither up and blow away" editorial (see chapter 11), declared that "we have been told—with such unnecessary and brutal over-emphasis—that no Catholic can occupy the White House."

Honey Fitz, like almost every Catholic in Boston, strongly supported the Smith campaign and was devastated by his loss. Joe Kennedy, however, was curiously noncommittal. The Kennedy family biographer Thomas Maier speculates that the politically astute and success-obsessed Joe may have seen the handwriting on the wall and deemed that the time was not yet ripe for a Catholic president. In any case, Catholics would have to wait a bit longer to see one of their own occupy the Oval Office.

After the move to New York, the story of the Kennedy clan was a roller-coaster ride of spectacular success and devastating catastrophe that has fascinated biographers ever since. In a decision with terrible consequences, Joe submitted Rosemary to a lobotomy in 1941, having been persuaded by doctors that it would cure her emotional volatility. Rosemary's personality was shattered irrevocably, and she would be institutionalized for the rest of her life. Joe Jr., a bomber pilot, died in action during World War II at the age of twenty-nine. In the same year, 1944, the war also claimed the life of Kathleen's husband, a British aristocrat. Kathleen died in a plane crash four years later.

Eunice married into an old Maryland Catholic family. Her husband, Sargent Shriver, was prominent in Democratic politics and instrumental in founding the Peace Corps under the Kennedy administration. In 1962, Eunice went to visit Rosemary in Wisconsin, an experience that inspired her to become an activist on behalf of the disabled. Archbishop Cushing had told Joe about St. Coletta's, a home for the mentally disabled run by Sisters of St. Francis in Wisconsin. Rosemary moved into St. Clare Cottage in 1949 and remained there for the rest of her life. The Kennedy family donated an Olympic swimming pool to the community, and swimming became one of Rosemary's favorite activities. Eunice and Sargent opened Camp Shriver in 1962; it would evolve into the Special Olympics.

Patricia married an English actor and had four children, but the marriage ended in divorce in 1966. Robert and his wife, Ethel, had eleven children. He enjoyed a successful political career as US senator and attorney general in his brother's administration, but his life too would be cut short by assassination in 1968. Jean married an American businessman and served as the US ambassador to Ireland in the 1990s. Like Jack and Robert, Edward (Ted) was elected US senator from Massachusetts, an office he held for almost forty years. But his own presidential aspirations were stifled by the scandal arising from the 1969 Chappaquiddick incident.[3]

And then there was Jack.

The First Catholic President

Joe's money had greased the Kennedys' ride into the political elite. He saw and backed a winner in Franklin Roosevelt, and was rewarded with a post as ambassador to Great Britain. Joe had presidential aspirations himself, but Franklin Roosevelt's decision to pursue a third term in 1940 put an end to those. Moving on, father Joe had planned for son Joe a career in politics, with an eye to the presidency as the culmination. Jack took up the mantle after his brother's death, and in 1946 he won election to the US House of Representatives. (On learning the election results, Honey Fitz predicted that Jack would become the first Irish Catholic president.) In 1952, he won his US Senate race, prevailing over Henry Cabot Lodge. That election was especially sweet for the Kennedy family, as a symbolic changing of the guard, from WASP to Irish Catholic.

In 1960, Senator Kennedy won his party's nomination for president. Thirty-two years after Smith failed against Hoover, a Catholic would try his luck against Richard Nixon.

In some ways, 1960 looked much like 1928. Detractors leveled many of the same charges regarding Catholicism's compatibility with the American political system that had been used against Al Smith. Protestant groups circulated pamphlets such as *How the Roman Catholic Church Would Change the Constitution*. The prominent preacher and author Norman Vincent Peale worried about the influence of Catholic officials on American policy: "It is inconceivable that a Roman Catholic president would not be under extreme pressure by the hierarchy of his church to accede to its policies."

Referring to his ambivalent attitude toward the Church, his wife, Jackie, allegedly joked that she thought it "so unfair of people to be against Jack because he is a Catholic. He's such a poor Catholic." But the politics of religion in 1960 meant that his personal belief and practice were secondary to his public persona. "Whether he liked it or not," Thomas Maier points out, "he became the uber-Catholic, a focal point for a discussion about the role of church and state in America, about tolerance and the rise of immigrant minority populations."

Kennedy decided to confront the religion issue directly. His first attempt, an interview in *Look* magazine in March 1959, was widely panned. Using imprecise language about the relationship between faith and politics, he managed to upset the Catholic commentariat without doing anything to mollify Protestant skeptics. He learned his lesson and, prior to his next major attempt, consulted thoughtful Protestant and Catholic advisors, who examined every word of the proposed statement. In what has been heralded ever since as one of the finest rhetorical performances in the history of presidential politics, Kennedy addressed the Greater Houston Ministerial Association on September 12, 1960. "I believe in an America where the separation of church and state is absolute," the candidate began,

> where no Catholic prelate would tell the President (should he be Catholic) how to act, and no Protestant minister would tell his parishioners for whom to vote—where no church or church school is granted any public funds or political preference—and where no man is denied public office merely because his religion differs from the President who might appoint him or the people who might elect him.

Kennedy invoked his Irish ethnicity openly and turned it against his detractors, arguing that an America with religious tolerance for all is "the kind of America for which our forefathers died."

The popular-vote margin was razor thin, but Kennedy beat Nixon 330 electoral votes to 219. At age forty-three, he became the youngest president ever elected. He had also destroyed the myth that the 1928 election had left in place—that a Roman Catholic could never be president. Kennedy had exorcised the ghost of Al Smith.

From the start, the press trumpeted the new president's religion. A few weeks after the election, *Life* magazine ran splashy photos of the baptism of John F. Kennedy Jr. in the chapel of Georgetown University Hospital. Even as he became the nation's most prominent Catholic, however, his own coreligionists were divided. Although Catholics voted heavily for Kennedy, there were important dissenters such as the rising conservative star William F. Buckley Jr. More galling to the Kennedys was the defection of Cardinal Francis Spellman of New York, a longtime family friend, who shifted his support to Nixon and became a vocal critic of the Kennedy administration's policy on public funding for Catholic schools.

In June 1963, Kennedy became the first sitting president to visit Ireland. During a speech in the Kennedy family's ancestral home of New Ross, County Wexford, he embraced the heritage that Rose and Joe had instilled during his early years on Beals Street. "When my great-grandfather left here to become a cooper in East Boston," the president reflected, "he carried nothing with him except two things: a strong religious faith and a strong desire for liberty. I am glad to say that all of his great-grandchildren have valued that inheritance."

The sickly Beals Street baby had grown up to lead the most powerful nation on the planet. In the process, he proved that even the Irish Catholic—once among the most downtrodden of Americans—could triumph in the land of the free.

Yet doubts lingered. Kennedy had successfully defused the religion issue, but at what cost? His promise of an "absolute separation of church and state" could mean an aggressively secular public square where Catholics would only be welcome if they agreed to "leave their faith at the door." The Kennedys had achieved the ultimate political prize, but had they achieved the respect they craved? While he was president, Kennedy complained to a companion, "Do you know it is impossible for an Irish Catholic to get into the Somerset Club in Boston? If I moved back to Boston even after being President, it would make no difference." The writer Gore Vidal expressed the enduring disdain of the elite in 1967: "The origin of the Kennedy sense of family is the holy land of Ireland, priest-ridden, superstitious, and clannish."

Moreover, triumph and tragedy usually went hand in hand in the Kennedy dynasty. Five months after his trip to Ireland, John F. Kennedy was dead, struck down by an assassin's bullet in the state where he had delivered his oratorical masterpiece three years earlier.

The Dynasty Continues

Joseph Kennedy, in decline since surviving a 1961 stroke, passed away in 1969, having witnessed his ambitions fulfilled in his presidential son but also having lived to see Jack and three other children suffer untimely deaths. Rose would live another twenty-six years, dying at the age of one hundred and four.

Kennedy family involvement in politics did not end with Joe and Rose's children. In the second generation, Jack's daughter Caroline served as ambassador to Japan in the Barack Obama administration. In Maryland, Eunice's son Mark was in the state legislature and Robert's daughter Kathleen was lieutenant governor. Robert's son Joseph II was a US representative from Massachusetts for twelve years, and Joseph's son, Joseph III—representing the third generation—began serving in the same body in 2012. Ted's sons Edward Jr. and Patrick have held electoral office as state representatives in Connecticut and Rhode Island, respectively, and Patrick served three terms in the US House as a representative from Rhode Island. Anyone born into the family is said to have "politics in their genes." Of their celebrity status, one great-granddaughter of Joe and Rose remarked, "I meet people who know more about my family than I do."

In 2020, Joseph III's bid for the US Senate came up short—the first time a Kennedy ever lost a political race in Massachusetts—leading some commentators to declare the end of "the Kennedy political dynasty."[4] Time will tell. The unquestioned premise underlying such proclamations is that there was a Kennedy political dynasty.

It all began in a modest home on Beals Street in suburban Boston, where Joe and Rose started an Irish Catholic family who, it would seem, had politics in their genes.

Sources

Carty, Thomas J. *A Catholic in the White House? Religion, Politics, and John F. Kennedy's Presidential Campaign.* New York: Palgrave Macmillan, 2004.

Casey, Shaun. *The Making of a Catholic President: Kennedy vs. Nixon, 1960.* New York: Oxford University Press, 2009.

Dallek, Robert. *An Unfinished Life: John F. Kennedy, 1917–1963*. Boston: Little, Brown, 2003.

Green, Steven K. *The Third Disestablishment: Church, State, and American Culture, 1940–1975*. New York: Oxford University Press, 2019.

Jensen, Peter. "Townsend Daughters Are Drawn to Service." *Baltimore Sun*, October 29, 2002. www.baltimoresun.com/news/bs-xpm-2002-10-29-0210290025-story.html.

Kennedy, Rose Fitzgerald. *Times to Remember*. Garden City, NY: Doubleday, 1974.

Koehler-Pentacoff, Elizabeth. *The Missing Kennedy: Rosemary Kennedy and the Secret Bonds of Four Women*. Baltimore: Bancroft, 2015.

Maier, Thomas. *The Kennedys: America's Emerald Kings*. New York: Basic Books, 2003.

Miller, Kerby A. *Emigrants and Exiles: Ireland and the Irish Exodus to North America*. New York: Oxford University Press, 1985.

26.

Peacocks and Provocative Prose

Andalusia Farm
2628 North Columbia Street, Highway 441 North
Milledgeville, Georgia 31061

*Did you know that Flannery
O'Connor's first bit of publicity came
at the age of six, when a newsreel
crew filmed her with a chicken she
had trained to walk backward?*

"I am at home every afternoon but Monday and would be most happy to have you come over. We live four miles from Milledgeville on the road to Eatonton in a two-story white farmhouse. The place is called Andalusia."

So wrote essayist, novelist, and short-story writer Flannery O'Connor in May 1955, in response to a letter about one of her stories. It was a typical invitation, welcoming a potential visitor to her pastoral retreat ninety miles southeast of Atlanta. Andalusia is where Flannery O'Connor spent her final thirteen years, sketching a remarkable array of "Christ-haunted" characters before her untimely death at age thirty-nine.

Irish, Catholic, Southern

Twentieth-century American Catholicism was graced with many outstanding fiction writers, including Paul Horgan, Caroline Gordon, J.
F. Powers, and Walker Percy. But none has attracted more attention
than the intriguing young woman who produced most of her work
while living on her family's farm in rural Georgia.

Mary Flannery O'Connor was born on March 25, 1925, entering
the world at St. Joseph's Hospital in Savannah, Georgia. The hospital,
founded and run by Sisters of Mercy, was a kind of family affair, as
its main benefactor was Katie Semmes, Flannery O'Connor's cousin.

Her parents' home in Savannah was located near the Cathedral of
St. John the Baptist, where Flannery was baptized three weeks after
her birth. Her family on her mother's side, the Clines, were prominent
citizens of Milledgeville, the town nearest to Andalusia. O'Connor
was descended from Irish Catholic immigrants on both sides of her
family. They fell into a long but tortuous line of Catholic presence in
Georgia. Spanish Franciscans and Jesuits evangelized what they called
the Guale missions along the Carolina-Georgia coast beginning in the
1560s. By the 1680s, however, Catholics had been pushed south, and
the early Catholic presence was long forgotten by the time Georgia
was handed over to James Oglethorpe and other trustees as a British
colony in 1732.

Oglethorpe envisioned the colony as a society of hard working,
white, Protestant farmers living in peace with their Native American
neighbors. To that end, hard liquor, slavery, and Roman Catholics were
prohibited at the outset. Economic demand caused the laws against
strong drink and slavery to be quickly abandoned, but the ban on
Catholics remained until the new state's constitution went into effect
after the Revolution.

With the introduction of slavery and the growth of cash crops
such as indigo and rice in the tidewater region, Georgia, like most of
its southern neighbors, developed into a slave economy. By the time of
American independence, the new state was split about evenly between
free whites and enslaved Blacks. In the nineteenth century, the spread

of tobacco and cotton production provided additional momentum for the slave system.

One interior town that grew in importance was Milledgeville, located near the center of the state on the Oconee River. The state capital from 1804 to 1868, it was the site of the 1861 state convention at which the delegates approved secession from the Union. The railroad center of Atlanta and the rich swath of land between it and Savannah would feel the brunt of the war when Sherman marched his marauding army across the state in 1864. The plantation at Andalusia was plundered by the Union troops, but the house was left standing.

By that time, Catholicism had returned to the state. French-speaking Catholics fleeing the Haitian Revolution had settled in the port of Savannah in the 1790s, forming the nucleus of the state's Catholic Church. About two thousand Irish fleeing the potato famine of the 1840s had also found their way to Savannah. On the strength of this immigrant community, the first Catholic diocese in the state was created in 1850.

It was into this community—Irish, Catholic, and southern—that Flannery O'Connor was born in 1925.

A Sojourn in the North

The future author began her formal education in 1931 at St. Vincent's School for Girls, run by the Sisters of Mercy. She did poorly in math and spelling but excelled in catechism. The Irish sister who taught Flannery composition complained that the student "always wrote about ducks and chickens." Her earliest writing instructor didn't perceive greatness. "Nothing remarkable about her as a student," she later reflected, adding that "she was a little forward with adults."

When O'Connor was thirteen, the family moved to Milledgeville, a more convenient location for her father's new job in Atlanta. There Flannery attended a progressive public school, a sharp departure from her previous experience. During the summer, she and her young cousins frolicked together at the family's 550-acre dairy farm a few miles out of town, Sorrel Farm. Later, Flannery learned from a descendant of the property's original owner that the place had been known as

Andalusia, after a region in southern Spain. She persuaded the farm's owner, her uncle Bernard, to revert to the older name.

After a brief stay in Atlanta, the O'Connors returned to Milledgeville, where Flannery's father died in 1941 of lupus. O'Connor began studies at Georgia State College for Women the following year. She joined the Catholic Newman Club and attended First Friday Mass with the rest of the Catholics at the school (about ten). She continued to struggle in math, but she also began to perfect the craft that would be her lifelong vocation. Initially, that meant humor pieces and cartoons for student periodicals. She also tangled with a professor who challenged the assumptions of her Catholic upbringing. Although the two remained at loggerheads over the merits of medieval philosophy, they had a mutually respectful relationship, and the professor encouraged her to apply to graduate school at his alma mater, the University of Iowa. She was accepted with the offer of a full-tuition scholarship in journalism.

At Iowa, Paul Engle was running the nation's first master of fine arts in writing program, the Writers' Workshop. While living in Iowa took some getting used to—Flannery's thick accent was, as a biographer put it, "routinely treated as a foreign language"—the Writers' Workshop set the aspiring author on the path to greatness. Engle was connected with a number of writers who would, along with its most famous representative, William Faulkner, come to be appreciated as the progenitors of a southern renaissance in literature.

In the course of her time at Iowa, O'Connor came into contact with renaissance writers John Crowe Ransom, Robert Penn Warren, Andrew Lytle, and Allen Tate (who would convert to Catholicism in 1950). She would later get to know Brainard and Frances Cheney and spend time at their home in Nashville, a nerve center for the literary revival.[1] At Iowa, she also took a class with Paul Horgan, a Catholic and later two-time winner of the Pulitzer Prize for history. She took to heart his advice to the fledgling writers to set aside a period every day dedicated to their craft, a habit that "became her lifelong regimen, the very soul of her artistic credo."

Her Iowa mentors cultivated O'Connor's potential. By the time she finished her degree, she had won an award from Rinehart Publishing that included an advance and first option on her first novel (*Wise Blood*, ultimately published by Harcourt, Brace). She would return to Iowa in the fall as a teaching assistant. In the meantime, she went home for the summer. Andalusia was now under the joint ownership of Flannery's mother, Regina, and her brother Louis.

Never at home in the Midwest, O'Connor was always at home in church. During her university days, she was a regular communicant at St. Mary's Church in Iowa City. "It was right around the corner and I could get there practically every morning," she remembered. "I went there three years and never knew a soul in that congregation or any of the priests, but it was not necessary. As soon as I went in the door I was at home." The spiritual intensity of this devotion went beyond a feeling of comfort at familiar surroundings. The Eucharist, she wrote later, "is the center of existence for me; all the rest of life is expendable."

At the end of her teaching year at Iowa, O'Connor won a fellowship to the Yaddo artist colony in Saratoga Springs, New York. The artists' retreat had been in operation since the 1920s. Writers and intellectuals such as Langston Hughes, Lionel Trilling, and Hannah Arendt had spent time there. Aaron Copeland composed music in one of its artist domiciles.

As a devout Catholic and a southerner, O'Connor never fit in very well with most of her fellow Yaddo guests. The dissolute lifestyle of some put her off. Determining that "the help was morally superior to the guests," she made friends with the Irish Catholic caretakers, traveling with them to Mass every Sunday in Saratoga Springs.

Although her Yaddo social life didn't thrive, her intellectual life did. She read and pondered the French Catholic philosopher Jacques Maritain's *Art and Scholasticism*, solidifying her inclinations toward the philosophy of St. Thomas Aquinas and gaining new insight into its relevance for her authorial vocation. She also made good progress on her novel.

An imbroglio at Yaddo in 1949 shut down the colony temporarily, and O'Connor ended up in Manhattan. There, Robert Lowell kindly introduced her to important figures in literary and publishing circles, including Robert and Sally Fitzgerald, who would remain lifelong friends. Robert was a Catholic who had returned to practicing his faith (a "revert"), and his wife was a convert. Their combination of artistic sophistication and devout faith suited O'Connor perfectly. She also met Robert Giroux, an editor at Harcourt, Brace at the time, who would remain a valuable professional and personal companion throughout the rest of O'Connor's life.

Andalusia

In December 1950, O'Connor left her friends in New York to return home for Christmas. She became ill on the way and, upon arrival, was diagnosed with lupus, the disease that had killed her father. Treatments for lupus had improved since the 1920s, but her relatively severe case was still a death sentence and the twenty-six-year-old O'Connor knew it. Although she would travel frequently over the thirteen years of life remaining to her, her unreliable physical capabilities required a stable residence and an on-site, dedicated caretaker. Andalusia would be her home, and her mother would be her constant companion.

Regina and Flannery moved into the "austere farmhouse" at Andalusia in the spring of 1951. "She is nuts about it here, surrounded by the lowing herd and other details," the daughter wrote about the mother, "and considers it beneficial to my health." From rocking chairs on the screened porch of the 1850s white frame house, they surveyed the pastures, rolling hills, and pine woods of the former plantation.

Flannery derived much of the inspiration for her stories from her life at Andalusia. The farm embodied a South in transition. As late as 1940, 65 percent of Georgia's population was rural and agricultural tenancy rates were high, especially for Black farmers. Andalusia's tenants, white and Black alike, are unmistakable models for many characters in O'Connor's stories. But by the time the O'Connors arrived at Andalusia, this way of life was fading in the face of social change and rapid economic development. More Georgians were employed in industry than agriculture by 1950, and by 1970, 60 percent of

Georgians lived in cities. Andalusia was gradually passing from a representation of southern life into a relic of its past.

That June, Harcourt, Brace accepted *Wise Blood* for publication. Robert Fitzgerald also put O'Connor in touch with another titan in the southern Catholic literary pantheon, Caroline Gordon (wife of Allen Tate), which inaugurated a years long correspondence by which O'Connor constantly honed her technique and her prose. The critical reception of her first novel, though not universally positive, put the young Georgian on the literary map.

At Andalusia, Flannery and Regina established apartments on the first floor of the main house, leaving the upstairs bedrooms for the numerous guests they would host over the ensuing years. Flannery's bedroom doubled as her study, where every morning she worked on writing projects. She rose early and prayed from her breviary, had coffee, and then drove to Sacred Heart Church with her mother for Mass. From nine to noon, she focused on her writing.

One of the symptoms of O'Connor's disease was fatigue, so afternoons were usually low-key. She fussed over her birds, sometimes using them as subjects for her hobby of painting. Afternoons were also the standard time for receiving the numerous guests who visited.

After dinner, Flannery's evening wound down quickly. She usually spent some time reading, often Thomas Aquinas. "I read a lot of theology because it makes my writing bolder," she explained. She read non-Catholic theologians as well, including Paul Tillich and Karl Barth.

Biographer Brad Gooch has documented the manifold ways in which O'Connor's life at Andalusia provided the material for her stories. One obvious example was the arrival in 1953 of a tenant farm family, the Matysiaks, driven from Poland during World War II. The American government and the Catholic Church were both active in resettling these "displaced persons," and Sacred Heart's pastor arranged for several Catholic families to live in the Milledgeville area. In 1954, O'Connor published the first version of her story "The Displaced Person," and an expanded revision appeared the following year.

O'Connor made one substantial journey away from Andalusia during these years: a pilgrimage to Lourdes with a group from Savannah. Aware of her literary prowess but oblivious to her reputation for unflattering treatment of her subjects, the monsignor who accompanied the pilgrimage suggested Flannery "write up" the trip for publication. "I don't think he has thought this through," she quipped. Of the famous Marian shrine, O'Connor wrote to a friend, "I prayed there for the novel I was working on, not for my bones, which I care about less."

In October 1952, O'Connor purchased a pair of peafowl who were destined to be, after the author herself, the most famous residents of Andalusia. O'Connor had always had an inclination to ornithology, and she had often kept some kind of birds—chickens, ducks, geese— around her. The peacocks, whose numbers mushroomed to as many as thirty at one point, were the crown jewels of her collection, and she frequently introduced them to visitors and wrote about them to her correspondents—and occasionally sent a splendid tailfeather as a gift.

Under Regina's management, Andalusia evolved over the years from a dairy farm with a sideline of Shetland ponies to a beef farm with extensive timber sales. As O'Connor's notoriety waxed, it also increasingly became a destination for admirers and writers, aspiring and established alike. Among those who visited to converse with O'Connor and gawk at the peacocks were Caroline Gordon, the Texas-born author Katherine Anne Porter, and O'Connor's publisher friend, Robert Giroux.

"The Whole Racial Picture"

Andalusia was home over the years to several African American tenants, and it's no surprise that Black characters and race-related themes make appearances in some of O'Connor's stories. Although race was not a central concern of her fiction, her racial views have come under scrutiny in recent years.[2] One book-length study encapsulates her attitude as "radical ambivalence."

Racial segregation was a widespread reality across 1950s America, north and south alike. As in many other places, Georgia Blacks labored under an array of Jim Crow laws. But legal segregation was only part of the story, as local norms, often backed up by local law enforcement, were usually the more burdensome restrictions. Black political resistance was largely impossible through the first half of the twentieth century, until the civil rights movement began in earnest in the 1950s.

In 1954, the Supreme Court's *Brown vs. Board of Education* decision began dismantling legal segregation. There was massive resistance in Georgia and elsewhere. Atlanta was a bastion of civil rights action and home to the Ebenezer Baptist Church of Martin Luther King Sr. and his more famous son.

O'Connor's racial views are hard to pin down. Some of her stories ridicule the bald racism of white characters, but some of her letters contain seemingly racist comments and language. One of the monks at the Trappist monastery in Conyers that she visited described her view of people of color: "It wasn't that she didn't know they were children of God and redeemed by the blood of Christ. Of course, she knew that. But the vocabulary she used was typical Southern white." Although "she avoided writing topical fiction as though it were poison," and even her letters manifest little interest in politics, her few comments reveal a position more open to change than that of most white Georgians. O'Connor was critical of civil rights activism that was in her view inadequately realistic, but she was in favor of racial progress. In 1963, as legal burdens on Blacks in southern states were being lifted, she wrote, "I feel very good about those changes in the South that have been long overdue—the whole racial picture."

"Catholicity Has Given Me My Perspective"

In the fall of 1963, O'Connor's health began worsening. Since the time of her diagnosis, she had often needed crutches; now she was nearly incapacitated. On the feast day of Christmas, the habitual daily communicant was too ill to go to Mass.

In late June 1964, she was released from the hospital, the doctors having concluded that nothing more could be done. She returned to Andalusia for her final days, continuing to write as much as she could. She had been working for several years on her last book, a collection of stories that would be published shortly after her death as *Everything*

That Rises Must Converge. On July 28 she wrote her last letter, but she never got a chance to send it. A few days later, she was rushed to the hospital, where she received last rites from the abbot of the Conyers monastery. Mary Flannery O'Connor died shortly after midnight on August 3 and was buried the following day after a funeral Mass at Sacred Heart Church.

At one point during her time at Yaddo, Flannery had written, "Were it not for my mother, I could easily resolve not to see Georgia again." The sentiment was fleeting. Rural Georgia remained her home throughout most of her productive writing period, and she paid tribute to the fact in a 1957 letter to a budding southern writer:

> It's perhaps good and necessary to get away from it [the South] physically for a while, but this is by no means to escape it. I stayed away from the time I was twenty until I was twenty-five with the notion that the life of my writing depended on my staying away. I would certainly have persisted in that delusion had I not got very ill and had to come home. The best of my writing has been done here.

Flannery O'Connor was a creature of the South, but her faith gave her an outsider's view. She once said as much: "Catholicity has given me my perspective on the South." Her stock lecture on the speakers' circuit was "The Catholic Novelist in the Protestant South." In a 1960 lecture, later published in a nonfiction collection, *Mystery and Manners*, she said, "I think it is safe to say that while the South is hardly Christ-centered, it is most certainly Christ-haunted." Unpacking the ideas in *Wise Blood* to a correspondent, she revealed her paradoxically intimate-yet-distant relationship: "The religion of the South is a do-it-yourself religion, something which as a Catholic I find painful and touching and grimly comic. . . . If this were merely comic to me, it would be no good, but I accept the same fundamental doctrines of sin and redemption that they do."

Although O'Connor observed Catholic disciplines without fail and defended Catholic belief in her voluminous correspondence, she admitted that faith was not an easy path. To a friend struggling with her own faith, O'Connor wrote, "I would like you to know that

I sympathize and I suffer this way myself. When we get our spiritual house in order, we'll be dead. . . . You arrive at enough certainty to be able to make your way, but it is making it in darkness. Don't expect faith to clear things up for you. It is trust, not certainty."

Nor was the application of faith to writing an easy process. O'Connor did not write stories about pious Catholics with happily-ever-after endings, but she insisted to skeptical correspondents that her faith was at the heart of her enterprise: "I write the way I do because (not though) I am a Catholic." She created shocking stories about grotesque characters because she sought to arrest the attention of a world increasingly oblivious to the transcendent. "The moral sense has been bred out of certain sections of the population, like the wings have been bred off certain chickens to produce more white meat on them," she observed. "This is a generation of wingless chickens, which I suppose is what Nietzsche meant when he said God was dead." To this audience, O'Connor offered a reacquaintance with reality. "The stories are hard," she explained, "but they are hard because there is nothing harder or less sentimental than Christian realism."

Interest in Flannery O'Connor and her stories has not waned in the years since her death. Robert Giroux arranged her short stories in chronological order and published them as *The Complete Stories* in 1972; the collection won that year's National Book Award in fiction.[3] Her reputation continued to climb in the twenty-first century. In 2009, the Modern Language Association counted 1,340 entries under her name, including 195 doctoral dissertations and 70 books. A journal, the *Flannery O'Connor Review*, is dedicated to study of her work. Andalusia, preserved through funding left by Regina O'Connor, has become "a literary shrine."

"There won't be any biographies of me," she once remarked, because "lives spent between the house and chicken yard do not make exciting copy." Yet the biographies keep coming. Andalusia's parochial setting did nothing to diminish the power of O'Connor's prose; on the contrary, it enhanced it. O'Connor was a woman with deep roots in a particular place, and she, like all good authors, wrote about what she knew. By doing so, she tapped into universal human experiences and longings in a way that appealed across time and place to reach atheists and Christians, Blacks and whites, southerners and northerners. Thus, while the rolling fields and modest farmhouse of Andalusia may seem an incongruous home for a world-famous author, they are in truth entirely appropriate. For Flannery O'Connor, Andalusia was a window to the world.

Sources

Amason, Craig R. "From Agrarian Homestead to Literary Landscape: A Brief History of Flannery O'Connor's Andalusia." *Flannery O'Connor Review* 2 (2003): 4–14.

Buttimer, Brendan J. "Catholic Church." *New Georgia Encyclopedia*, December 10, 2005. www.georgiaencyclopedia.org/articles/arts-culture/catholic-church.

Coleman, Kenneth, gen. ed. *A History of Georgia*. Athens: University of Georgia Press, 1977.

Fitzgerald, Sally, ed. *The Habit of Being: Letters of Flannery O'Connor*. New York: Noonday Press, 1979.

Foss, Jerome C. *Flannery O'Connor and the Perils of Governing by Tenderness*. Lanham, MD: Lexington Books, 2019.

Gooch, Brad. *Flannery: A Life of Flannery O'Connor*. New York: Little, Brown, 2009.

Murray, Lorraine V. *The Abbess of Andalusia: Flannery O'Connor's Spiritual Journey*. Charlotte, NC: St. Benedict Press, 2009.

O'Donnell, Angela Alaimo. *Radical Ambivalence: Race in Flannery O'Connor*. New York: Fordham University Press, 2020.

Rubin, Louis D., comp. and ed. *The Literary South*. 1979; rpr. Baton Rouge: Louisiana State University Press, 1986.

Wood, Ralph C. *Flannery O'Connor and the Christ-Haunted South*. Grand Rapids: William B. Eerdmans, 2004.

27.

A Cold Warrior in the Space Program

The Moon Room
Central Catholic High School
2550 Cherry Street
Toledo, Ohio 43608

Did you know that Gene Kranz's white vest from Apollo 13 is part of the collection of the Smithsonian National Air and Space Museum?

Just north of downtown Toledo rises Central Catholic High School, a stately brick building erected in 1919. Within its library is a unique room dedicated to a unique subject: the moon. The room's most prominent feature is a display of a small chunk of rock—"a lunar sample returned by *Apollo 17* Astronauts who traveled to the moon in December 1972." How the moon rock ended up in a high school library requires telling the story of a kid who walked the halls of Central Catholic in the 1940s.

A Boy with His "Head in the Clouds"

No Catholic has occupied a more key position in the American space program than Gene Kranz. From Toledo's Central Catholic High

School, Kranz went on to Saint Louis University, the US Air Force, and eventually, NASA's mission control center, where he most famously directed the *Apollo 11* and *Apollo 13* missions.

"I always wanted to fly," says Kranz in his book-length account of the space program. "As a boy in Toledo, Ohio, I had my head in the clouds and my heart followed."

Kranz's paternal grandfather emigrated from Germany, founded a successful savings and loan company in Toledo, and was then wiped out in the Great Depression. Kranz's father, who had been a medic during World War I, died of a bleeding ulcer when Gene was just seven. Gene regretted not having the chance to know his father as he grew up, but he always admired his dad anyway—and imitated his military photo by sporting a crew cut for "most of my life."

With the burden of supporting the family falling on Gene's mother, she moved them to a better neighborhood in West Toledo and then "turned our home into a boarding house to pay the bills and she ran it like a drill sergeant." Servicemen lived there during World War II, and Kranz became fascinated by the many facets of war, especially the air force. As a teen, he snapped up aviation magazines and became obsessed with both the science and the glamour of flight. He wrote his high-school thesis on "The Design and Possibilities of the Interplanetary Rocket," concluding, "An examination of the current technical and industrial development demonstrates the high probability that the moon will be shortly conquered by man." It was confident visionaries like this who would eventually build America's space program.

The tough work ethic instilled at Kranz's home was reinforced in Catholic schools, where he "absorb[ed] the lessons and discipline" of the nuns who taught him. Across the country in the early twentieth century, dioceses established "central" high schools to achieve the enrollment and financing scale necessary to provide a top-notch secondary education. The nearly two thousand students of Central Catholic in Toledo were taught by a variety of lay teachers, diocesan and religious priests, and sisters from five different congregations.

Kranz was proud and delighted when he won a naval ROTC scholarship to the University of Notre Dame and congressional appointment to the Naval Academy, but his dreams were crushed when he failed the physical due to high blood-sugar levels. Kranz instead enrolled at Parks Air College, East St. Louis. He graduated in 1954 with a commission in the Air Force Reserve and landed a job at McDonnell Aircraft Company in the flight-test department.

Stars and Stripes Forever

Patriotism suffused Kranz's worldview. Early in his career, when he was faced with fear after a difficult, solo cross-country flight, he was emboldened by hearing John Philip Sousa's popular military march, "Stars and Stripes Forever." He collected more than twenty different recordings of the piece and listened to it regularly: "It became a key element in my way of life."

Kranz's next stop was Lackland Air Force Base in San Antonio, where he went on active duty in March of 1955. In Texas he met Marta Cadena, and the two were married in April 1957. After serving a tour of duty in Korea, Kranz went back to work for McDonnell but soon applied for the new government space program, Project Mercury, headquartered at Langley Air Force Base in Virginia. He was hired immediately.

The Mercury program was run from Langley, but missions were launched seven hundred miles south, on the coast of Florida. When Kranz first arrived at the mission control center at Cape Canaveral, he was surrounded by the primitive technology of the early days of the space program. Dominating the room was a big world map, across which a "toylike spacecraft model" moved, suspended by wires. There were boards on each side of the map, with beads like an abacus for plotting critical measurements. Monitors, computers, and digital systems were in the future, but for now "we were in the Lindbergh stage of spaceflight."

The American space program was in a catch-up phase. Immediately following World War II, the USA and the USSR began vying for dominance in world affairs. The erstwhile allies both benefited from rocket technology confiscated from the Nazi V-2 program; in addition, the United States gained key German personnel such as Wernher von

Braun. Even so, the American space program lacked urgency through the 1950s. When news of the flight of *Sputnik 1* reached the United States in 1957, it stunned the nation. Senator John F. Kennedy of Massachusetts gained national attention by complaining of a "missile gap," with American technology lagging dangerously behind the Soviet Union's.[1] The space race became a focus of Kennedy's political life.

After Kennedy won election as president, the Soviets followed up by sending the first man into space, Yuri Gagarin, in April 1961. A few days later, the debacle of the Bay of Pigs invasion added insult to injury, as US-sponsored Cuban exiles were overwhelmed on the beaches of Cuba in a failed attempt to overthrow Fidel Castro's Communist regime.

Patriotic pride and national security concerns combined to stoke the heated competition with the Soviet Union, which in turn drove the space program forward. "I find it difficult today to convey the intense frustration and near despair as we picked ourselves up after each setback, determined to break the jinx on the program," Kranz wrote about the early American efforts.

But the revamped American program, with Kennedy appointee James Webb at its head, lurched forward. With the country watching, the Mercury project was both stressful and exhilarating. Astronauts were "instant celebrities," Kranz recalled. Americans followed closely the selection and training of the original seven astronauts, a group who were later immortalized as having "the right stuff" in book and film. On May 5, 1961, the program notched its first major accomplishment, when Alan Shepard rode a rocket to make *Mercury-Redstone 3* the nation's first manned space flight. For this and other early flights, Kranz had the critical job of formulating the "go/no-go" procedures that governed decision-making during the missions.

An Ultimatum

The program was given additional energy and pressure when President Kennedy issued an ultimatum in his noteworthy speech of May 25, 1961. In an address to a joint session of Congress begging for funds for national priorities, the president articulated the first priority: "Before this decade is out . . . landing a man on the moon and returning him safely to the earth." He argued that "no single space project in this period will be more impressive to mankind, or more important for the long-range exploration of space."

The 1969 deadline issued by Kennedy came as a shock to almost everyone in the space program. "Has he lost his mind?" one of Kranz's colleagues wondered. For his part, Kranz was thrilled: "I had always yearned to be involved in an undertaking that would challenge the imagination of man. Any doubt I ever had about moving into space vanished."

Plunging ahead, Kranz and his colleagues achieved their second huge success in February 1962, when the *Mercury-Atlas 6* flew into orbit with Kranz's fellow Ohioan John Glenn aboard. The Glenn flight underlined the extreme risk of the space program in its early years. The project had little experience with orbital flight with unmanned craft, and those few flights had included several failures. "We were rolling the dice in a way that would not be allowed in today's space programs," Kranz reflected later.

Kranz was reminded of that risk in May 1962, when *Mercury-Atlas 7* took Scott Carpenter and Shepard into space. A fuel problem required adjustment of the atmosphere reentry, which put the astronauts' safe return in jeopardy. During blackout—the period during reentry when communications between the spacecraft and mission control are impossible—Kranz "muttered a silent prayer to St. Christopher, the patron saint of travelers." It became a habit. With nothing to do but wait during the nerve-racking blackouts, "I always said a prayer for the crew at this time." Carpenter and Shepard made it safely back to earth.

The breakneck speed of space flight progress continued. During the summer following Glenn's triumph, the Manned Spacecraft Center (MSC) moved from Langley to Houston, Texas. There the program enjoyed expanded land, water, and human resources. From a staff of 750 at Langley, MSC staff more than doubled each year through the early sixties, reaching six thousand by the time Gemini operations began in 1964.

Shortly after the move to Houston, President Kennedy reaffirmed his commitment to the space program in a widely hailed speech at Rice University. In response to those asking why go to the moon, Kennedy replied,

> They may well ask why climb the highest mountain. . . . We choose to go to the moon in this decade and do the other things, not because they are easy, but because they are hard, because that goal will serve to organize and measure the best of our energies and skills, because that challenge is one that we are willing to accept, one we are unwilling to postpone, and one which we intend to win.

Kennedy would not live to see his dream turn into reality. Kranz was at work in his office in Houston on November 22, 1963, when the news of the president's assassination broke. The NASA team, with the rest of the country, was stunned. "John Kennedy had inspired us with his vision," Kranz wrote. "One by one we left work to grieve in private. The flag was at half-staff in our hearts." Kennedy's death, Kranz averred, only steeled the resolve of those striving to reach his goal: "At Mission Control and throughout NASA, in our hearts we resolved to honor John Kennedy's memory by meeting the challenge he had set for us."

Good Guys Wear White

By 1965, Kranz was a flight director, the head of one of several mission control teams. The teams were color-coded, and Kranz's was "White Team." During preparations for *Gemini-Titan 4* in 1965, Marta had an idea. She had made scarves for Gene's squadron during his air force days, and now she suggested making a white vest for Gene as a kind of team insignia. "Somewhat skeptical," he recalled, "I told her to give it a shot." Recognizing the value of team camaraderie, Gene did wear it during the Gemini flight.

Marta had created a NASA icon. "She was quietly pleased that I had worn her vest and told me that she would make me a new one for each succeeding mission. Later on, if my team did especially well, I would ask her to make me a splashy one for the landing shift." Usually the vests were white, but Marta got creative for *Gemini 9* in 1966. After the launch had been scrapped twice, "Marta made a splashy vest of gold and silver brocade over white satin. She thought I needed a bit of good luck for my third launch try." The flight was successful.

During the Gemini phase, it became clear that the massive resources devoted to the space program were paying off. By 1965, when *Gemini 6* and *Gemini 7* achieved the first manned rendezvous of two spacecraft, it seemed that the Americans had outpaced the Soviets. The patriotic Kranz reveled in victory: "I mentally savored the moment of America's triumph like a fine wine." NASA needed all the good publicity it could get; by that time, polls showed the American people thought the space program was absorbing too great a share of the federal budget.

For the most part, life at mission control was a matter of mastering technical details that had little to do directly with Kranz's Catholic faith. But aspects of his duties did resonate with his religion. There were, for example, the penitential sessions following each flight, when mistakes were identified. "As a Catholic," Kranz reflected, "I found debriefings were almost like confessing my sins to a priest—except that this was done over a microphone, so the whole 'congregation' heard my mea culpas."

In 1959, attracted to the Catholic fraternal organization's code of "charity, unity, fraternity, and patriotism," Kranz joined the Knights of Columbus. As much as possible, Kranz integrated his life as a Catholic with his professional duties. "Blessed by my mother with strong faith," he wrote, "during almost every mission, I find a way to get to church and pray for wise judgment and courage, and pray also for my team and the crew." The pastor at his Houston parish, Fr. Eugene Cargill, "was invited to the Cape for launches and was a familiar face at the crew's splashdown parties." Fr. Cargill followed the program closely and always offered Kranz a special blessing at the morning Mass preceding a mission.

In the late 1960s, NASA's push toward the moon faced strong headwinds. In 1967, the inauguration of the Apollo program was marred by the deaths of three astronauts in a fire during a training exercise—a stark reminder that the quest to explore outer space was not costless. Gus Grissom was one of those killed. Asked in an earlier interview about facing the dangers of space flight, Grissom had said, "We hope that if anything happens to us it will not delay the program. The conquest of space is worth the risk of life."

The country itself seemed to be falling apart. The annus horribilis of 1968 saw the assassinations of Martin Luther King Jr. and Robert Kennedy. Riots tore through Chicago, Detroit, and Washington. The space program was targeted by protests and bomb threats. Even so, Kranz always believed America would pull through, and that the space program was more necessary than ever: "Apollo was a bright glow of promise in a dark and anxious era."

With *Apollo 8*, human beings left the earth's orbit for the first time. The evening before the launch, Charles Lindbergh stopped by mission control, a meaningful event for Kranz. The aviator's visit "told you something powerful, something historic was taking place." It was "a kind of laying on of hands. I felt that he had handed the stick and rudder over to the astronauts."

As the craft began orbiting the moon, astronaut William Anders read from the book of Genesis. "In the beginning God created the heaven and the earth. And the earth was without form, and void; and darkness was upon the face of the deep. . . . And God said, Let there be light: and there was light." For Kranz, it was a transcendent moment. Tears welled as he listened to the creation story. "I was enraptured, transported by the crew's voices, finding new meaning in the words from Genesis. For those moments, I felt the presence of creation and the Creator."[2]

To the Moon

The next step was landing a human being on the moon. Cold War competition had not dissipated. With its successful mission in early 1969, the Soviets' Soyuz program appeared to have caught up with the American effort. Kranz was ecstatic when he learned that his control team had been assigned to the shift during which Buzz Aldrin and Neil Armstrong would descend onto the surface of the moon in their lunar module.

The launch took place from the Kennedy Space Center in Florida on July 20, 1969. The day before, Kranz attended Saturday evening Mass with Fr. Cargill. On the twentieth, as Kranz made his way to mission control, he had his "usual vague feeling that somehow my entire life has been shaped by a power greater than me to bring me to this place, at this time."

The atmosphere of the mission control room was anything but anti-septic. The staff smoked copiously, "and soon the usual pall of blue smoke hung in the air over the consoles. Stale cigarette butts, cold coffee, and day-old pizza made the scent of Mission Control." Most of the controllers were in their mid twenties; Kranz was a comparatively old thirty-five.

There were, as usual, some tense moments, but the moon landing came off as planned. As the *Eagle* was in its final seconds of descent, Kranz recalls, "I cross myself and say, 'Please, God.'" Across the coun-try and around the globe, six hundred million people were watching or listening as Armstrong set foot in the lunar dust.

After the success of *Apollo 11*, Kranz "thank[ed] God for being an American." He "was more teary-eyed in the months after *Apollo 11* than at any time in my life. Every time I heard the National Anthem, or looked at the Moon, or thought of my team, I got misty." Kranz wasn't alone in his sentiment. In a recent history of the moon landing, the historian Douglas Brinkley observes that this patriotic fervor was the principal impetus for the whole project: "The story of the American lunar landing wasn't wrapped up in any idealized aspiration to walk on the moon surface; instead, it was all about the old-fashioned patriotic determination to fulfill the pledge made by President Kennedy."

Wrapping Up Apollo

The *Apollo 13* landing was supposed to touch down at Fra Mauro, a formation named after a fifteenth-century monk-cartographer. During the eventful mission, Kranz was on duty when astronaut Jim Lovell issued his understated distress call following an explosion in the ser-vice module's oxygen tank: "Okay, Houston, we have a problem." Kranz dealt with the situation in the immediate aftermath, then handed the reins over to a relief crew. He described the period as "the longest hour in my life." He came back on for the final shift, when the crew made their triumphant reentry into the earth's atmosphere. With the astronauts and other flight directors, he rode in a ticker-tape parade in Chicago a few weeks later.

Gene Kranz's final mission as a flight director was *Apollo 17*. Marta again surprised him with a memorable vest. "It was a spectacular creation, and the favorite of all my vests, made of a metallic thread with broad red, white, and blue stripes." Kranz imbued the garment with symbolism: "For me the vest stood for America, President Kennedy, outer space, the many firsts, and the Brotherhood of Flight Control."

He would go on to finish his career at NASA, rising to become director of Mission Operations. After he retired in 1994, he kept a busy schedule of public speaking, reminiscing about his time in mission control but also exhorting his audiences to recover the spirit that had fueled his commitment to the space program.

On December 6, 2007, NASA bestowed on Gene Kranz an Ambassador of Exploration Award, which included a small portion of the more than eight hundred pounds of lunar samples collected over the course of the Apollo program. The awards ceremony was held at Central Catholic High School, which Kranz had chosen as the location to display the prize. The Moon Room is a fitting tribute to America's space program, and especially to the white-vested patriot who was a fixture at mission control.

Sources

Brinkley, Douglas. *American Moonshot: John F. Kennedy and the Great Space Race*. New York: HarperCollins, 2019.

Kranz, Gene. *Failure Is Not an Option: Mission Control from Mercury to Apollo 13 and Beyond*. New York: Simon & Schuster, 2000.

Nelson, Craig. *Rocket Men: The Epic Story of the First Men on the Moon*. New York: Viking, 2009.

Ramos, James. "A Mission from Above." *Columbia*, March 1, 2019, www.kofc.org/en/columbia/detail/mission-from-above.html.

Spiers, Edward F. *The Central Catholic High School: A History of Their History and Status in the United States*. Washington, DC: Catholic University of America Press, 1951.

Zuniga, Jo Ann, and James Ramos. "'We Need a Habitat on the Moon,' Says Former NASA Flight Director Gene Kranz." *The Dialog* (Diocese of Wilmington), July 19, 2019.

Notes

Introduction

1. John Paul Meenan, "Why Not Go on a Pilgrimage?" *Crisis Magazine*, July 10, 2018, https://www.crisismagazine.com/2018/not-go-pilgrimage.

2. Cited in Henri de Lubac, *Catholicism: Christ and the Common Destiny of Man*, trans. Lancelot C. Sheppard and Elizabeth Englund (San Francisco: Ignatius Press, 1988), 273.

3. "On Pilgrimages," trans. William Moore and Henry Austin Wilson, from *Nicene and Post-Nicene Fathers*, ed. Philip Schaff and Henry Wace, 2nd ser., vol. 5 (Buffalo, NY: Christian Literature Publishing, 1893).

4. Wilfred M. McClay and Ted V. McAllister, eds., *Why Place Matters: Geography, Identity, and Civic Life in Modern America* (New York: New Atlantis, 2014), ix.

5. Benedict XVI, Address at the Cathedral of Santiago de Compostela, Spain, November 6, 2010, Vatican website.

1. The First Parish of an Emerging Nation

1. One beneficial result of Drake's raid was the creation of the oldest extant map of the town, produced by the privateer's cartographer. Thanks to Drake, we know what old St. Augustine looked like.

2. There is a longstanding effort among Florida Catholics to document, recognize, and attain beatification for more than a hundred missionaries and laypeople, Spanish and Native American, who shed their blood for the faith in Florida during the sixteenth, seventeenth, and eighteenth centuries. See MartyrsoflaFloridaMissions.org.

3. Unfortunately, St. Augustine's legal troubles had only begun. The parish would be one site for the trustee conflicts that rankled so many American Catholic churches in the early nineteenth century.

4. Another renovation and addition occurred in the 1960s, which brought the structure to its current form and appearance.

2. The Catholic Plymouth Rock

1. This fear was a foreshadowing. The *Dove* never made it back to England, sinking with its load of furs on the return trip in 1635.

2. Historian Maura Jane Farrelly points out that even as King James I cracked down on Catholicism within England, he tolerated the conversion of his wife, Anne, to the faith and raised a number of Catholics, including George Calvert, to the ranks of the nobility.

3. The Gunpowder Plot is sometimes called the "Jesuit Treason" for the alleged involvement of Jesuit priests—though Fr. White was not involved in any way. The thwarting of the assassination attempt gave rise to a holiday named after one of the conspirators (Guy Fawkes), which was for hundreds of years thereafter the excuse for an annual explosion of English anti-Catholic vitriol.

4. There are discrepancies in the sources concerning who joined the expedition at the Isle of Wight and why the ships stopped there. Some accounts name more than one Jesuit priest among the travelers.

5. It was known during the seventeenth and eighteenth centuries as St. George's River.

6. Ingle also captured four other Jesuits, three of whom he abandoned in Virginia in hostile country on his way to England. Their fate remains unknown.

7. A small monument to Fr. Andrew White stands just north of St. Mary's City along State Route 5.

3. The Abenaki Tribe and Fr. Rale's War

1. Mutual misunderstanding, exploitation, and outright fraud were unfortunately common characteristics of white/Indigenous land bargains, here and throughout the British colonies.

2. The dictionary was donated to Harvard College forty-two years later and is still there, housed among the rare books and manuscripts in Harvard University's Houghton Library.

4. A Franciscan Adventure in Alta California

1. Because of his association with the colonization of North America, Serra has long been a figure of controversy. The cause for his canonization exhaustively examined the issue and found in favor of Serra's sanctity. Debate was nonetheless reignited as part of the widespread movement to remove objectionable monuments from American public spaces. During the summer of 2020, a statue of Serra in San Francisco was knocked down, eliciting a response from Archbishop Salvatore Cordileone. See "Statues of Saint Junípero Serra Deserve to Stay," *Washington Post*, June 30, 2020.

5. Catholic Gateway to the West

1. Fr. John Carroll, who would go on to become the first American bishop as bishop of Baltimore, joined his cousin Charles Carroll, Benjamin Franklin, and Samuel Chase in the unsuccessful diplomatic mission to Canada.

6. Ground Zero for Catholic New York

1. In that same year, Fr. Edward Sorin, having arrived from France en route to Indiana (see chapter 11), said his first Mass in the United States at St. Peter's.

8. Prompt Succor for Andrew Jackson

1. The contract is reproduced in Heloise Hulse Cruzat, "The Ursulines of Louisiana," *Louisiana Historical Quarterly* 2 (January 1919), http://www2.latech.edu/~bmagee/louisiana_anthology/texts/cruzat/cruzat--ursulines.html.

2. The Baratarians, whatever their ethical deficiencies in other respects, proved their patriotism by rejecting an earlier British proposition of alliance.

9. Catholicism on the Bourbon Trail

1. This limestone filter also plays a role in two other features of the Kentucky landscape. First, it erodes unevenly, creating underground caverns of astounding dimensions. Second, "it is the same bone-strengthening water that is a contributing factor in producing million-dollar racehorses" (Fulkerson, "America's Native Spirit").

2. Spalding would later become the bishop of Louisville (1850–1864) and then the archbishop of Baltimore.

3. The other three dioceses established in 1808 were Boston, New York, and Philadelphia.

10. A Hurricane Survivor on the Gulf Coast

1. By comparison, about 1,800 people died during Hurricane Katrina in New Orleans in 2005.

11. Faith and Football at Our Lady's Lakes

1. A traditional but unverified account has it that the Jesuit missionary Fr. Claude Allouez founded a mission there in the seventeenth century and named it Sainte-Marie-des-Lacs—Saint Mary of the Lakes.

2. The origin of the moniker "Fighting Irish" is not exactly known. It was likely rooted in the press's anti-Catholicism expressed against athletes from a small, private, Catholic institution. University president Fr. Matthew Walsh, CSC, officially adopted the "Fighting Irish" nickname in 1927.

12. "No Holier Place in the World"

1. The largest collection of relics in the United States is on display at St. Anthony's Chapel in Pittsburgh, Pennsylvania.

2. Having processed through affiliation with the Benedictines, Trappists, and the Propaganda Fide—not always with the requisite approvals—Brunner had a complex, irregular canonical situation that even his meticulous biographer could not sort out definitively. See Knapke, *American Province*, chap. 8.

3. The pope's gift, the relic of St. Cruser, can be found at the shrine today.

4. The inscription is in German with a slightly different English translation etched below. The translation used here is taken from Sr. Octavia Gutman, *Not with Silver or Gold*, 223.

13. The Puzzle of the Pope's Stone

1. This was Daniel Carroll of Rock Creek, whose nephew, the second Daniel Carroll of Duddington, owned much of the land on which Washington was built. Daniel of Duddington and Pierre Charles L'Enfant had a rancorous dispute when, during the city's construction, L'Enfant demolished a new house being built by Duddington. George Washington intervened to smooth the waters. (For help in sorting out names within the venerable Carroll family, I am indebted to the creators of the family tree posted at the website O Say Can You See, https://earlywashingtondc.org/families/carroll.)

14. A Christmas Riot at the Corner of Eighth and Plum

1. Bedini referred to Gavazzi as "the apostate" in his report to Rome.

2. Local Catholics who helped to defend the cathedral gained legendary status. Sr. Mary Agnes McCann, a historian of the Sisters of Charity of Cincinnati, recalled seeing a relic from the event in her family's home: "The sword-cane [my] father carried on that memorable occasion was an object of great interest in the family."

15. The First Architect of the Northwest

1. Sr. Joseph Pariseau was present at the cathedral in Montreal when François Blanchet was consecrated as the first bishop of Oregon in 1845.

2. Some accounts report that the American Institute of Architects (AIA) bestowed this title on her. The AIA has no record of such an official designation. It is possible, as one account suggests, that Mother Joseph won the accolade in an informal vote of members at an AIA meeting in the 1950s. See Ellen Perry Berkeley, ed., *Architecture: A Place for Women* (Washington, DC: Smithsonian, 1989), 289.

17. A General Absolution before Battle

1. A duplicate of the Gettysburg Corby statue stands in front of Corby Hall on the campus of the University of Notre Dame.

2. Catholic priests were thus a small percentage of the total number of Civil War chaplains, estimated to be nearly 3,700.

18. A Catholic Conspiracy to Kill a President?

1. In his fugitive diary, Booth claims to have injured his leg in the jump, and that account was long accepted. Michael Kauffman makes the case for the riding accident theory in *American Brutus* (2004).

2. Surratt had attended the diocesan minor seminary of St. Charles, not the Jesuit college at Georgetown. The correspondent either confused him with Herold or was simply mistaken.

3. Various versions of this "last-minute stay" attempt have circulated. One version has the priests enlisting the aid of Archbishop Spalding of Baltimore, who wrote to President Johnson; this account, at least, seems to be false, based on the absence of any record of such correspondence. See Zanca, *The Catholics and Mrs. Mary Surratt*, 87.

19. A Sister of Charity in the Wild West

1. Titled *At the End of the Santa Fe Trail*, it has been reprinted several times.
2. A variation of the winged cornette was made famous by the *Flying Nun* television series of the late 1960s.
3. This is one incident in the diaries that has been checked for accuracy by a professional investigator in the course of Blandina's canonization cause.
4. The wounded outlaw never recovered, dying later that year.
5. Blandina returned to Albuquerque briefly a few years later to assist in founding a hospital.

20. The Murder of an Archbishop in Alaska

1. The last is an Italian name, but the explorer Alessandro Malaspina sailed in the service of the Spanish Empire.
2. The gun could be seen in the cathedral at Victoria until the 1990s, when it was moved into archival storage.

21. A Catholic Mission and an Indian Tragedy at Wounded Knee

1. The Sioux Nation was a confederation of seven divisions, including the Teton Sioux, to which the Oglala and Brule bands belonged. The Sioux were also divided by language dialect into three groups: Lakota, Dakota, and Nakota. The Oglalas and Brules were Lakotas.
2. The Jesuit order was abolished by order of the pope in 1773. It was reinstated by Pope Pius VII in 1814.
3. There has been speculation that Sitting Bull was himself Catholic, but that remains unverified.
4. There is much debate about the details of Black Elk's life, including his religious views. See the introduction in Clyde Holler, ed., *The Black Elk Reader* (Syracuse, NY: Syracuse University Press, 2000), and the preface to Michael F. Steltenkamp, *Nicholas Black Elk: Medicine Man, Missionary, Mystic* (Norman: University of Oklahoma Press, 2009).

22. "There Are No Bad Boys"

1. At least one account claims that Tracy wanted to keep his trophy and the one at Boys Town is a duplicate, but Boys Town officials affirm that the one in their museum is the original.
2. The phrase originated with a nineteenth-century Presbyterian minister.

23. The Churches of Quincy, Illinois, and the First Black Priest

1. Tolton was the first American Catholic priest who publicly identified as Black. The three Healy brothers of Georgia—James, Patrick, and Alexander—were the sons of an enslaved mother and an Irish father and were all ordained priests before Tolton. Their physical features were not noticeably African, and they did not identify as such. See James M. O'Toole, "Passing: Race, Religion, and the Healy Family, 1820–1920," *Proceedings of the Massachusetts Historical Society* 108 (1996): 1–34.
2. For a summary that appreciates the complexity of Catholic thinking, see chapter 2 of John T. McGreevy, *Catholicism and American Freedom* (New York: W. W. Norton, 2003).
3. It is known today as the Congregation for the Evangelization of Peoples.
4. "Augustus" was Tolton's baptismal name, though it was often rendered afterward as "Augustine." His cause for canonization and other more recent usage has favored the baptismal name.

24. The Saint of Immigrants

1. Stereotypes concerning Italians' proclivity to crime persisted through the twentieth century and beyond. During World War II, Italian Americans—like Americans of German and Japanese descent—were subject to suspicion and sometimes relocated to internment camps.

25. The Birth of a Political Dynasty

1. Some accounts have given the fathers' political rivalry as the reason for their disapproval of the courtship, but in her memoir, Rose downplays that suggestion and stresses the couple's young age as the chief objection.

2. The University of Pennsylvania sociologist E. Digby Baltzell coined the term WASP (white Anglo-Saxon Protestant) to describe the group who dominated elite American institutions through the middle of the twentieth century (*The Protestant Establishment: Aristocracy and Caste in America* [New York: Random House, 1964]).

3. After leaving a party on a Friday night on Chappaquiddick Island off the coast of Massachusetts, Kennedy drove his car into a pond. He escaped unharmed, but his passenger, a young woman, died. He left the scene and failed to report the accident to the police until late the following morning.

4. Among many examples: Leah Barkoukis, "The Kennedy Political Dynasty Is Over," Townhall, September 2, 2020, https://townhall.com/tipsheet/leahbarkoukis/2020/09/02/kennedy-concedes-to-markey-n2575508.

26. Peacocks and Provocative Prose

1. The feeling of camaraderie among southern revival writers might be glimpsed in a congratulatory 1962 letter to fellow Catholic Walker Percy, in which O'Connor says, "I'm glad we lost the War and you won the National Book Award."

2. Against those who have reduced the value of O'Connor's fiction to their analysis of her racial views, O'Connor scholar Jerome Foss rightly warns against "the danger of interpreting art through the biography of the artists"—a method that O'Connor herself criticized repeatedly ("Flannery O'Connor and the Terrors of American Sentimentality," *Law & Liberty*, July 16, 2020).

3. Giroux reported later that at the award ceremony a famous author asked him, "Do you really think Flannery O'Connor was such a great writer? She's such a Roman Catholic."

27. A Cold Warrior in the Space Program

1. Kennedy exaggerated the gap between the two countries' capabilities. In fact, President Eisenhower had not been idle, and the US program was making substantial progress. It was Eisenhower who created the National Aeronautics and Space Administration (NASA) in 1958.

2. Atheist activist Madalyn Murray O'Hair sued NASA after this religious moment was broadcast publicly. As a result, the crew of *Apollo 11* kept their moon-landing prayer service private.

Index

Kevin Schmiesing lectures on Church history for Mount St. Mary's Seminary and School of Theology in Cincinnati, Ohio, and serves as director of research at the Freedom and Virtue Institute. He served as a research fellow at the Acton Institute for the Study of Religion and Liberty from 1999 to 2020.

Schmiesing is cohost of the podcast *Catholic History Trek* on Spotify and YouTube and has contributed to *Catholic World Report* and *Crisis Magazine*. He is the author of *Merchants and Ministers* and *Within the Market Strife* and editor of *One and Indivisible, Catholicism and Historical Narrative,* and *The Spirit Matters.*

He earned his bachelor's degree from Franciscan University of Steubenville and a doctorate in United States history from the University of Pennsylvania.

Schmiesing and his wife, Anne, have seven children and live near Dayton, Ohio.

Facebook: Kevin Schmiesing
YouTube: Catholic History Trek

Mike Aquilina is the editor of the Reclaiming Catholic History series and the author of *A History of the Church in 100 Objects, History's Queen,* and *The Church and the Roman Empire (301-490).*